D1535480

THE LITTLE PACKAGE

Books by Lawrence Clark Powell

Lawrence Clark Powell

THE LITTLE
PACKAGE

Pages on Literature

and Landscape

from a Traveling

Bookman's Life

CLEVELAND AND NEW YORK

THE WORLD PUBLISHING COMPANY

Acknowledgment is gratefully made to the following
for permission to reprint these essays and addresses:
Bibliographical Society of America, Book Club of
California, Carnegie Institute of Technology, New
American Library, New Mexico Historical Society,
Rodgers Library, Southern California Historical
Society, University of Arizona, Ward Ritchie Press,
*Arizona and the West, Arizona Highways, Library
Journal, Minnesota Libraries, New York Times
Book Review, Saturday Review, Southwest Review,
Wilson Library Bulletin.*
"On the Malibu Coast" appeared first in 1958
as part of *The Malibu,* written by W. W. Robinson
and L. C. Powell, illustrated by Irene Robinson,
and printed in a small edition at the Plantin Press
for Dawson's Book Shop.

Published by The World Publishing Company
2231 West 110th Street, Cleveland 2, Ohio
Published simultaneously in Canada by
Nelson, Foster & Scott Ltd.
Library of Congress Catalog Card Number: 64-12063
FIRST EDITION
The woodcut on the title page is by Ellen Raskin.
WP264

To the Big Family Package

FAY   NORMAN   WILKIE

PIPPIN   JOEY   JUNIOR

BESA   EMILY

Preface

By MEANS OF these essays and addresses, most of them written in the years since I left library administration for teaching, I have spoken to readers in and out of libraries and in many parts of the United States, Europe, and Asia, proving anew that the book-man's world is one world.

In a new era of electronics and automation, mine is an old-fashioned voice, speaking time and again of books, new and old, and of the magic they work for those who take them in hand and read them.

I have gone everywhere with books in my baggage or in memory alone, and although these pages from my life at home and abroad were written for a variety of occasions and publica-tions, their constant theme is of the rewards that come to the read-ing traveler, the traveling reader, of the riches that fill and over-flow the heart and mind when one lives on a balanced diet of life, literature, and landscape.

This book, then, is in praise of life, and is also a thanksgiving for what life has given me.

L. C. P.

School of Library Service
University of California
Los Angeles

Contents

CONTENTS

III. *Books and Writers*

IV. *Music and Travel*

V. *Bookman in the Southwest*

CONTENTS

Part I

LIBRARIANS AND LIBRARIES

What's Wrong with Librarians?

THE ANSWER depends upon whom you ask. A library user might say that librarians are austere and unapproachable, that they lack the human touch, are timid, and, worst of all, dull. Ask a librarian and he will say that librarians do too much clerical work, and that if only someone else would do the dirty work, then librarians could be the professional people they really are.

I shall never forget my wife's response when one day in the Depression I came home from my job in a bookshop and announced my intention of becoming a librarian.

"You a librarian?" she exclaimed.

"Why not?" I asked, defensively.

"You're too lively. Besides, you read books."

Then I had to explain that the idea had come from a librarian, not from me; and from Los Angeles's leading librarian, Althea Warren, head of the Public Library, who had interrupted my sales talk when I called at the library to sell books with a sales talk of her own, and had persuaded me that liveliness and bookish bent *were* the things library work needed. Miss Warren was herself lively, bookish, and so persuasive that I quit my job, borrowed money, and went back to school to add a library credential to

17

my other degrees, which were proving useless in those bad times. Neither administration nor research was my goal. All I wanted was a job with books and people that would pay $200 a month. I never got one. I started in a public library at $125, went on to a university library where in six years I rose from $135 to $185. Then I became head librarian of the university at $500. I have always had a feeling of intermediate failure.

Althea Warren was right; my liveliness and my bookishness proved assets. My wife modified her opinion of librarians as she came to know them better, but she has never overcome her first impression that librarians, like many others who are completely immersed in their own work, are more interested in rules and penalties and having things tidy than they are in giving people their own way, are in fact unable to see patrons as they see themselves. She derived this early and ineradicable impression from a prim librarian who could not see the library for the rules and routines.

I was luckier in my first impression of librarians. It was formed by a little gray-haired lady in the town library of South Pasadena, where I grew up. She seemed always to be behind the desk, making the date stamp smoke. I never saw anything but the upper half of her, particularly her twinkling eyes; but she saw all of me, and realized that I was a swift reader.

By the age of twelve I was through Tom Swift and the Rover Boys, the Texan and Civil War series of Joseph Altsheler, devouring Zane Grey, and moving on to D. H. Lawrence. All of this was apparent to dear deaf Nellie Keith, and for me she waived the rules that to this day make many librarians nay-sayers rather than yea-sayers. A library should have as few rules as possible, someone (not a librarian) once said, and break them all whenever necessary. Mrs. Keith let me take out any books, regardless of the color of the stars on their backs, and in quantities limited only by the number I could carry home. When I appeared with a laundry basket wired to the back of my bike, she let me fill it with books and pedal off to my idea of an orgy.

Thus my philosophy of librarianship was formed by my good fortune in knowing these two good librarians whose favorite word was *yes*. Even though a librarian is going to have to say *no* in the end, for example, to a patron who wants to take the library's only unabridged dictionary home with him, it should be said this way: "Certainly you may, if we only had a duplicate. Why not get someone to give us another, then you can take this one home."

Patrons don't like to be asked *why* they want a particular book. The cynical librarian believes that people usually don't know what they want or how to explain what they want. Patrons hate librarians who are condescending. Although I would not urge surrealism in reference work, I do like to see a blithe spirit on the public desk. Something of the lightheartedness with which Henry Miller taught English in a French high school. Remember? About the love life of elephants. You will find it in *Tropic of Cancer,* but you may not find that book in your library. It is often banned; *Lolita* is not.

To be inquiring without being nosy is a fine art. How absurd to proclaim librarianship a science! It is an artful craft, a crafty art, to be practiced with a trinity of talents: hands, head, and heart.

I have long been at odds with the library intelligentsia who believe that by gloving themselves from physical contact with books, librarians thereby enhance their status. What makes a librarian professional, in my book, is his devotion this side of fanaticism to the cordial service of people who want and need books. A good librarian knows, serves, believes. He ignores clock and calendar, and the caste which deifies the administrator and degrades the book-handling (and reading) rank and file as untouchables.

The public expects two things of a librarian: that he be bookish and that he be cordial. Call me simple if you will, but I believe that any worker in a library, regardless of rank, who is not both bookish and cordial is in the wrong work. And by "bookish," I mean informed about the contents of whatever library he works in.

No day should pass in any library when every librarian therein, no matter his rank, should not lay hands on books. I am not a biblio-mystic, and yet I do believe that in library work the hands are as important as the eyes. Having a *feel* for books is just as important as having a *feeling* for them.

You have only to watch a bookman at work, in a library or bookstore, to know what I mean. I remember seeing Ernest Daw-son, a great antiquarian bookseller, appraise a collection of books as he handled every book he thought he might buy—a real vir-tuoso performance, as he pulled them off the shelf and piled them around the room. Likewise, when William A. Jackson of Harvard's Houghton Library, one of our greatest bibliographers, visits another library, his hands work equally with his eyes in examining the collection.

It goes back to the myth of Hercules and Antaeus. When the latter lost physical contact with the earth, he lost his strength. Likewise, when a librarian loses physical contact with books, then he is no longer a strong librarian.

Thus, I believe that a good librarian is approachable, affirma-tive, inquiring, both a reader and a handler of books. There are librarians who do not think it imperative for librarians to be both bookish and humane. Some believe that administration is a science and that its universal laws apply to all areas of manage-ment, and therefore that a head librarian is better trained in a school of personnel administration than in a bookstore or library. They see Riesman's Law as supreme, whereby an inexorable upward movement leads administrators to higher salaries and narrower spans of control, and which is taking some top libra-rians out of library work into education, foundations, govern-ment, and industry. Whatever "law" is operating, I say that these emigrés should never have been librarians in the first place.

There is another group which finds bookish humanism out of date, and with whom I have engaged in controversy. They are the devoted special librarians who have arisen to serve the ex-panding needs of business, industry, science, and government. They have to deal with the masses of non-book data spawned by the scientists. Known as documentalists, rather than librarians, they "search literature" and "retrieve information," employing coded cards and machines. Most library schools have retooled to train for this expanding field.

To communicate with each other, and with their machines, the documentalists have developed acronymic "languages" which on occasion rise to the realm of poetry. Among the finest are SOAP (Symbolic Optimum Assembly Program) and BACAIC (Boeing Airplane Company Automatic Internal Compiler). UGLIAC, a routine for the Datatron 205, is neat, as are CHIP, FLAP, FLIP-SPUR, MISHAP, RAWOOP-SNAP, and IT. A group of computer personnel has amalgamated as SHARE (Society To Help Alleviate Redundant Effort).

If librarians are stereotyped as prim, austere, timid, nondescript, dull, superficial, petty, and tyrannical technicians who yearn for the status of ministers, doctors, lawyers, and architects, what is library education doing to change this popular conception which, incidentally, has come to be believed of themselves by many librarians?

Library schools are trying to train people for a variety of jobs by grounding them in the importance of libraries in society and at the same time giving them basic technical knowledge. Many of the later failures on the job can be blamed on librarians themselves having sent the wrong kind of recruits to the library schools.

In any case, the public is never concerned with these inner troubles of librarians, or with where a librarian went to school, any more than persons sick in body and soul ask of their doctor or minister what they studied at medical school and theological seminary. The public comes to the library for the books or the facts; nothing else matters.

And there is our dilemma. Who are we? Professionals, craftsmen, salesmen, teachers, or a bit of all? I have been trying to answer this question as best I can in the new library school at UCLA, which was opened in 1960.

"Powell was a bad boy," one library educator is said to have declared wryly, when he heard about the UCLA library school. "And his punishment was in his being given a library school."

We have sought to teach students about books and other forms of recorded knowledge, about the importance of libraries in a free society, and about the responsibilities of librarians in defending man's right to read all sides of all questions. We instruct them in the arts and skills of acquiring books and of employing them usefully, in the planning and operation of buildings; and first, last, and always, in ways of consummating the next greatest of all earthly unions, that of a man with a book.

A good librarian is not a social scientist, an educationalist, a documentalist, a retrievalist, or an automaton. A good librarian is a librarian: a person with good health and warm heart, trained by study and seasoned by experience to catalyze books and people.

We expect our graduates to know, and to know how to impart knowledge and, most important of all, to want to do this more than anything else, and to believe that this act of serving others who want books almost as much as they want food and love is a calling, a dedicated way of life that can approach the ministry and medicine in its selfless devotion.

Quality of teaching, not the curriculum, makes a school great. Ask a graduate of any school what he found memorable, and he will usually recall a teacher, not a course. We need another Grundtvig, that great reforming Danish bishop who believed that the personality of the teacher is always more important than what is taught. Overconcern with the form of education, made a business by professional educationalists, has killed the spirit.

Let me give an example of what this has done to the simple act of reading. At a conference sponsored by a library school, the subject was children's literature, and the participants were asked to give their criteria for evaluating such books. One young librarian, the father of a six-year-old, gave as his only criterion for a certain book that his daughter liked it. Swiftly fell the sword of the executioner, as the chairwoman said in all seriousness, "I cannot imagine a poorer criterion by which to judge juvenile literature. What should be asked is, How well does it integrate with today's culture-pattern?"

People's patience with this nonsense is running out, as witness the uproar when an administrative librarian gets himself into the position of "suggesting" that some of the old favorites like the Oz books be withdrawn from his library because they are unfit for today's children.

When students meet teachers who know and believe and are able to impart their belief, then are they converted, then will they go forth as servants of the book, convinced that the greatest good they can do is to aid old readers and make new ones. Thus it may be that a position in the children's room of a town library, a seat beside the driver of a bookmobile, a job in a hospital library or overseas information center, no matter where, as long as there is contact with books, partnership with people, and animation by the ideals and the knowledge, the arts and skills learned from teachers, from reading, and from field work—this is what should be taught as the goal of librarianship, not frittering in an office, designing forms, pinning up charts, memoizing, administering by remote control, gowned and gloved against the dust and dirt of the workaday book world, blindly sterile, and certain of success because administrative eminence and top salary have been attained. Tinkertoy librarians, they have been called.

In my fight against non-bookism in library work and with unsocial scientists, I have rallied many librarians and laymen to the cause, in a revival of reading. Sick of jargon, and of surveys which spin out what we already know, of so-called human engineering and the decision-making process, of the flight into techniques of those unbelievers who will do everything to a book but read it, these lonely librarians and readers have rallied to the old-fashioned gospel that books are basic, books are best, books are to be read and shared, world without end.

Librarians need a return to the faith of their founders—to Melvil Dewey and John Cotton Dana, to James L. Gillis and Sydney B. Mitchell, to William Warner Bishop and Herbert Putnam, to Miriam Tompkins and Althea Warren—to invoke some of the saints of library service.

I do not want to leave the impression that out in the field things are bad. Among the 60,000 librarians in the land, many are shattering the stereotype by proving to be normal, attractive, courageous, alert, and friendly individuals, no matter the size or kind of library they work in. Poor education cannot spoil a good person, nor can a bad person be transformed by degrees.

Good things are happening in libraries, particularly where the new architecture, featuring ready access to books, and comfort, has replaced the forbidding old structures.

Recently I asked a western photographer who uses libraries for historical background, "What's wrong with librarians?" My question astonished him.

"What do you mean what's wrong with librarians? Nothing's wrong with them. I love librarians. Couldn't live without them. Do you want to know how well my local library in Ventura treats me? I'll tell you. They let me bring Suzie in with me."

"Your baby daughter?" I ventured.

"Baby daughter, my eye! Suzie's my dog!"

The Elements of a
Good Librarian

AFTER THIRTY-FOUR YEARS of giving out and getting in books, UCLA's head circulation librarian retired. Most of those years and for seven days a week this strong woman was on her feet, making fast connections between books and people and keeping her files nailed, and her sense of humor.

A few years ago, before going to an American Library Association Conference, I planned to interview an applicant for a loan desk position, and so I asked Deborah King what to look for.

"Good feet," was all she said.

Are there any other elements of a good librarian? A paragon might be formed as follows:

> *A good librarian is energetic.* (I get lazier as I grow older, and want to dream more and do less.)
>
> *A good librarian is honest.* (I once stole a book and sneaked it back in, when my first job was in the library from which I had taken the book ten years before.)
>
> *A good librarian has an encyclopedic mind.* (I flunked geometry, had a hard time with French, got a C in cataloguing, and never could deal with Dewey.)

Address to Indiana and Ohio Library Associations, French Lick, 1959.

A good librarian is selfless. (I have always had to fight against being self-centered.)

A good librarian is patient. (I have a do-it-now compulsion which is shortening my life and those of the people around me who have not learned how to protect themselves.)

A good librarian is orderly. (My desk is. At home my books are crudely classified.)

A good librarian is tolerant. (I despise librarians who don't read, and people who show their slides. I also have a bad name for being bookish to the point of blindness.)

A recent visitor demonstrated to me my bad name in librarianship. As he came timidly into my office, he stopped near the door and said, "I am a documentalist." I was speechless, as he approached cautiously and sat on the edge of his chair. He was such a nice man, he almost made me ashamed of the things I have said about non-book librarians.

In short, I am a man who would be a good librarian, but who falls short because of the limitations of my own character.

I can only describe what I value most in a librarian—what I myself strive to be—and in terms of librarians whom I have seen exhibiting these elements of goodness.

One Sunday we were lunching at a neighbor's upcoast from us, an enchanting house near the sea cliff in the midst of semi-wild foliage—mesembryanthemum, sweet alyssum, rosemary, and salt bush—looking out on the waters sailed by Drake and Dana.

We were eating on trays in the living room, whose front wall was all windows and whose wall in back of where I was sitting was all books. I could feel, but not see them at my back, a thousand or more volumes reflecting the educated mind of their owner.

Politeness kept my attention on the conversation, as we ate a good meal and talked about the beaches of Baja California and the craters on the moon, about the Ponte Vecchio and the Rainbow Bridge. My left hand, however, roamed behind me over the backs of the books on the bottom shelf, practicing biblio-osmosis, and kept returning to a single book, wondering what it was, for it was taller and thinner than the rest, a modern book with a jacket, in the midst of older books in calf and cloth.

My mind became obsessed with this invisible volume and, as soon as the luncheon was over, I got up and heaved aside the overstuffed chair in which I had been sitting, dropped to my knees, and seized that tantalizing book.

It proved to be a volume of reproductions of paintings and sculptures by different artists of all periods and lands, with captions, called *The Quiet Eye, A Way of Looking at Pictures,* compiled by Sylvia Shaw Judson, and published in 1954 by Henry Regnery of Chicago.

"This book is not meant to teach," the preface said, "it is intended as an experience. The illustrations represent a long and happy search. They are admittedly the choice of one woman who is conditioned by her own life."

This Quaker woman, Sylvia Shaw Judson, who compiled *The Quiet Eye,* chose her examples to reveal a sense of "divine ordinariness, a delicate balance between the outward and the inward, with freshness and a serene wholeness and respect for all simple first-rate things, and which are for all times and all people." Pictures ranged from Dürer to Brancusi, captions from St. Augustine to Aldous Huxley.

She achieved her aim. The effect on me was that of an experience. I was not the same for having looked at and read it. It cleared and deepened my vision. The caption for a picture by Henri Rousseau set me on a path I had not walked since boyhood. It read: "All things were new; and all the creation gave another smell unto me than before, beyond what words can utter."

The words are those of George Fox, founder of the Society of Friends, who lived from 1644 to 1691. They are from his Journal, published three years after his death.

When we had returned home, I went to my study and laid hands on an old book which had been a family fixture since boyhood and to which I had become so accustomed that I never saw it, even when my eyes were on it.

Looking at Sylvia Judson's *The Quiet Eye* cleared my cloudy vision, and I spent that evening reading in this family copy of the first edition of George Fox's Journal, an ancient book bearing the successive signatures of my forebears who in turn had owned it.

This led to my ordering the definitive text of Fox's Journal, published by the Cambridge University Press in 1953, and to a widening interest in the faith to which I had been born.

A good librarian is curious.

In 1954 I dedicated my *Alchemy of Books* to Nellie Keith, city librarian of South Pasadena during the book-hungry years of my boyhood. The library was a wonderful one. No one ever bothered me with "readers' advisory service." I knew what I wanted. I never wasted my time in the children's room. My earliest reading was Grimm's grim *Fairy Tales, Tom Sawyer,* and the *Book of Knowledge,* which I never thought of as children's books. I liked compact books with dense type pages, because I read fast, and those silly picture books with a few words to a page lasted about two minutes.

I went to the library on my bicycle after dinner, first of all to play a game called "Ditch" with my cronies, around the library park and in and out of the library building. This we could do with safety as long as we kept out of Mrs. Keith's sight, for she was deaf. We used to crawl by the loan desk from one side of the building to the other on our hands and knees.

When exhausted from play, I would select my books and leave. Sometimes she caught me. Then the punishment was no books that night. Gradually she broke me of my wild ways, at least in the library.

I don't know a thing about Nellie Keith in the way of her formal education for librarianship or where she had worked before she came to South Pasadena. I suspect that her education and experience were limited. I don't even know if she read books or knew anything about the history of libraries and learning.

And yet, Nellie Keith had at least one of the elements of a good librarian. She was perceptive of my exceptional reading ability, and my hunger for books was not interfered with by her annoyance at my noisy play habits. She perceived my need and she met it, and thereby unknowingly determined my ultimate fate; for, twenty years later, when Althea Warren asked me why I didn't declare for librarianship, I thought back to the first librarian I had known, and the image of Nellie Keith came before my eyes—stamping out books, with a twinkle in her eye, sending a small boy out of the building with his arms full of books.

The book stamping Nellie Keith did was clerical, but the important thing is that she carried out this task at the key point in the library, past which people came and went. And she saw them, knew them, talked with them, observed what they read, and was the symbol of service to the citizens who used the public library.

Abdicate this key position in a library to a clerk who does nothing but the charging routines, or to a machine, and you have abdicated your standing as the one who delivers more than the books.

A good librarian is perceptive.

We live in a perilous time. The advantages of mass communication are many in keeping people informed by newspaper, radio, television, films, of all that is happening everywhere every day. There is a sense of excitement and wonder engendered by the front page of the morning paper. And there is also danger in it, when pressure groups exploit these media to create public hysteria. Not only groups—single men. I was teaching at Columbia University at the time of McCarthy's heyday, and I saw what unscrupulous conduct can do to injure people.

It was a year or two before this that we saw what a single librarian allied with a journalist could do by attacking the work of a good teacher of librarians. I refer to the distorted review of Helen Haines's *Living with Books*. The index of *Library Literature* is nearly devoid of reference to this incident. The exception is the strong reply made by Elinor Earle of Akron in the *ALA Bulletin*.

I recall another case, which at the time was tentatively considered by the American Library Association Intellectual Freedom

Committee and not dealt with because it was held that the issues were cloudy. They are clearer now. I could not find any reference to the case in the index of *Library Literature*. I refer to the case of Mary Knowles, librarian of the Plymouth Monthly Meeting of the Society of Friends, in Plymouth, Pennsylvania.

In 1953 Mrs. Knowles had been dismissed from a position in Massachusetts because in 1948 she had been a member of an organization on the Attorney General's list of subversive groups, and would not reveal the names of associates and was opposed in principle to loyalty oaths. In 1954 the Pennsylvania Quaker group employed her as librarian, satisfied that she had renounced her former left-wing association and was in fact a loyal American and a competent librarian. Both she proved by word and deed to be.

But patriot groups and congressional investigators would not let Mrs. Knowles's past be forgotten, and a storm of controversy was blown up and kept turbulent. The Plymouth Meeting itself was divided, but the sense of the Meeting was to support their appointment. When the Fund for the Republic made a grant of $5,000 to the Plymouth Meeting for its support of democratic principles, the storm reached gale force. In 1956 Mrs. Knowles was again called before a congressional committee and, upon her refusal to recognize the committee's right to compel her to reveal details of past associations, was convicted of contempt of Congress.*

Whereupon, the Library Committee of Plymouth Meeting issued this public statement on January 24, 1957:

> A committee of Congress has just spent virtually a whole day ventilating the unhappy internal affairs of a small religious group, Plymouth Meeting of the Religious Society of Friends. Not a single fact has been developed that was not known before.
>
> Mrs. Knowles has sworn that she has had no subversive association since 1948, and no evidence has been produced to the contrary. Unless, or until, evidence is produced indicating activity inimical to our democratic form of government, we envision no change in our relationship with her.

* In 1961 the United States Supreme Court reversed her conviction.

As individual members of the Religious Society of Friends, we reaffirm the supremacy of conscience. We recognize the privileges and obligations of citizenship; but we reject as false that philosophy which sets the state above moral law and demands from the individual unquestioning obedience to every state command. On the contrary, we assert that every individual, while owing loyalty to the state, owes a more binding loyalty to a higher authority—the authority of God and conscience.

In a pamphlet entitled "The Plymouth Meeting Controversy, a Report prepared for the Civil Liberties Committee of the Philadelphia Yearly Meeting of the Religious Society of Friends," we read the following:

> A basic religious issue has been raised: the Christian belief in the power of truth to unfold in every human heart and in the possibility for every person to change and develop. This implies accepting individuals for what they are at face value rather than chaining them to a past, alleged or actual.
>
> Friends' interest in these issues is rooted in long experience. From the first generation of Quakerism, Friends have been concerned to champion personal liberty and the freedom of conscience for their own members and others. Plagued in the seventeenth century by test oaths and informers, they suffered fines and imprisonment until major legal reforms were made. But in different forms the issues of religious and civil liberties rise anew in every generation.

I do not know Mrs. Knowles, either in person or by correspondence, but I do know that for a librarian to take an unpopular stand such as she took, based on principle and conscience, and to maintain it steadfastly in the face of hostility and indifference, requires the element I have been all this time leading up to.

A good librarian is courageous.

When individual courage and competence are matched by courageous support from a librarian's board, as in this case, the entire profession is benefited. A study of school library censorship in California, undertaken by Marjorie Fiske, on a grant from the Fund for the Republic, and sponsored by the

University of California's School of Librarianship and the California Library Association, was opposed at first, and Library Association support nearly caved in. The courage of Dean J. Periam Danton, Chancellor (now President) Clark Kerr, and Professor Frederic Mosher, chairman of the California Library Association's Intellectual Freedom Committee, saved the day.

The results of the study, published as *School Libraries and Censorship*, indicated that censorship in California's school and public libraries is usually self-imposed by timid librarians who are trying to avoid controversy. They are timid because they cannot count on the support of their professional colleagues when controversy arises.

We are haunted by the question, Are we members of a profession or are we self-glorified housekeepers? I am suspicious of those who define professional people as those who in doing the brainwork direct others beneath them to do the handwork. Thus for them it is necessary to rise administratively in order to achieve status professionally. The establishment of standards for positions and libraries has of course improved the status of people and services. The trouble is that essentially nonprofessional librarians have a way of decking themselves out in fancy standards—degrees, surveys, charts, etc.—and proclaiming themselves as the elite.

It is the ancient matter of form versus spirit. If the desire to serve and to learn is in a person who works in a library, that person is truly a librarian, no matter what his formal qualifications or how he is classified. The desire to serve others is perhaps the most important of all the elements that make up a good librarian. The desire to learn can be instilled in a person. Knowledge can be acquired. Curiosity and courage can be strengthened by example. The desire to serve is inborn.

Take this latter quality, this desire to serve others before one's self—and there must be added to it learning and technique and psychology, and the other refinements of education, before one gets a librarian deserving of the label "professional"; one who places the needs of patrons and his profession above his own needs and the needs of his family.

I once had visits, a month apart, from the head of a library and from a clerical employee in that library's order department. The one has a Ph.D. in so-called library science, having written a dissertation on library housekeeping; the other has a B.A. Each asked a question.

The Doctor of Philosophy asked, "How is your multiple order form working?"

The Bachelor of Arts asked, "How do you stimulate faculty members to order books in areas where the library is weak?"

Which of the two is professional?

Suppose you are the head of a small library, and at closing time on a day when you are due to hurry home and take your wife to a social engagement there arrives a person who has come a distance in urgent need to use a special collection and who has been delayed by an accident. What do you do? The answer you give will tell me whether or not you are the member of a profession.

What is this element?

A good librarian is dedicated to the service of others.

To be a good servant, one must be more than a knower; one must be a believer. Believe in what? In the goodness of mankind and life on earth. He must be an optimist. And then he must believe that his work, library service, is *the* work of works. Inner belief cannot be concealed; it is outwardly visible. The students at Cambridge who tried in vain to pull George Fox off his horse shouted, as they saw his radiant face, "See, he shines, he glistens!" He was not wearing armor. George Fox wore a suit of leather.

If believing is elementary in a good librarian, then it is even more essential in one who would teach librarians. I met Miriam Tompkins only once, when I was at Columbia. She had the office next to mine, on the highest floor of the Butler Library. Soon after I had arrived, there came a knock on my door and a woman entered. I didn't know who she was, but light shone from her face as she held out her hand and said, "Welcome to Columbia. I am Miriam Tompkins." If I ever saw a believer's face, it was hers. A week later Miriam Tompkins was dead. But what she was—her belief—lives in her students, and in me, to whom she transmitted it merely by a smile and the touch of her hand.

Can beginners be taught these elements? Can young men and women be taught to be curious, perceptive, courageous, dedicated, and believing? Yes. In only one way. By example. Not by saying; by doing.

"What you are," said Emerson, "stands above you and thunders so loudly, I cannot hear what you say." Thus it is with teachers, whether they be in library schools or in libraries. It need not be only by their own example. Library history is peopled with great librarians, by those who in their deeds were curious, perceptive, courageous, and dedicated.

The study and emulation of good librarians should be the constant concern of those who would likewise be good librarians. We need more biographies of them, more histories of their works. If one is the head of a library, his is a sacred obligation to set an example to his staff. This is the hardest thing on earth to do, for it means the wearing away of one's life in trying to be a good librarian.

The good librarian sets an example just short of fanaticism. A single librarian of such stature does more to give librarianship professional status than a thousand play-it-safe and take-it-easy free-riders.

A generation ago Charles F. Lummis, newspaper editor and first Southwest booster, found himself librarian of the Los Angeles Public Library, a position he held for only five years, from 1905 to 1910, and yet in that time this fanatically dedicated little Yankee, without either library training or experience, changed the character and direction of the library. His annual reports are the most exciting library reports I have ever read.

The same generation in California also produced James L. Gillis, founder of the state-wide county library system and teacher of a band of county librarians whose dedicated zeal has never been seen again in the West. Gillis came to librarianship from the unlikely position of lobbyist with the Southern Pacific. When a new governor asked him what he wanted as his share of the patronage, Gillis chose to be State Librarian—and the rest is library history.

Every state in the Union can recall librarians who are likewise memorable in their dedication to service, and whose preparation for librarianship was unorthodox. Today's librarians in every region and town should think continually of their librarians who were truly great. They teach us by their example. Let us not follow any lesser leaders than those who went all the way, who gave their lives in the going, and who advanced librarianship along the road behind the ministry and medicine. And let us never forget that the education of a good librarian may or may not include library school training.

And finally, a favorite book of mine is called "Fischerisms; being a sheaf of sundry and divers utterances culled from the lectures of Martin H. Fischer, professor of physiology in the University of Cincinnati," and printed privately by C. C. Thomas of Springfield and Baltimore.

Let me quote a few of these medical aphorisms in the tradition of Hippocrates; they illuminate for me what it is to be a professional person.

Unless you overwork you underwork.

Expect an early death, it will keep you busier.

The heart is the only organ that takes no rest. That is why it is so good.

A doctor must work eighteen hours a day and seven days a week. If you cannot console yourself to this, get out of the profession.

Earth, air, fire, and water are the elements of physical matter. Curiosity, perception, courage, service, and dedicated belief are the elements of a good librarian. O Lord, help us be such!

On the Grindstone

Two THINGS PEOPLE SEEK and too few find are faith and security. We need to have faith in something or someone, and to believe therein with all our heart. There is our need also to feel secure in the present and the future, so that energy for our work is not sapped by fear and worry.

Many have found faith and security in library work. People turn to books for all that books hold for people: knowledge and power, distraction, delight, strength, and solace. Some need no help, no intermediaries. More, however, do need help, need librarians as guides.

"Is *this* a good book?" we are asked, time and again.

"What's it about?" the child asks, and stays for an answer, will not leave until answered, sees through the thin answer.

Slick answers can be given by librarians who read only the reviews. One can even be a passing fair librarian without reading many books. The answer that stays with the questioner, however—the reply that may change his life—is made by the librarian who has X-rayed every book in sight, by the librarian who has a reservoir of answers accumulated from reading.

This faith in the necessity of librarians, this belief in our

36

meaning and usefulness, are things which sustain us and which we must tender to young idealists who seek to give themselves without reserve.

Books in numbers compound my security. It has been so since childhood, when I preferred the public library to the public schools, and the forest of the stacks was a place without perils. Later in library school it was the stacks of the university library that served as sanctuary when assignments were menacing.

And now, with time to read and reflect, and troubled by the state of the world, I go daily to the stacks, in the way some people go every day to church. Often it is for specific books, or again just to roam among a million volumes, many of which I once collected throughout the world, handled in shops and upon arrival, and even read. There in the stacks I gain security from identification with all mankind, from the cave-painters of Lascaux to the bomb-builders of Los Alamos.

Down in that subterranean world those ranges of red cloth are the library of Arthur Chuquet, French military historian, mostly on the revolution of 1789, bought en bloc from Champion of Paris. Those linear feet of three-quarter red moroccos are John Fiske's books, another collection acquired intact, each and every one of which I once examined for Fiske's marginalia, twenty years ago when I was writing a paper on the American historian.

On every level, along every aisle, regardless of the classification, from *A* to *Z*, I am among friends and fellow bookmen, all alive and life-giving for me, regardless of the dates on their catalogue cards faraway upstairs. Chance encounters also occur that lead to friendships with books new to me. Once I was down among the *D*'s—European history and travel—looking for a book on Salzburg in preparation for a Mozart pilgrimage, and was on my way back to the stairs, passing the *DC*'s, when a single book stayed my progress. There was nothing occult about the experience; the reasons were obvious: The subject was rivers, the locale France, the publisher Faber, all forming a massive roadblock.

Three Rivers of France by Freda White, published in 1952, is a handbook that ripened long in the author's experience, study, and thought before it was written. Unlike some modern "quickie" books, concocted to cash in on a trend, this Scots-woman's book about the Dordogne, the Lot, and the Tarn, those rivers of southwestern France that rise in the Massif Central and flow into the Atlantic, is aged and mellow.

Its pages are saturated with the author's catholic interests: history, folklore, landscape, fauna and flora, architecture, gastronomy; and her guidebook and its photographs and map convey the ambience of an ancient land, swept over repeatedly by warring men. Its dedication reads: "To the French Resistance of the River-Country: to those who died and are remembered and to those who live and remember."

No matter what library I am in, from the mighty Widener to that humble quonset hut in Tokyo's Washington Heights, I always experience this sense of recognition and discovery, of satisfaction and security. I suppose the data-processor feels this way among the winking lights of his computers, the banker in his vaults, the miller in a grain elevator, even the owner of a wrecking yard. Each man needs, seeks, and, if fortunate, finds faith and security. As a librarian I find mine among books and the infinity of service they contain.

II

I never knew that modern Maecenas, Frederick P. Keppel, president of the Carnegie Corporation, but I like evidences of the imaginative things he did. Presidents of today's foundations with their giveaway millions should emulate Keppel. More of the advances in librarianship are due to individual genius than to committees, although I will grant that organizations are often the fuel that puts the individual into orbit.

These observations are due to my rereading a short book published in 1939 by the American Library Association. Years ago when I first read it in a library copy I had little experience by which to evaluate it. Now I own my own and am free to annotate it marginally, as I like to do the books that move me. I found my copy in a secondhand bookshop at the bargain price of $2, a copy doubly prized for its having belonged to the late Robert O. Schad of the Huntington Library.

American Librarianship from a European Angle by Wilhelm Munthe is an example of Frederick Keppel's imagination in transcending the bureaucratic procedure which brakes down so much library activity today. By the mid-1930s the Carnegie Corporation had poured a pot of money into American librarianship. With what results? President Keppel wondered. Instead of setting up a board of inquiry, he asked one of Europe's most eminent librarians, the Norwegian Munthe, to have a look-see and a say-so.

Dr. Munthe came not as a greenhorn, having made several trips to the United States. When he told an American colleague that he was going to swing around and cut across the U.S.A. in three months and write a report for the Carnegie Corporation, he got the response you might expect. "Do people take you for a commission? Or have you supernatural powers?"

This gave Munthe pause only for a moment; then he recalled Keppel's charge: "See what you like! Go where you like! Don't worry about statistics! Read our professional literature or let it alone. Talk with whomever you like, but don't trust anyone. It is your own personal impressions we are after."

So off went Wilhelm Munthe on his odyssey. East coast, west coast, and all around the land, he covered the continent in a way that few American librarians (Keyes Metcalfe excepted) have done, using eyes and ears, and bringing to bear on everything he saw and heard his own rich experience of a lifetime in libraries.

Upon returning to Norway he thought he had better check his data with library literature, but he soon realized the folly of trying to wade through it. "So I stopped short, took my notes and a few handbooks and retired to a country cabin about 100 miles from Oslo, and there this report took shape."

What a good report it is!—at once confident and cautious, olympian and humble, sounding just the right note on every page. Encyclopedic too. The works. Munthe covered it all:

reading habits, book trade, public and academic libraries, regional developments, buildings, library education, feminism, and so forth. As critical as he is admiring, Munthe wound it up by hanging out the classic sign: "Don't shoot the pianist, he's doing his best!"

The book is out of date in some respects, of course. Federal aid and automation, for example, are now major factors in librarianship. Most of it, however, is still pertinent. *Plus ça change* . . .

We need more such virtuoso performances. We should invite more foreign librarians (correction, there is no such thing as a *foreign* librarian) who have seeing eyes, suitcase stamina, experience by which to measure, and courage to say, and send them roaming around the U.S.A., Munthe-Gunther-wise, going by Greyhound rather than Silver Falcon, the only requirements being that they produce a report for publication.

Name names? Readily. Preben Kirkegaard, long-time public librarian and now head of the Danish State Library School, who has made several trips to the U.S.A., a man with a sharp eye, fluent tongue, and facile pen; Roy Stokes, also a former public librarian turned educator, now head of the Loughborough Library School, a courageous critic of the status quo, with teaching experience in the library schools of Syracuse, Illinois, and UCLA, an atypical Englishman never seen to drink tea or carry a rolled umbrella; Robert L. Collison, librarian of the British Broadcasting Corporation, long-time reference librarian of the city of Westminster and prolific author of reference works, like Roy Stokes a great looker, asker, and writer.

Why didn't some organization finance John Wakeman in a swing around the land to write a terminal report on American librarianship before he left the *Wilson Library Bulletin* to return to his native England? I'll tell you why. Because the organization has no imagination. Only the individual has imagination.

I suggest a moratorium on organizational probing and peeking. The dead sea of library literature has had enough surveys and reports of facts and findings dumped into it. Writing lasts only when it receives life from the individual. The gift to breathe life into prose is given only to a few. Why not find them and fund them?

III

I have observed evidences of a reaction against librarians becoming too bookish. *Cult of the book, bibliophilic sentimentality, obsession with smells of paper and ink and feel of bindings, ivory towerism, retreat from reality*—are some of the words used to castigate the cultists.

The reactionaries should go back to Melvil and deploy Dewey against those who harp on books. "Mr. Dewey was primarily an organizer, secondarily an educator, rather than a bookman," Josephine Rathbone recalled. "I won't say he never read, but I never remember hearing him speak of a book."

They could also quote from Dewey's talk, "Our Next Half-Century," given in 1926 at the semicentenary conference of the American Library Association, in which he predicted the obsolescence of the book: "I am not at all sure that the library of fifty years from now will not have outgrown the book and that it may go back into the museums like the inscriptions on clay."

Whatever 1976 may hold for the book as a means of recording, transmitting, and preserving knowledge, as of now the public still thinks of a library as a place of books. Those who worked at Century 21 library exhibit at the Seattle World's Fair tell me that people went to the books, not to the gadgets, as horses go to water. Men, women, and children persist in coming to libraries for books, for information about books and their contents; and they expect librarians to be authorities.

How does a librarian get to be an authority? By study, in or out of school; by retaining some rub-off from every book handled and person served; by hiving up the honey of knowledge and experience. Lloyd P. Smith said it back in 1876 at that epochal meeting in Philadelphia out of which came the American Library Association. In speaking on "The Qualifications of a Librarian," he enumerated them as follows:

1. A love of books and learning
2. Academic training
3. A sense of order
4. A passion for collecting
5. Courtesy.

All of this can't be taught in library school, even in the utopian ones. These attributes can be encouraged and refined, but actually the best librarians are born not made.

One way of increasing librarians' bookish authority might be by library schools and foundations working out post-M.L.S. internships in bookstores, new and secondhand. Here could be learned answers to such questions constantly asked of librarians, as "What is this book worth?" "How do I go about getting a manuscript published?" "Where can I buy these out-of-print books?"

Bookshops are the best places to meet and learn from book collectors. I have as lifelong friends book collectors whom I first met thirty years ago, when I worked in new and antiquarian bookstores.

Such internships would lend proprietors bookish librarians, whose sense of order could prove useful, and would offer interns the opportunity of learning the economic facts of the book trade—a trade which can be of great usefulness to librarianship, as every wise librarian doth know.

Go Forth and Be Useful:
A Valedictory Address

GRADUATION IS AN OCCASION of ambivalent feelings, mostly joyful yet with an undertone of sadness. It is the last time we will meet as a group, we who have lived together for a year in this mighty, believing little community. We will hold alumni reunions as long as we live, but so widely dispersed will you be in the profession you now join that the odds are against us all ever coming together again at the same time and place.

And so I wish to observe the rareness of the occasion by speaking some common words, to say what I expect of you, and hope for you.

If we are not destined to meet again as a class, yet so lastingly have we been welded together in this small school in a large library on a great campus, that I can also say to you that never again, as long as you live and practice what we have learned together, will you be alone. You will be one with not only your teachers and fellow graduates, but will also join the ranks of Callimachus, Naudé, Panizzi, Putnam, and a thousand nameless, unsung librarians who have loved learning and served people.

As you live out your daily lives in libraries and spend your

Address to the Class of 1962, School of Library Service, UCLA.

43

nights in the refreshment of friend and family, of food, books, and sleep, you will make company with fellow librarians, it matter not that they lived and died long ago; for one of the rewards of librarianship is that you escape Time's hold on people.

You have heard Seymour Lubetzky speak of Anthony Panizzi, you have heard Frances Sayers recall Anne Carroll Moore, and in their words and recollections those two inspiring librarians achieve their immortality.

Take unto you your own patron saints from the library hierarchy, those who in the words of Everyman will go with thee by thy side, in thy most need to be thy guide.

Go where? To a library where you can give, where what you are and what you have will be needed and wanted. This is the ideal to seek. If you fail to achieve such a situation, if you find yourself merely getting, in a job which does not tax you to your utmost, which is just a job, a salary, a day's work, without challenge or trouble or demands which make you give till it hurts and make you grow by stretching; if, I say, you are not changed by what you do, then you are one of the living dead who haunt librarianship and make it sterile as a graveyard.

Go to work each morning, asking, What am I needed for? What is there for me to do today? Dress at home, then undress on the job. Walk naked. We have tried to toughen your skin. Be yourself. If called on to write, reach for Fowler and Webster. If asked to speak, bounce your words off the back wall. Write to be understood, speak to be heard, read to grow.

And if you are not already given to prayer, learn to pray. For what? Humility, and courage. If you stand for truth, sooner or later you will be called upon to defend it; and if you are called to the stand, remember you do not stand alone. For company you will have Milton and Jefferson, Thoreau and Emerson. Because you are a reading believer, a believing reader, they and all other defenders of truth will be there with you, far more real than today's shadowy, shady politicians.

This is not mysticism. This is reality—but only if you are a believer.

Try not to be snobbish. Remember that the hands are also capable of learning. Let no day pass, regardless of your title or classification or responsibility, that you do not lay hands on books. Then let the eyes have them, followed by the mind and heart. There is no machine on earth can do what man can do.

Strive to be a librarian in whom the trinity of head, heart, and hands are co-equal.

Let your pride be no greater than your usefulness to others. Distinguish between service and servitude. Avoid fancy names. When asked who you are, reply with two one-letter words, one two-letter word, plus one longer word, which go to make the declarative sentence, *I am a librarian.*

Now that the cord is cut, go forth and be loving and useful, whether you be followers or leaders. Be librarians.

Up Near the Source

I CAME HERE because of a couple of my obsessions. Relief is had by talking about them. Room is thus made for more obsessions to move in. I hope I won't disappoint anyone when I say that neither obsession has to do with books.

What then is there to talk about? Clues are in my title, "Up Near the Source." The first should not be hard to guess. Rivers. River talk. Lake Itasca to the Delta and the Gulf. Mississippi talk. All my life I have been obsessed by the flow of water. My parents were born on opposite shores of the Hudson. I was born on the shore of the Potomac. And one of the sorrows of my life is that most of it has been spent in an arid land whose rivers are dry rivers, and I have had to settle for that body of water without any directional flow called the Pacific Ocean.

Here where we meet, up near the source of the Mississippi, I feel the power and the strength of this symbolic location, and my mind teems with river recollections, of all the crossings I have made by train and plane and car, seeing the river's snaky signature on the land; and of all the river reading I have done throughout my life—Mark Twain, Lyle Saxon, T. S. Eliot,

Address to Minnesota Library Association, Rochester, 1962.

46

William Faulkner, culminating in a paperback, *The Mississippi River Reader*, compiled by Wright Morris. Let me read from his preface:

> When and where I was a boy, in the Platte Valley of Nebraska, the word Mississippi was an ornament for spelling bees, a tongue twister with the hissing lisp of the river itself. In time I learned that the Platte flowed into the Missouri—it did if there was water in it—that the Missouri flowed into the Mississippi, and that the Father of Waters, having no other course, flowed into the sea. My discovery, that is, though a bit late, paralleled all of those made earlier, being a mishmash of hearsay and legend slowly merging into fact. It is this *fact* that we see on the map, dividing the continent like a bolt of lightning, but that which lingers, like the topsoil of the delta, is the hearsay and the legend—a blend of impressions into which the facts dissolve.
>
> Two rivers, therefore, are open to discovery—the one that flows, as it must, to the sea, and the one that man has empowered to flow in reverse, out of time the river, into himself. This river bears not merely the topsoil of legend, but the stamp of national character. It is no accident that the raft of Huck Finn first drifted out on its waters, and that no craft of equal importance drifts on it today. The bird of dawning does not sing, as he once did, in the canebrakes, and the modern Huck Finn takes his ease at the wheel of a hotrod. Of time and the river there is now very little; it does not swim by, according to Huck's reckoning, but flies, leaving only the dissolving plume of the jet. It is now more relevant, than irreverent, that the first white man to set eyes on the river, Hernando de Soto, should have hardly seen it at all. He had his gaze on plunder. It was one more river to cross. . . . So it has once more become, as the traffic whines, like an alternating current, across the great bridges, affording clipped glances at the muddy water below. What river is it? One where the traveller pays his toll. Thus the river has come full circle, it has had, like man, its rise and its fall, and man's love affair, intermittent and capricious, has run its course. Like the planet itself, it now awaits rediscovery.

In the topsoil of this *Mississippi River Reader* my reading flourished. I went upriver, rather than down, to Schoolcraft, not Faulkner, to the crystal source, not the muddy delta. I read everything I could find about Henry Rowe Schoolcraft and his discovery and naming of Lake Itasca—*veritas caput*, the true source; and now I have the prospect of a visit someday to the State Park which Minnesota has wisely made of Lake Itasca.

The farthest downriver I will go again is to St. Louis, birthplace of T. S. Eliot, and solely to see "The Meeting of the Waters," that beautiful fountain by Carl Milles which symbolizes the union of our two greatest rivers.

I am a believer in the recognition and the marking of these significant places, of tangible signs and symbols which give us a focal point for recognizing and honoring momentous events and great people.

This is partly an intellectual belief that a people need such evidence of their national heritage, need tangible means of identifying themselves with the forces and the heroes who have made us what we are. In the arid West, where water is life, I have urged every city and town and school and library to erect fountains, to create shrines of shining water to teach the young to respect and to honor this life force, and to give the old a place to give thanks.

An intellectual belief, yes, and also a primitive superstition based on fear and respect of the element that can destroy life as well as sustain it.

This feeling is what moved T. S. Eliot to write these lines about his natal river:

> I do not know much about gods; but I think that the river
> Is a strong brown god—sullen, untamed and intractable,
> Patient to some degree, at first recognized as a frontier;
> Useful, untrustworthy, as a conveyor of commerce;
> Then only a problem confronting the builder of bridges.
> The problem once solved, the brown god is almost forgotten
> By the dwellers in cities—ever, however, implacable,
> Keeping his seasons and rages, destroyer, reminder
> Of what men choose to forget. Unhonoured, unpropitiated
> By worshippers of the machine, but waiting, watching, and waiting...

So much for my first obsession, with running water, of where it starts, where it goes, what it does, and what we owe it in the way of recognition and honor.

My second obsession also has to do with sources. *Our* sources as librarians, yours in Minnesota, mine in California, of ours as American librarians who have inherited the books and are charged by the code of our profession with being honest and fearless, imaginative and ingenious, cordial and useful to those in need of knowledge and delight.

Whom did we come from, what were our origins, our sources of strength and inspiration in the relatively short years we have regarded ourselves as a profession? This has always interested me since I became a librarian and on through my working years, but never deeply. I took it mostly for granted that we had pioneers who broke the ground, cleared the woods, and wrote the laws by which we live today. But as I grew older and did less and thought more, particularly in the years that I have been trying to teach younger people the elements of good librarianship, this interest in our library forebears has become an obsession.

In my introductory course there is a section called Library Leaders, in which students are sent back to the years, not so long ago, when there were giants on the earth. Wasn't Ole Rolvaag an adopted Minnesotan?

There is in us a need for identification with gods and goddesses, with librarians who were truly great and who, in Spender's words, "left the vivid air signed with their honour." The need becomes greater as our standards are lowered, our ethics tarnished, and we look on the prospect before us as De Soto stared beyond the river, his eyes on plunder—ours on the highest salary the quickest, the fringe benefits, the coffee breaks, and the gimmicks.

In this time of plenty, of easy pickings, we need to pilgrimmage to our more austere past when those with less did more. This is not a popular doctrine, but my experience has convinced me that there are many among us, including the young, who believe in it and who will follow leaders who will lead.

How do we learn about our library past? How do we make an unnatural about-face, swim upstream? How do we resurrect our giants, make them come to life and walk the earth again? It can be done by the oral tradition, by hearing the spoken word, the personal recollection and reminiscences. Have you ever heard Frances Clarke Sayers speak of Anne Carroll Moore? It also can be done by the written word—by reading. An example of the oral tradition is the series of reminiscences of library pioneers which have been presented on the American Library History Round Table programs.

If you were fortunate, you heard David Mearns at the Minneapolis ALA Conference in 1954, working magic with language to portray Herbert Putnam's Minneapolis years, a young male librarian so handsome that the ladies came to the library merely to gaze upon him.

Or heard Howard Haycraft recalling the Minneapolis origins of the H. W. Wilson Company, telling a story of the old founder working at his roll-top desk in sub-zero weather, "hat on head, overcoated, fur collar turned up around his ears against the piercing cold."

Or heard Bernard Van Horne's moving resurrection of Mary Frances Isom of Portland, Oregon, in which he told of a "young trainee assigned to work on Christmas Eve. Miss Isom came down to take her place, saying, 'You have a family. I have none. Go home and enjoy the holiday.'"

In 1924 the ALA commenced the series of monographs, edited by Arthur Bostwick, called American Library Pioneers. It included eight volumes, issued intermittently over a thirty-year span. Upon Bostwick's death in 1942, the editorship went to Emily Miller Danton. The series petered out in 1953 with a final volume made up of brief sketches of library pioneers.

To learn why this series had lapsed, I wrote to Mrs. Pauline J. Love, director of the ALA's publishing department, and was told that in 1955 it was "voted that the Editorial Committee would not continue actively to initiate projects for specific biographies nor seek authors to write them; that it would always be interested in good biographies of distinguished librarians, living and dead; and that when a biography was found worthy of publication it would then be added to the American Library Pioneers."

Mrs. Love went on to say that the committee's action was based on the apparent lack of interest of librarians in the series as reflected in far below average sales. "While sales figures are by no means the final word on the value of any publication to the library profession," she wrote, "the figures are indicative of the interest and use of this series and their contribution to library literature."

To which I say, No, a thousand times no. To have correlated the sales of this series with its importance to librarianship was a mistake.

Fortunately the advancement of biographical library history does not depend upon the ALA and its kiss-of-death Editorial Committee. It was furthered by Wayne Shirley and Louis Shores in their American Library History Round Table; and the idea of biographical sketches, as carried out by Emily Danton in the final volume of the ALA series, produced a score of biographies-in-miniature read at the Round Table and collected by John David Marshall in his *American Library History Reader,* published by the Shoestring Press.

Let it not be assumed from my strictures that I am an anti-organization man, that I am in favor of dissolving the American Library Association and starting over. The ALA is the bulwark behind which we are building our profession. I merely want to call for a re-evaluation of our values, of our professional ideals. We must emerge from the cellar of routines, leave the ground floor of housekeeping, climb and stretch and grow taller. Our great library giants had their feet on earth, surely, as we must have, but they had towering minds and their visions were sky-high.

Last summer I made my way upstream through the underbrush of committees and proceedings, to the Lake Itasca of the ALA, to the *annus mirabilis* of 1876, when, prompted by a Minnesotan, Thomas Hale Williams, Librarian of the Minneapolis Athenaeum, ninety men and thirteen women, led by twenty-five-year-old Melvil Dewey, met at the Centennial Exposition in Philadelphia, starting on October 4, and formed the American Library Association.

Thanks to Sarah Wallace I have a copy of T. H. Williams's letter of August 3, 1876, to John Eaton, U.S. Commissioner of Education—a most wonderful letter which should be printed in full, so full is it of common sense and idealism.

The proceedings of this four-day meeting were published in Volume I of the *Library Journal,* which for a number of years was the official journal of the ALA.

I should like to see this fateful meeting of 1876 and its proceedings made the subject of a book similar to the one by George C. Utley on an earlier librarians' conference, at Providence in 1853, published, I am glad to note, by the ALA. It would include "Saint Melvil's" ringing editorial "The Profession," which concluded:

> It is in the interest of the modern library, and of those desiring to make its influence wider and greater, that this journal has been established. Its founders have an intense faith in the future of our libraries, and believe that if the best methods can be applied by the best librarians, the public may soon be brought to recognize our claim that the free library ranks with the free school. We hold that there is no work reaching farther in its influence and deserving more honor than the work which a competent and earnest librarian can do for his community.
>
> The time *was* when a library was very like a museum, and a librarian was a mouser among musty books, and visitors looked with curious eyes at ancient tomes and manuscripts. The time *is* when a library is a school, and the librarian is in the highest sense a teacher, and the visitor is a reader among the books as a workman among his tools. Will any man deny to the high calling of such a librarianship the title of profession?

I hardly need tell Minnesotans that in a double sense they *are* up near the source. The river rises north northwest. The great flow of power and glory that made *Huck Finn* and Faulkner and one of the *Four Quartets* begins in Minnesota.

As for Minnesota librarians who were truly great, what a roll call there can be! Herbert Putnam, James K. Hosmer, Gratia Countryman, Carl Vitz—the first four librarians of the Minneapolis Public Library, who all became presidents of the ALA.

I remember University Librarian Frank K. Walter, one of the wisest (and as I can testify to from once having sat next to him at a dinner meeting) one of the sweetest men who ever lived.

I recall H. W. Wilson—along with Leypoldt and Bowker and Frederick Melcher—one of the non-librarians who, by all that he did to make librarians more useful, took his place among our saints of library service. How fitting that his successor as president of the company, Howard Haycraft, is another Minnesotan.

Some of the best librarians of our time have come to us from other disciplines, as indeed they did in the past, and have become eloquent spokesmen for us. From History came Stanley Pargellis. Here is what he said at a Library History Round Table:

> No young doctor, reading the lives of the great doctors who are gone, but can take inspiration from the quality of their devotion and the play of their imaginations. In the same way librarians can take inspiration from the lives and achievements of the great librarians of the past and from their concepts of the purposes of libraries. We talk wistfully of librarianship as a profession. Any profession must have a kind of code of its own . . . a sense of the significance of the profession which does not change as it is handed down from generation to generation.

We must pilgrimage repeatedly to where we have been tonight, *up near the source;* we must link up with our founders in the great chain of our profession, and feel the shock of recognition that runs back and forth along the chain.

Building, with Books

MY TITLE DEMONSTRATES the importance of punctuation, of the little mark called the comma. Unpunctuated, it would seem to herald an inspirational talk on the building of character in the educational process by means of books. I was shocked by another variant, which read *Building on Books,* giving the imagination a picture of a structure reared on a foundation of old folio volumes.

What I really meant is *Building comma with Books*—that a library building without books is no library. I'm not being merely rhetorical. There are some modern libraries which are *Buildings comma without Books.* The donors were satisfied with outward appearances, in the way that some Hollywood beauties present the façade of a fine figure with neither mind nor character in back.

This is no time or place to question the generosity of Andrew Carnegie and his gift of more than two thousand library buildings throughout the land; and yet too many towns have been content with their library building and failed to fill it with good books.

Out in the Southwest the words over the door, "Carnegie Free

Dedication address, Hunt Library, Carnegie Institute of Technology, Pittsburgh, 1961.

54

Library," are sometimes taken literally. In Las Vegas, New Mexico, a trustee of the Carnegie Library told me that their chief difficulty is in getting the Spanish Americans to return the books they borrow, for they believe the word "free" to mean what it says.

I grew up in South Pasadena, California, in a library building given by Andrew Carnegie, and into which the librarian, Nellie Keith, kept pouring books till it overflowed. I have reason to revere the great Scotsman's memory.

I have been in libraries throughout the world which had more books than building. I remember the Fifth Air Force Library at Washington Heights in Tokyo, jam-packed into a quonset hut. After long absence from Paris, I returned to my favorite eating place, the Café Restaurant Voltaire in the Place de l'Odéon, and found it turned into the U.S.I.S. library, teeming with hungry readers. I have seen a mud-coated bookmobile in northwestern New Mexico pull up before a school of Spanish American and Indian children, and a small stampede ensue.

And there can be a library without *any* kind of building. I am thinking of the Winifred Martin Memorial Library of Brookville, Kansas, whose sole staff member and trustee is its founder, Mr. Lynn Martin. Let me read from his prospectus:

> Our books-by-mail program is quite like rum mincemeat; the experience of it even more exciting than its promise.
>
> The library is named for a Kansas village high school teacher who talked book-reading all her life; at her death in 1958 it was decided to extend her influence.
>
> Fifty books about the West were ordered from university and regional presses. These were mailed to selected readers, with the question, "Who else, anywhere in the United States might like to read this book?"
>
> A suggested new reader for the library's books-by-mail service is still the best gift a patron can offer us. There are no charges of any kind: no fees, no dues, no fines. References are not required and money is never begged. The library pays the postage one way and a library materials label enclosed with every book permits its return for approximately 5 cents.
>
> The ideal reader is one living on a farm, or on a ranch, or in a

mining camp, or in a small town, or in an isolated area, or one who is shut in from unfortunate causes. Readers who have little normal access to usual public libraries, or who shun the folderol of Application Blanks, Replacement Guarantees, and all Administrative Protocol, are the cream of our patronage.

The Martin Library now has a thousand volumes in circulation. It will not refuse gifts of good books.

When the conjunction occurs of fine building, good books, and librarians who are able and willing then is the closest I've come to heaven on earth. Caesar's architect, Vitruvius, as paraphrased by an Elizabethan, said a building must have commodity, firmness, and delight; or, in today's English, utility, stability, and beauty. The best library has all three, plus books and people, to give it mind and heart, to animate it.

I will not have much more to say about library buildings. Thanks to your donors and planners and builders: to Mr. and Mrs. Roy Arthur Hunt, to President J. L. Warner, to Librarian Kenneth Fagerhaugh and his staff, and to architects Lawrie and Green, Deeter and Ritchie, and contractor George Fuller and Company, you have here a library building in which the necessary elements, from Vitruvius to our time, are wedded.

I might comment on the metallic trinity represented here today: Carnegie *steel*, Hunt *aluminum*, and Clark *copper*, for I come from a memorial library built with that somber metal from Montana and Arizona.

More precious than all, however, is the *gold* of books about which I shall talk now. Whose books? Native daughter Gertrude Stein's? No, for I do not talk about books I have not read. Or should I say, Cannot read? The books of native son Robinson Jeffers? Yes, for I have been reading them with pleasure and profit ever since my college days. Jeffers was born in Sewickley; his father was president of Western Theological Seminary. Jeffers was educated in Europe and California, and for most of his life he lived on the Pacific Coast at Carmel. He also took a forestry course at the University of Washington, and his poetry abounds in precise botanical observations.

When writing my dissertation on Jeffers, as a student at

Dijon in Burgundy, I was aroused by a statement made by the late Henry Seidel Canby in an editorial in the *Saturday Review of Literature*, which said that one of the troubles with modern American poets was that they didn't know one flower from another.

My reply was an article on Jeffers' knowledge of botany as revealed in his poetry. Dr. Canby did not publish it. I enumerated many wild flowers, flowering vines, and bushes which Jeffers described, including yellow and lavender sand verbena, blue beach aster, wild lilac, maidenhair fern, sage, lupin, poppy, purple iris, brown and ruby lichen, thistle, blackberry, saw grass, water cress, bitter sorrel, coltsfoot, wake-robin, yellow violet, Solomon's-seal, bronze bells, satin bell, golden broom, deerweed, white globe tulip, flag flower, Indian paintbrush, and the golden baeria of Point Joe.

There are other bonds between Pittsburgh and the West which I have encountered in my literary ramblings. I am thinking of Haniel Long, who taught English at Carnegie Tech from 1909 to 1929. He retired then to Santa Fe, New Mexico, and founded the co-operative publishing venture called Writers' Editions.

In the twenty years Haniel Long spent on this campus, he sought to understand and to write of Pittsburgh in the same earnest way he became a Southwestern spokesman in his last incarnation. His book *Pittsburgh Memoranda*, in the form of a Whitmanesque prose poem, is an illuminating vision of this city.

Thomas Wood Stevens, the founder of Carnegie's School of Dramatic Arts, was another Pittsburgher who emigrated to the Southwest. As the papers of Haniel Long found their last repository at UCLA, so have the Stevens papers been preserved in the University of Arizona Library, in Tucson, where Stevens spent his final years; and there they have recently been catalogued and made available for scholarly use.

Still another example of the fertile interchange between Pittsburgh and the West is that of Porter Garnett, the San Franciscan who founded the Laboratory Press. Its revival as the New Laboratory Press, directed by Jack Werner Stauffacher from San Mateo, California, is promising.

With all respect to other leading technological institutes, in Massachusetts, Georgia, Illinois, and California, none of them has surpassed Carnegie's record in the creative arts.

I shall speak now of a creative art, of which today's celebration is the fruit—the reason why there is a new library, a building with books, and why I am here to speak in honor of the occasion. I mean the art of book collecting, in which Rachel McMasters Miller Hunt has excelled. It is an art which few women have mastered. Perhaps the reason for this is that to collect books in a creative and lasting way, as done by Morgan, Brown, Huntington, Clements, Clark, Folger, Lilly, and Barrett, for example, calls for determination and persistence, wedded to knowledge and taste. No one disputes women possessing the latter; men are more usually noted for the former. All must be present before one has a great book collector. And let us not overlook the role of sympathy and encouragement and understanding played by Mr. Hunt. Books and boys are the fruit of this marriage.

I heard of Rachel Hunt and her collection long before I met her. Certain names and fields are associated in the book world. Folger and Shakespeare, Huntington and Renaissance literature, Clements and Carter Brown and American History, Clark and Dryden, Morgan and Illuminated Manuscripts, Waller Barrett and American Literature, Hunt and Horticulture.

Then I received a letter from Mrs. Hunt, written spontaneously after she had read one of my books, which led to friendship and my being here today—and all because of our mutual interest in the art of book collecting. She ended it as follows: "Forgive such a long letter from a stranger—no, not that, for there are no strangers when it comes to book-lovers."

I am a bookman, yes; and, if not actually a botanist or a collector of horticultural books, I have in my veins, because of my family heritage, some sap blended into the blood stream which orients me toward botany. My Grandfather Powell was a developer of the New York State Agricultural Extension

Service. My father took his Master of Science degree at Cornell in 1895 under Liberty Hyde Bailey, was in the Bureau of Plant Industry of the United States Department of Agriculture and, because of his field work in California on the blue mold and the prevention of decay in citrus fruit caused by it, was made general manager of the Sunkist co-operative.

In my orange-grove boyhood, I trudged miles after my father, as he led Professor Bailey and David A. Fairchild down the long rows of dark green trees. My eldest brother went off to South Africa as a young horticulturist to help develop the citrus industry down there. And my mother, also a Cornell graduate, taught me to know and to love all green and growing things, as well as the wedding of nature and design in landscape architecture. I love parks and fountains, neither of which distinguishes the American Southwest, where nature has done pretty well by herself—I mean the Grand Canyon.

It was not until I was a student in Europe that I came to appreciate the humanizing of nature. The aqueducts and the fountains of Rome. The parks and public gardens of Italy and France. And the work of Lenôtre, France's great landscape architect. In Dijon, the public park was designed by Lenôtre in the seventeenth century. I loved to bicycle and to walk its leafy ways, and rest awhile on a bench by the river. Years later, reading Henry James's *A Little Tour in France*, I came with delight upon his closing paragraph, which told me that nothing had changed in the years between his going and my coming:

> I think the thing that pleased me best at Dijon was the little old Parc, a charming public garden, about a mile from the town, to which I walked by a long, straight autumnal avenue. It is a *jardin français* of the last century—a dear old place, with little blue-green perspectives and alleys and *ronds-points*, in which everything balances. I went there late in the afternoon, without meeting a creature, though I had hoped I should meet the President de Brosses. At the end of it was a little river that looked like a canal, and on the further bank was an old-fashioned villa, close to the water, with a little French garden of its own. On the hither side was a bench, on which I seated myself, lingering a good while; for this was just

the sort of place I like. It was the furthermost point of my little tour. I thought that over, as I sat there, on the eve of taking the express to Paris; and as the light faded in the Parc the vision of some of the things I had enjoyed became more distinct.

So it is a deep appreciation I bring to Rachel Hunt's accomplishment in uniting botany and books. My reading tastes in this field are literary rather than scientific, run to Thoreau rather than to Linnaeus. I like to be outdoors amidst growing things with a book in my pocket, to loaf amid leaves, flowers, and grasses, and read. Sometimes scientific botanical descriptions are a kind of free verse. Once I found myself reading aloud the following; and it sounded more truly poetical than most of what passes today for poetry:

> Slender, branching, submerged,
> Fresh-water annual herbs,
> The branches forming either open and diffuse
> Leaves linear, usually spiny-toothed,
> Apparently opposite but each pair consisting of a
> Lower leaf and an upper leaf
> On opposite sides of the stem,
> Or leaves seemingly whorled
> Or appearing fascicled
> Because many are crowded in the axils.
> Leaf bases dilated, forming conspicuous sheaths,
> The shoulders of these truncate,
> Obliquely rounded, or drawn out
> Into auricles of various lengths,
> A pair of minute, hyaline, cellular scales
> Often present within the sheath.
> Flowers monoecious or dioecious,
> Usually solitary in the leaf-sheath axils,
> But sometimes several together.
> Staminate flowers consisting of a single stamen
> Usually enclosed by a perianth-like envelope
> Ending above the anther in two thickened lips.
> The anthers one- or four-celled,
> At first nearly sessile but becoming
> Short-stalked at maturity.

Pistillate flowers naked,
Consisting of a single ovary,
Tapering into a short style
Bearing two-four linear stigmas.
Fruit a nutlet,
Enclosed in a loose and separable
Membranous coat.

I need not tell the botanists that the foregoing is a description of Najadacae, of the Water Nymph family, taken from *A Flora of the Marshes of California* by Herbert L. Mason.

The art of book collecting does not end with the assembling of a collection, and then leaving its future to chance. Dispersal of a collection by sale or auction, or giving it away piecemeal, is not unfortunate if it is a heterogeneous lot of rarities and high spots, for such collections have no real coherence or meaning or usefulness to scholarship and posterity. Such a collection was A. Edward Newton's, and its dispersal at auction in 1941 benefited individual and institutional collectors who wanted examples of this or that in various fields.

It is a joy to round out this tribute to Rachel Hunt as the perfect book collector by praising the wise provision she has made for the housing, staffing, and development of her collection. Extremely important, in my opinion, is the collection's affiliation with an established and respected seat of learning such as the Carnegie Institute of Technology. I could go around the country (but won't) and point out examples of collections which were established separately and in isolation from educational centers and which, again in my opinion, have correspondingly reduced usefulness.

Thus we see the elements which constitute the art of book collecting: knowledge, taste, determination, persistence, generosity, social altruism, and forethought for the preservation, the development, and the usefulness of the collection.

Now the responsibility for the Hunt Collection is in the hands of Carnegie Tech, of Director George Lawrence and his staff, and the advisory committee, which includes, I am pleased and proud to note, my UCLA colleague Professor Mildred Mathias.

Librarians with the competence to serve in such special collections as the Hunt are in short supply. There is, I am glad to observe, a new awareness of the need. Library schools are now making an effort to teach librarians the importance of the three *h*'s.

What are they? First, *head.* A good librarian knows, has knowledge, an inquiring mind. Second, *hands.* A good librarian can handle books, strongly, surely, delicately. Is even a binder. Third, *heart.* A good librarian feels loving toward people, is motivated to serve others, is a yea-sayer.

By these definitions, plus the initial of her name, Rachel Hunt is truly a 4-H librarian.

Part II

BOOK COLLECTORS AND READERS

John Fiske—Bookman

JOHN FISKE WAS A BOOKMAN during most of his fifty-nine years. The only exceptions are those of his infancy. By the time he was in preparatory school he owned several hundred carefully chosen books. Later he served as Assistant Librarian of Harvard College, in charge of thousands of volumes. He wrote a score of books of his own. At the end of his life he left a private library of 7,500 volumes. He loved books both for their content and their format. His career is one with the books he collected, loved, worked with, and created.

In this essay I propose to make a bibliographical excursion through Fiske's life; to note the first evidences of his bibliophilism; to report his adventures with books, his collecting habits, his experience as librarian, the use he made of libraries in the writing of his own works; and finally to examine the collection which he formed during fifty years of collecting and which, since 1926, has been a part of the Library of the University of California at Los Angeles. About Fiske as historian and philosopher I shall have little to say; about him as bibliophile, much.

John Fiske was born at Hartford, Connecticut, on March 30,

1842, the only child of Edmund Brewster Green, a Whig newspaperman of Philadelphia Quaker stock, and Mary Fisk Bound of Middletown, Connecticut. Theirs was not a happy marriage. When the lad was only eight years old his father joined the gold rush; en route he stopped off in Panama and founded the Panama *Herald*. There he died of cholera two years later. In the meantime the mother was earning a living by teaching school in New York. From the time he was four years old the boy had lived with his maternal grandparents in Middletown and when, in 1855, three years after her husband's death, his mother married Edwin W. Stoughton of New York, the grandparents bribed the child to take the name of his great-grandfather, John Fisk.[1] The change was legalized by an act of the state legislature. Five years later, in his first year at Harvard, through a clerical error, a final *e* was added to his name in the college catalogue. Instead of objecting to the error, John "thought it looked better and more finished." [2] Thenceforth he was "John Fiske."

Books were an essential part of the furnishings in the Middletown home. If there had not been any, doubtless the boy would have introduced them. It took no conditioning to make him a bibliophile; he was born one. No one had to teach him to read; he taught himself. Thereafter his educational progress was almost incredibly precocious.

At seven he was reading Caesar, and had read Rollin, Josephus, and Goldsmith's *Greece*. Before he was eight he had read the whole of Shakespeare, and a good deal of Milton, Bunyan, and Pope. He began Greek at nine. By eleven he had read Gibbon, Robertson, and Prescott, and most of Froissart, and at the same time wrote from memory a chronological table from B.C. 1000 to A.D. 1820, filling a quarto blank book of sixty pages. During the next two years he read the whole of Virgil, Horace, Tacitus, Sallust, and Suetonius, and much of Livy, Cicero, Ovid, Catullus, and Juvenal. At the same time he had gone

---

[1] *Letters of John Fiske,* edited by his daughter, Ethel F. Fisk (New York, Macmillan, 1940), p. 7.
[2] *Letters,* p. 50.

through Euclid, plane and spherical trigonometry, surveying and navigation, and analytic geometry, and was well on into differential calculus. At fifteen he could read Plato and Herodotus at sight, and was beginning German. Within the next year he was keeping his diary in Spanish, and was reading French, Italian, and Portuguese. He began Hebrew at seventeen and took up Sanskrit the following year.[3]

This remarkable passion for acquiring knowledge was accompanied by an equally ardent desire to own books. These came by gift and by purchase. He sold a pair of skates in order to buy a copy of Euclid. A note written in his copy of Liddell and Scott's *Greek-English Lexicon* tells how he acquired the volume when he was twelve years old:

> By the beginning of 1854 I had read most of the Collectanea Graeca Majora with the aid of Schrevelius' Lexicon in which the meaning of the Greek words was given in Latin. This I found very inconvenient and I longed for a good Greek-English dictionary; but my grandmother thought five dollars a great sum for so unpractical a luxury as Greek. I then began to earn money. Among other things I learned that an Irishman, named Hennessey, would buy old bones at 37 cents a barrel. I picked up bones here and there until I had got five barrels which brought me $1.85. In other ways I raised my fund till it amounted to $3.40, when my grandmother, seeing my determination, suddenly furnished the remainder of the $5.00 and in June 1854 I became the jubilant possessor of this noble dictionary, which I have ever prized most highly, as I count the knowledge of Greek one of my most spiritual possessions.

When he was thirteen Fiske entered Betts's Academy in Stamford. There he found that his own library of 116 volumes was larger than that of the Academy! Books were more important to him than clothes: "If you will bring me Anthon's Xenophon's Anabasis $1.25," he wrote to his mother, "I will value it more than the broadcloth suit." [4] He developed early an appreciation of bindings. When writing home for books to

[3] Edwin D. Mead, "John Fiske, a Sketch of his Life and Work," *Christian Register*, LXV (April 15, 1886), 228–29.
[4] *Letters*, p. 5.

be sent to him, in addition to giving the titles, he would describe the volumes as "bound in black cloth with morocco back," "in blue muslin," "in yellow leather," "in green muslin, with red morocco back." [5] In 1858 on a visit to the Yale library he was moved to ecstasy by an edition of the Latin classics "bound in rich red Turkey morocco and loaded with gilt."

His unorthodox philosophy was revealed early in his choice of books. By the time he was eighteen and ready to enter Harvard he had given up going to the Middletown Congregational Church. Thereupon the minister came to see his grandmother, to get some light on the cause of his "backsliding." The grandmother stoutly declared that the boy could not be an infidel, and for proof took the minister in to see John's library. In a letter to his mother the youth told what happened: "There Taylor found, side by side with books of sound orthodoxy, many ancient classics and the works of Humboldt, Voltaire, Lewes, Fichte, Schlegel, Buckle, Cuvier, La Place, Milne, Edwards, De Quincey, Theodore Parker, Strauss, Comte, Grote, Gibbon, and John Stuart Mill. Grandma asked him what he thought of them, but his only response was to shake his head." [6]

By the time Fiske entered Harvard as a sophomore, in 1860, his library numbered 266 volumes. When one of the older students called on Fiske to see his books he wrote to his mother:

> I never was more struck with the character of my library than when, after looking awhile in silence, McCarthy exclaimed: "You're hell-bound I see!" I laughed like thunder; the upshot was that I went to walk with him and on our return went in and took a look at his books. By that time I knew about what he was. He has Carlyle, Emerson, Grote, and Demosthenes—that is pretty much all his library. . . . He is very poor and cooks his meals on a portable stove, cost $1.25. His housekeeping costs only $2.00 per week. . . . A good way to live I think. I have a mind to try it, and if I like it to stick to it and save $104 a year for books.[7]

[5] *Ibid.*, p. 9.
[6] *Ibid.*, p. 31.
[7] *Letters*, p. 41.

Fiske soon became a bookshop and library frequenter. While browsing in Ticknor and Fields's Old Corner Book Store he came upon the original prospectus of Herbert Spencer's system of philosophy, together with the announcement of that author's plan to issue by subscription a series of his positivist works. The cost was $2.50 per year. His subscription marked one of the most decisive acts of Fiske's life.

In Little, Brown's bookstore he observed a literary curiosity —the complete works of Voltaire in a single volume of 6,000 pages, "a horrid looking book." Letters to his mother contained frequent references to his purchases, with emphasis upon the bargains he had made. Mrs. Stoughton was not entirely in sympathy with her son's bibliomania. Coming upon one of Quaritch's catalogues, he ordered through Sever, the Harvard bookseller of that day, the following titles: Donaldson's *Varronianus* and his Greek grammar, Wilson's Sanskrit grammar, Bleek's Persian grammar, Stewart's Arabic grammar, Mill's *Logic,* Van Bohlen's *Genesis,* and Saint-Hilaire's *Histoire des Anomalies de l'Organisation.* When the bill came it amounted to $45—and his mother gave him a severe chiding for what she thought was a wholly needless purchase. Fiske patiently and dutifully pointed out how essential the books were to the line of thought he was pursuing and the help they would be in giving him enlarged views in his college studies. But for months afterwards he practiced little economies, in order that "money might be saved towards that dreadful book-bill."

With his best friend and roommate, George Litch Roberts (1836–1929), he visited the public and private libraries of Boston and Cambridge. From the venerable George Ticknor, Fiske received permission, "since I was an earnest scholar," to come to his library whenever he chose and borrow any book. Nor did he neglect the treasures of the college library. "I went into the Harvard Library the other day," he wrote, "and there was a whole alcove full of Asiatic books: Sanskrit, Persian, Prakrit, Arabic, Turkish, and all sorts . . . and so many other books that I was driven nearly wild by the sight of them. . . . Dr.

Sibley, the genial old librarian, is very obliging—gave me the key to the case where these books were and let me overhaul them." [8]

It was natural that a lad of eighteen as precocious and learned as Fiske would be set somewhat apart from his fellows. He complained that hard study was considered disgraceful and that the normal course was to do just enough to get by. Even at Betts's Academy Fiske had been distinguished by his reluctance to take the usual morning and afternoon recesses for exercise; and when his tutor insisted that he stop studying and go out on the playground with his fellows, the boy would don his overcoat and stand out of the wind in a sheltered spot.[9] His being different, however, gave Fiske no concern; in fact it pleased and amused him, as revealed in this excerpt from a letter written during his first year at Harvard:

> The other day when reading over his Whateley's Rhetoric, a fellow called out to me, "Fiske, what the devil is an enthymeme?" "Why," said I, "it is a syllogism with the major premise suppressed." "Well what in hell is a syllogism?" was the hyperastonished reply. Great Zeus I thought I should split. There's a specimen of Harvard scholarship! One of the fellows again exclaimed, "Fiske I don't see what the deuce you ever came to college for, you must have been through the whole course before you came." At Harvard a good recitation is called a "squirt," and some of the fellows have undertaken to call me Squirty. . . . Vague rumors are circulating to the effect that I can speak 17, 25 or 40 languages, while others swear that I know all about medicine and have "even read such stuff for the fun of it." Nevertheless they all seem to like me tolerably well.[10]

Fiske had a normal capacity of reverence for his superiors. For example, after a visit to Emerson, he wrote to his mother: "I have never before seen a man whose works had made him immortal, and I listened to him as to an oracle. I thought him the greatest man I ever saw. . . . Of all the men I ever saw, none

[8] *Letters*, pp. 41–42.
[9] F. W. Osborne, "John Fiske as a School Boy," *Education* (Dec. 1901), 206–08.
[10] *Letters*, p. 55.

can be compared with him for depth, for scholarship, and for attractiveness." [11]

Harvard in the early 1860s was reacting strenuously to the Darwinian heresy. The authorities were on the side of orthodoxy, and Fiske earned himself a public admonishment for reading Comte during Sunday service in Christ Church. The anti-Darwinians, led by President Felton, urged a more severe punishment, while Professors Gurney and Peabody defended the sinner. The outraged president wrote to Fiske's mother: "We never attempt to control the religious opinions of young men. But I consider it a great and lamentable misfortune to a young man, when, in the conceit of superior wisdom, he openly avows himself an infidel." And he added, "Any attempt to spread the mischievous opinions which he fancies he has established in his own mind will require his removal." [12]

Fiske's reaction to this state of affairs was not that of Shelley at Oxford; he did not pen a pamphlet on the necessity for atheism. Instead he busied himself with his private studies, collected books, and enjoyed his friends. When at graduation he inscribed his autobiography in the class album, no bitterness is evident; it is typically good-natured, as the last paragraph shows:

> My life has been fraught with romantic adventure, never exceeded in strangeness by any novel, but I am not at liberty to recount my adventures. Should it ever become desirable, full information may be obtained from copious autobiographical matter in my own possession. I have the unfailing hereditary mark of the Fisk family—a crooked little finger. I have a marked fondness for the study of Philology, which is likely to be my life study. My plans of life are soon told—they are to write books, supporting myself by teaching.[13]

There is today in the Fiske collection an album of photographs

[11] *Ibid.,* p. 52.

[12] S. E. Morison, *Three Centuries of Harvard* (Cambridge, Mass., Harvard Univ. Press, 1936), p. 308.

[13] Harvard University Archives. I am indebted to William A. Jackson for enabling me to obtain this and other material from the archives. Fiske's reminiscences of Harvard are found in his "Oration" in *Cambridge Fifty Years a City,* 1897, pp. 41–44.

of the Class of 1863, including the officers of government and instruction. Some bear contemporary autographs and dates of birth, and under many, Fiske, some years after graduation, wrote their names, home towns, comments, and dates of death. His own picture shows a serious freckle-faced youth, wearing oval steel-rimmed spectacles, his broad forehead framed by an aureole of bushy, curly hair, and balanced by a full lower lip —the face of a lover of good things to eat and to drink, as well as of knowledge.

It was not until six years after graduation that Fiske published his first book, although he did distinguish himself as a writer while an undergraduate. In the course of his associate editorship of the *Harvard Magazine*, during his senior year, he contributed such articles as "Ye Vital Principle," "A Very Old Tale," "Diatribe on Archbishop Whateley," "The Life and Teachings of Gotama Buddha," and "Colonial Rights, Ancient and Modern." [14] He also wrote the class supper ode. His most remarkable accomplishments, however, were two scholarly essays written and published during his first and last years. The first was a review of Buckle's *History of Civilization in England*, 1857–1861, called "Fallacies of Buckle's History," which appeared in the *National Quarterly Review* for December, 1861. The other was a philological review of three books, by Müller, Renan, and Spencer, called "The Evolution of Language"; this appeared in the *North American Review* for October, 1863. In 1939 copies of these two essays, bound and interleaved with manuscript corrections by Fiske, and bearing the autograph of his friend George L. Roberts, came on the market and were added to the Fiske collection in Los Angeles.

Upon graduation Fiske was unable to secure a tutorship at Harvard, or even a teaching position in a high school. His avowed agnosticism had made him suspect in the quarters where such appointments originated. All through his college course his mother, and stepfather, who was one of the leading patent lawyers of New York, had urged him to the study and practice

[14] The contributions are anonymous; in his copy Fiske signed those which he wrote. Vol. IX, 1862–63.

of law. Now he was inclined to take their advice. Accordingly he entered Harvard Law School, and in the summer of 1864 was admitted to the Boston bar.

He duly hung out his shingle, but his heart was never in it. The whole tenor of his thought was centering around the evolutionary philosophy. The two articles which he had published had attracted wide and favorable attention. Within a year he reluctantly disapointed his parents and abandoned law for free-lance writing and reviewing. He was now married and blessed with a daughter. A few years later, when their first boy was born, Fiske's preoccupation was reminiscent of Mozart's, who had composed one of his most heavenly string quartets while in the next room his wife was laboriously giving birth to a child. Fiske wrote to his mother: "Our little boy was born at 10 o'clock. He roars and kicks tremendously, and seems to be in every way healthy and vigorous. I was reading Büchner when the youngster arrived; but you see I didn't expect him to come before the middle of the afternoon." [15]

Fiske's first book was a piece of polemical criticism, which today is almost forgotten. In 1868 the noted biograper James Parton, who was a crank on diet, smoking, and drinking, published a temperance tract entitled *Smoking and Drinking*.[16] Fiske was commissioned to write a review of it for the New York *World*. In a subsequent gust of enthusiasm he expanded this into a 162-page book called *Tobacco and Alcohol. I. It Does Pay to Smoke. II. The Coming Man Will Drink Wine*.[17] Fiske had given much attention to the effect of narcotics upon the human body, and he thought the great importance of temperance could be more convincingly shown through a popular scientific presentation of the laws of physiological action in regard to the two narcotics than through the heated assertions of ignorant social reformers. Accordingly he trained the big guns of scholarship on Parton's little book, and so completely blasted it that no rejoinder was attempted. This was a bit of a disappoint-

[15] *Letters,* p. 162.
[16] Boston, Ticknor & Fields, 1868.
[17] New York, Leypoldt & Holt, 1869.

ment to Fiske, for, as he wrote to his mother, "I should have enjoyed nothing better than the job of sitting down and demolishing any answer which he might have written. In the language of the poet I might have warned him, 'Don't you believe there's no more fat. Lots in the kitchen, as good as that.' " [18]

Fiske's book was a complete success; it sold several thousand copies and elicited many tributes from the medical profession. Although at the time Fiske was gratified by his victory over Parton, twenty years later he refused to allow Harper to reprint the book.

These were some of the prime years of Fiske's life. "I live in my library, walled with books, like a mollusc in his shell," he wrote to Herbert Spencer, "writing six hours, reading six, and sleeping nine, all days except Sunday; always well, and hardly ever more than pleasantly weary; and have reason, therefore, to believe that I am seeing my best days." [19]

Harvard meanwhile had trimmed its sails to the new winds of science. Under the newly appointed President, Charles W. Eliot, a series of public lectures on philosophy was inaugurated. Emerson was the first lecturer. Then Fiske, who only eight years before had been threatened with dismissal if caught talking Comteism with anyone, was invited to expound Comteism to the College. From 1869 to 1872 he served as lecturer in philosophy, then as acting professor of history. Though championed by Eliot, there was bitter opposition to Fiske from the reactionary members of the Board of Overseers. He was never able to obtain an appointment as regular professor of history. The blame for this has been laid entirely to Fiske's advanced ideas. Another interpretation is advanced by Professor S. E. Morison, in a letter to the present writer, to the effect that what were said to be Fiske's unpunctual habits, irregular hours, and fondness for Bohemian ways unfitted him in the eyes of the administration for an appointment which demanded first of all regular and comforming habits. This information came to Professor Morison

[18] *Letters*, pp. 182–83.
[19] *Ibid.*, p. 176.

from Ellery Channing (1818–1901), who maintained that it was the reason why Fiske never obtained from Harvard a teaching position commensurate with his ability as a philosopher and historian. According to W. R. Thayer, Fiske's relations with Harvard always remained desultory because he did not have the temperament to work ploddingly, nor to serve the fixed hours for exercises that have to be observed in an institution whose primary object is teaching.[20] In short, we may conclude that John Fiske was simply not the collegiate type as it existed in the latter part of the nineteenth century. He was more what someone has called Balzac, "a force of nature."

As a sort of consolation prize Fiske was given the position of Assistant Librarian, which had been left vacant by the resignation of Ezra Abbot. The idea was given to President Eliot by Fiske's stanch friend, Professor Gurney. It was hoped thus to pave the way for his advancement to a professorship. In May, 1872, Fiske received the library appointment at a salary of $2,500; the action was concurred in by the Board of Overseers, with one dissenting voice.

The Head Librarian, John Langdon Sibley, who had been cordial to Fiske as an undergraduate, was feeling the weight of his sixty-eight years, and the position of Assistant Librarian was virtually equal to that of Acting Librarian. Fiske held the post for six years. It was not the sinecure most writers on Fiske have called it. Although George Parker Winship states that the library tradition in his time as a graduate student was that Fiske cleared his desk of all regular official matters on Sunday forenoons, when he could work undisturbed, and for the rest of the week devoted himself to his own studies,[21] the actual evidence does not support the tradition. If Van Wyck Brooks is not altogether justified in stating that Fiske "worked wonders for the library," [22] it is true that Fiske put his talents unreservedly into the work, and accomplished as much as was possible under the circumstances.

[20] "Sketch of John Fiske's Life," *Harvard Graduates Magazine,* X, 33–38.
[21] Letter to the present writer, December 14, 1940.
[22] *New England: Indian Summer,* p. 263.

Let us examine the record. In 1872 the Harvard Library numbered 160,000 bound volumes, and was housed in Gore Hall. As Assistant Librarian, Fiske was in charge of the technical processes of ordering and cataloguing. In 1861 Ezra Abbot had commenced the first card catalogue, containing author, title, and subject entries, and at the time of Fiske's succession the project was still far short of completion. Upon assuming his duties in October, 1872, Fiske evolved plans to hasten the catalogue to a finish. These included hiring an extra corps of clerical workers to augment the present staff of ten girls. Before this could be realized a cruel blow fell. The great Boston fire of November, 1872, cost Harvard over $500,000 of assets. It seemed at first necessary to cut salaries, and Fiske was resigned to losing $500 of his. Although this was avoided, the library was forced to trim $3,000 from its budget. This made it not only impossible to hire more girls, but obliged Fiske to dismiss three of his regulars. "It has been a black day with me," he wrote to his mother. "I don't know what to do. The poor library girls get scanty pay at best, and have nothing to look to but their meagre salaries. I don't know which ones to cut off; it is quite heartbreaking to think of it. I am all the more anxious to see my new reforms got under way—which will serve the college more than the salaries of two or three girls—and so, as you can imagine, I am very busy." [23]

By the following spring he had made enough progress to win the commendation of President Eliot, who, Fiske wrote to his mother, "spoke to me with enthusiasm about the system which I had introduced into the Library and the quickness with which the work is dispatched. The *quickness* is the result of the *system*. And he told me that so long as I continued to like the place, just so long would he be only too glad to keep me in it. Gurney and 'Stubby' Child say I am doing a great deal more than Ezra Abbot did, and more than is expected of me. All right; it will bear fruit in the long run; Eliot is a man who appreciates that sort of thing." [24]

23 *Letters*, p. 220.
24 *Ibid.*, pp. 220–21.

Then in the summer of 1873 a wealthy woman who had heard Fiske's earlier lectures on philosophy provided him with money to go to Europe, especially to meet Spencer. Fiske had little hope of being able to secure leave from the library; to his surprise Eliot urged him to take advantage of the opportunity, and at a meeting of the Corporation he was not only given leave of absence, but was unanimously confirmed for life in his place in the library.

In Europe Fiske made a point of visiting libraries. "They are in the dark ages compared with us as to cataloguing," he wrote home, "and the more I see of these things, the more I appreciate the greatness of what Ezra Abbot has done for Harvard Library." [25] His visits included the University and the Advocates libraries in Edinburgh, the University Library at Cambridge, the Bibliothèque Nationale, and the National Library in Florence. Each successive stop further convinced him that Ezra Abbot was the world's foremost library technician.

Back at Harvard in the fall of 1874 Fiske took up his library work with renewed zest. He added Russian and Finnish to his linguistic accomplishments so that he could catalogue works in those languages. One Sunday, for example, he packed his lunch and worked all day at the library, revising the cataloguing of 416 books and 57 pamphlets. Other days he spent in Boston, buying books for the library. To the *Atlantic Monthly* he contributed an essay called "A Librarian's Work," which remains to this day a model of lucid exposition of the necessity for minute and accurate bibliographical cataloguing, in order to reveal to scholars the treasures otherwise lost in a library the size of Harvard's. The essay was intended as an answer to those who were in the habit of congratulating Fiske on his "sinecure office." [26]

In the summer of 1876, when Gore Hall was undergoing extensive alterations and additions, Fiske was faced with the problem of shifting thousands of volumes without interrupting

[25] *Letters*, p. 255.
[26] *Atlantic Monthly*, October, 1876; reprinted in *Darwinism and other Essays*, 1879.

service. Whereas old Sibley was the acquisitive watchdog type of librarian, Fiske was primarily interested in seeing that the books in his custody were made available for use with the least possible delay. In this instance his concern was that the faculty should not be disturbed by the removal. From President Eliot he secured plenary power to carry out the plan he had devised, and on June 20 he reported,

> The book moving at College Library goes on with beautiful quiet and regularity; it begins to seem so simple that any jackass might have done it. We have carried about 19,500 volumes over to Boylston Hall, and filled all the shelf room there, and have moved some 15,000 within the Library itself, besides shifting the entire stock of nearly 200,000 pamphlets. There has been no disturbance beyond the sound of carpenters' hammers. Books have been taken from and returned to the migrating divisions without perplexity.[27]

Old Sibley was not in favor of these alterations. Because of his advancing infirmities his annual reports during the final years of his tenure were brief, and have never been printed. An ever-recurring theme in them is Sibley's strictures on Gore Hall as a library building. In the 19th report, for 1873–74, his case is eloquently stated:

> Every year's experience in Gore Hall strengthens my conviction of its unsuitableness for a library, that all attempts to make it so are worse than worthless, that all expenditure of money beyond what is absolutely necessary to provide temporarily for accessions is an evil, and that measures should be taken at once for a comfortable fireproof building, with double walls, to accommodate the hundreds of thousands of volumes which will accumulate in the course of a century, and the millions which will be gathered in two or three centuries; and which, moreover, because of its peculiar excellences, shall tempt persons to prefer this library to any other, as a depository for special collections on which they have expended

---

[27] *Letters*, p. 349. The history of Gore Hall is given in *The Library of Harvard University; descriptive and historical Notes*. 4th ed. (Cambridge, 1934), pp. 20–24; also in C. E. Walton, *The Three-Hundredth Anniversary of the Harvard College Library* (Cambridge, 1939), pp. 33–44.

money, time, and labor, and which have become to them like household gods.[28]

In addition to his work as technical supervisor, Fiske had
undertaken to catalogue the outstanding items in the collection
of 3,700 volumes bequeathed to the library by the statesman
Charles Sumner upon his death in 1874. With the aid of two
assistants Fiske performed this task. A report upon the result
was made recently by Charles K. Bolton, Ex-Librarian of the
Boston Athenaeum, which stated:

> Mr. Fiske's catalogue of the Sumner collection of books, in the
> Harvard Library, is a test of learning that few librarians are called
> to meet. It shows his familiarity with early calligraphy, with the art
> and history of printing, with binding and illustration. It covers
> also the difficulties involved in cataloguing and annotating rare
> books, and indirectly proved that Mr. Fiske loved the text as well
> as the dress. The bibliographical notes, by their discrimination,
> variety and detail, show both erudition and clarity of mind such
> as we now associate with German scholarship.[29]

Yet in spite of these technical and bibliographical successes,
Fiske found himself less and less firmly rooted in the library.
Although his salary had been raised to $3,000—the same as
Sibley's—it was not enough to support his growing family. On a
trip to Baltimore, where he received $400 for a two-week course
of lectures on philosophy at the Peabody Institute, he visited
Johns Hopkins, with the result that he was offered a teaching
position there. Fiske did not want to give up residence in
Cambridge. In common with many others who have lived there-
abouts, he regarded it as the intellectual hub of the world.

Things began to come to a head in the summer of 1877. Fiske
had his eye on the chair of Medieval History left vacant by
Henry Adams's resignation. Then to complicate matters, on
July 2 Sibley resigned. Fiske wrote to his mother of the situation:

[28] Harvard University Archives. In 1941 the University Library numbered
4,250,000 volumes.
[29] *Letters*, p. 341.

It is intended to put me into the history department at Harvard next summer when the term expires of two young instructors who were appointed for a year on Henry Adams's resignation. Meanwhile Sibley's resignation on July 2 came unexpectedly to everybody; and things being thus it occurred to Eliot that now, just as we are about to remodel things here, would be the nick of time to make a grab for one of the big Boston librarians. So it was voted at once to offer the place, first to Justin Winsor, chief librarian of Boston Public Library, and then to Cutter, chief librarian of the Boston Athenaeum. The whole move affects my present position and salary in no way, it only indicates a different line for the future. It is not very likely that either of these gentlemen will accept and Eliot does not think they will. A rumor has just come in that Winsor will accept. The city of Boston instantly raised Winsor's salary to $4,500; and probably the Athenaeum will do similarly with Cutter. Sibley holds till a successor is appointed.[30]

Winsor, who was Fiske's senior by eleven years, received the appointment. It would seem that he had little subsequent use for Fiske. The younger man is mentioned by name only twice in Winsor's annual reports. In his first report, for 1878, Winsor printed Fiske's synoptical account of the cataloguing performed from 1872 to 1878. In his report for the following year, upon listing the publication of the Sumner catalogue, Winsor gave Fiske no credit for the work, terming it merely as having been "prepared by the joint labors of several members of the library staff." And in the same report Winsor noted the resignation of Fiske, which occurred on December 31, 1878, in the rather unusual form of a tribute to his successor.

> By the resignation of Mr. Fiske the immediate charge of the catalogue work passed April 1st into the hands of Mr. Samuel Hubbard Scudder, a gentleman of experience in bibliographical work, from whose care and discernment we may expect much in the elucidation of the present card catalogue.[31]

It is difficult to avoid the conclusion that Winsor was jealous of Fiske and was glad to be rid of him. The Sumner catalogue,

[30] *Letters*, p. 366.
[31] p. 11.

which was published in 1879 by the University, bore on the title page the words "Bibliographical Contributions. Edited by Justin Winsor." Fiske's name appeared nowhere in the catalogue. He was angry at having credit for his work usurped in this way. In his copy he wrote on the title page "Catalogued by John Fiske," and on the opposite blank page:

> This catalogue of the Sumner Collection, a work involving much laborious research, was entirely made by me, with the assistance of Miss Anne Eliza Hutchins and Miss K. V. Smith, in 1876 and the early part of 1877, before Mr. Winsor came to Harvard College Library. Mr. Winsor had nothing whatever to do with it. John Fiske.

As to the events of the autumn of 1878 which precipitated Fiske's resignation, we are mostly in ignorance. On November 12 he wrote to his mother, "I am beginning to feel my usual energy and enthusiasm awakening again and I hope another year will free me from the blasted old Library which has throttled and suffocated my original work for now nearly seven years of my life. I seriously contemplate resigning." [32] This he did, a month and a half later, in a letter which he left at President Eliot's house. The details were included in a letter to his mother, who at that time was in Saint Petersburg, where her husband was the Ambassador to Russia. The letter was never received.

John Fiske now stood on the threshold of his great career as the most popular lecturer and writer on American history ever known in this country. It was chance that turned him in this direction. His avowed interest was in medieval history, and he confessed to "an extreme longing for the place which Adams left vacant." [33] In March, 1879, he opened a course of six lectures on American history at Old South Church in Boston, arranged by another patron. "This affair of American history is not strictly within my line," he confessed. "I took it up to please Mrs. Hemenway." [34] In these fateful six days the pattern of

[32] *Letters*, p. 375.
[33] *Ibid.*, p. 379.
[34] *Ibid.*

Fiske's remaining twenty-two years of life was unalterably cut. From an evolutionary philosopher, a philologist, and a bibliographer, he was changed into a historian. Let him tell it in his own words:

> This was the worst of nasty March days—pelting snow, slush up to your knees, dark as Egypt—a day when ordinarily nothing would have tempted me to leave the house; but the Old South Church was *packed full* of the very cream of Boston, in spite of the weather. I felt every pulse quickened by the fact; and they say I was so eloquent as to seem almost like a new man. The applause was great; I felt the sense of having the people drinking in every word and tone with hushed breath and keen relish. Half unconsciously I deepened and intensified my voice and began to lose myself in the theme with which I was greatly bewitched myself. I had a sort of sense that I was fascinating the people and it was delicious beyond expression. . . . This thing takes the people, you see; they understand and feel it all as they can't when I lecture on abstract things. The fame of it is going about briskly and I believe I shall get full houses all over the country. The Centennial has started it, and I have started in at the right time.[35]

It was not without regret that he entered this new and triumphant epoch of his life. "I only write about [American history] because I can and people ask me to and pay me for it. If I were worth $1,000,000 I should spend the rest of my life in studying early institutions and the growth of European society." [36] Eight months later, however, Fiske wrote, "Youmans says I am absolutely dead sure to sweep all before me after another two years, and haul in money hand over fist." [37]

This is exactly what happened. We can understand Fiske's choice when we know that he had no income apart from that earned by his lectures and writings, and that dependent upon this money were his wife and their six children. From his wealthy stepfather, who was jealous of him, Fiske never received any benefits other than his minimum college expenses.[38] The lecture

35 *Letters,* p. 378.
36 *Ibid.,* p. 379.
37 *Ibid.,* p. 427.
38 Autobiographical notes, Huntington Library manuscript.

triumphs also richly compensated Fiske's personality, which had been only meagerly rewarded by his various Harvard experiences.

His knowledge of American history came out of his library years. In the preface to his *American Revolution*, 1891, he acknowledged this as due to his having overhauled what was called the "American room" and having superintended the cataloguing of 20,000 items relating to America. "In the course of this work," he went on to say, "my attention was called more and more to sundry problems and speculations connected with the transplantation of European communities to American soil, their development under new conditions, and the effect of all this upon the general progress of civilisation."

In this same preface Fiske revealed how free he was from any grudge, by the tribute paid to Justin Winsor's work in the same field. In fact, Fiske was accustomed to call upon Winsor for recommended books, whenever he was ready to take up a new period in American history.[39] This is one of the finest traits of Fiske's character: his glad recognition of outstanding ability, even when it was possessed by one who might be called a rival. As to Winsor's opinion of Fiske as historian we have less evidence. In the *Narrative and Critical History of America* there are a dozen or more citations to Fiske's works, only one of which takes critical issue, and then only mildly.[40]

There is no doubt as to what that third Americanist, Henry Harrisse, thought of Fiske. In Harrisse's copy of the latter's *Discovery of America*, now in the Clements Library, there is a marginalium, dated July 4, 1896, at the point where Fiske asserts Harrisse's American nativity; this is worth quoting:

> Withal, at no time was it possible to find a publisher in America for any of my works; although in every instance I offered the mss. for absolutely nothing. Nay, when by dint of effort I succeeded in having them printed in Europe, they scarcely ever found purchasers in the United States; and when occasionally men-

[39] S. S. Green, *Reminiscences of John Fiske,* American Antiquarian Society, *Proceedings,* n. s., XIV, 421–28.
[40] V, 533.

tioned in American reviews, it was generally with expression of ridicule. The conduct of my countrymen towards me in that respect is shameful! And when we see the unmitigated trash which commands their admiration, I, for one, feel humiliated to an inconceivable degree! [41]

Perhaps it would have mitigated Harrisse's scorn if he had known that the copies of his books in Fiske's library had been uniformly bound in sumptuous dark red three-quarter morocco, gold-ruled, with marbled boards and end papers! All are devoid of marginalia, but it is obvious from the manner in which he had them bound that Fiske prized the books.

As his fame as a lecturer grew, Fiske's income steadily increased. Among his manuscripts in the Huntington Library is an account of his earnings and expenditures for the month of February, 1886. This is how it reads:

LECTURES

Worcester	$200.00
Lewiston	91.00
Concord	75.00
Tremont Temple	45.00
Salem	21.50
TOTAL	433.00

on this paid commission to J. W. Black of $125.00

[For lecture expenses he listed:]

Steam cars	39.40
Cabs	8.40
Hotels & restaurants	22.70
Telegrams	8.38
Advertising	14.00
Reading lamp	5.00

[41] Courtesy of Dr. Randolph G. Adams, Director of the William L. Clements Library, to whom I am also indebted for several fruitful suggestions in the writing of this paper. Harrisse was equally contemptuous of Winsor; see R. G. Adams's essay on Harrisse in his *Three Americanists* . . . 1939.

[Other expenses for the month included:]

Clothes for family	18.38
Medicine for family	14.90
Fuel	16.50
Laundry	3.51
Stationery	2.00
Postage	3.54
Allowance to boys	7.36

[And two last items:]

Books	18.41
Beer	2.30

Five years later, in 1891, Fiske was earning more than $10,000 a year.

The man who as a youth had been a tall wispy bookworm was now filled out, until in the nineties he weighed over 300 pounds. He once described his dimensions as "72 x 56 inches." This caused his friend Howells to remark that "the slender youth I had once known was incredibly lost in the vast bulk which he himself seemed to regard at times with an alien and somewhat puzzled glance." [42]

This increase in flesh did nothing to diminish Fiske's enormous capacity for work. From Alaska to Scotland he traveled, lecturing several hundred times during a season of a few months. As Van Wyck Brooks wrote, the Fiske season came to equal Barnum's as an attraction! In the intervals at home in Cambridge, Fiske would shut himself up in his library for days and nights at a time, having his meals shoved in at the door; the result each time was a new book on American history.

In addition to his own library and that of Harvard, Fiske utilized many other libraries in the writing of his books. On his tours he made it a point to examine local repositories in search of source material. For example, on days when he was to lecture at Worcester, he would go early in order to work in the Anti-quarian Society Library and the Worcester Public Library. In

[42] *Harper's Weekly*, XL, 732.

New York he toiled in the Astor Library on the portraits of Washington, and at the Lenox Library he reported finding the Emmet collection all in one room and easy to consult. "Took a cursory glance," he wrote, "and am satisfied that I have struck a gold mine." [43] In Baltimore he was given a private room in the Peabody Library, where he worked a whole day, too busy to go out to lunch, on Chapter II of *The Discovery of America*. In Chicago he examined sixteenth-century books at the Newberry Library, and dined at the home of Edward E. Ayer—a dinner which was equal in quality, he reported, to the Ayer collection of early Americana. He visited the university libraries of Cornell, Howard, Kansas, and Minnesota, and at the Minneapolis Public Library he called on his friend Herbert Putnam, whose great Library of Congress career was still ahead of him. In St. Louis he worked at the Mercantile Library on old files of Missouri newspapers. In Oregon he examined the collection of the Library Association of Portland, and from the Washington State Library in Olympia he wrote to his wife, "I am in the midst of books you see. Came around here this morning to look over some old Spanish volumes on the early history of this coast." [44]

Once when he was due to lecture in England, he wrote in advance to Henry Stevens to inquire about the Americana resources of the British Museum. Stevens's reply was characteristic of the Green Mountain Boy:

> I think you will find the Library of the British Museum a little better place for study on early American history, as well as *late*, than even Harvard College Library and the Boston Public Ditto thrown in, though it may be hard to convince any Massachusetts man of this fact, until he has seen something outside the hub and its surroundings. . . . Do pray come over here and do your work here, where roast beef, American cheese, and strong beer may be had and taken ad libitum. *The Tree of Knowledge* grows now in the centre of the Reading Room of the British Museum in a huge pot. You have only to shake it and down the ripe fruit drops. So pray take an affectionate leave of your large family, pack up your

[43] *Letters*, p. 654.
[44] *Ibid.*, p. 607.

ideas, leave your sins behind, and embark for Bloomsbury, with your American gold-pen and your Yankee energy.[45]

Fiske took this advice, and was not disappointed. Richard Garnett, the Keeper of the Reading Room, cut red tape and gave him the run of the library.

These instances of Fiske's use of libraries have been cited in order to show that he was continually on the alert for source material. He not only knew of the obvious collections of Americana, and used them, but he was accustomed on his travels to explore lesser-known libraries, on the chance of finding new materials.

There has never been a more energetic bookman in our history. How he kept going year after year on a schedule of traveling, lecturing, and writing that would exhaust even a modern college president in a short time was a source of wonder to his friends. Once when asked for his system of health, he replied:

> Always sit in a draft when I find one; wear the thinnest clothes I can find, winter and summer; catch cold once in three or four years, but not severely, and prefer to work in a cold room, 55 to 60 degrees. Work the larger part of each 24 hours, and by day or night indifferently. Scarcely ever change a word when once written; eat when hungry, rarely taste coffee or wine or smoke a cigar, but drink two or three quarts of beer each day, and smoke a pipe all the time when at work. Never experienced the disinclination for work, and, therefore, never had to force work. If I feel dull when at work, a half hour at the piano restores normal mental condition, which is one more argument for the hygienic and recuperative effects of music.[46]

Fiske's library revealed the orderly mind of its owner. He arranged it by subjects and would speak of the philosophy corner, the folklore section, the philology shelves, and so forth. When writing home for a book while he was away on a lecture tour, he would direct his wife to the very spot where it was

[45] *Letters,* p. 479. Fiske's letter to Stevens is among the Henry Stevens papers acquired by UCLA in 1963.
[46] W. R. Thayer, *op. cit.*

shelved. He kept track of his books too, and once we find him writing with polite firmness to one of his friends: "I don't want to be fussy, but have you volume four of Challamel's 'Mémoires du Peuple Français' which you were reading when last here? I merely want to keep track of it, for I think it is out of print." [47] His bookplate was a simple one; it bore "John Fiske" in Gothic lettering on a small white rectangle, with a fine black-ruled border, and in the corner a place for entering the chronological accession number. Today his books bear in addition the University of California bookplate with Fiske's name and the names of the donors.

When his mother built a house in Cambridge, which was ultimately to come to him, he drew up the specifications for the library, with minute attention to the details.[48] At the time of his death from heart failure, on the Fourth of July, 1901, Fiske was in the midst of transferring his books to this house, which stood on the corner of Brattle and Ash Streets. The library measured fifty by twenty feet. Its walls were paneled in antique oak, and its floors were of quartered oak. The windows were of leaded glass, set in diamond shape. At one side of the room was a great fireplace, with a sandstone hearth, over which was a slab bearing Fiske's motto: *Disce ut semper victurus; vive ut cras moriturus*—"Learn as if to live forever; live as if to die tomorrow." [49] Upon his death the library went to Fiske's widow, and for twenty-five years it remained in the Brattle Street house as a memorial to him.

In 1926, after the death of Mrs. Fiske, the library was purchased en bloc by a group of citizens of Southern California, inspired by Ernest Carroll Moore, and presented to the University of California at Los Angeles.[50] Earlier in the century the near-by Huntington Library had acquired Fiske's manuscripts at several

[47] *Letters*, p. 665.
[48] Huntington Library manuscript.
[49] See "John Fiske's Library," in *Cambridge Tribune*, August 3, 1901, 2:1–2.
[50] The chief donor was Seeley W. Mudd, assisted by George I. Cochran, John R. Haynes, James R. Martin, Meyer Elsasser, William L. Honnold, and Mrs. Joseph F. Sartori—most of them Regents of the University.

auction sales. At the time of the Fiske acquisition the library of the newly founded southern branch of the state university contained only 75,000 volumes.

The Fiske library included approximately 7,500 volumes, about half of which were history and biography. Philosophy and religion, linguistics and literature, geography, folklore, classics, and orientalia made up the rest. It is in the field of Fiske's dominant interest—early American history—that the library is strongest. These works, acquired for the most part during the last twenty years of Fiske's life, when he was increasingly affluent, include the rarest and most valuable items. It is, however, essentially a scholar's working library, rather than that of a collector. Fiske cared little for editions, issues, and points. Two things he liked: subject matter and leather bindings. His later purchases were nearly all bound by McNamee of Cambridge, except for very old books which he preferred to leave in their original bindings. There is a manuscript card catalogue of the library made when it was put up for sale. Fiske apparently never catalogued his books; his prodigious memory doubtless included his entire library; certainly he knew where to lay hand on each and every item.[51]

Fiske's biographer, Clark, states that a respect for books "always restrained him from marking or in any way defacing them. In his Cambridge library the volumes that were his constant companions bear only the marks of respectful usage."[52] As a conscientious librarian I can hardly refuse to endorse Clark's pious sentiment; yet on the other hand, annotations in a work by such an eminent bookman as Fiske are of the greatest interest and value. A detailed examination of the entire library brought to light four categories of marked books: presentation copies to and from Fiske; books containing sentimental inscriptions by Fiske, giving the time and place of their acquisition; books with

[51] See Howells' testimony as to Fiske's remarkable memory. This, and Fiske's kindness, are the two qualities which most impressed Howells, *op. cit.*, p. 732.
[52] J. S. Clark, *Life and Letters of John Fiske* (Boston, Houghton Mifflin Co., 1917), Vol. I, p. 28.

notes on their cost, rarity, bibliographical points; and finally—most interesting of all—works in which Fiske inscribed critical notes.

Presentation copies to Fiske include several from his friend Howells, from Darwin and Huxley, and from Wilberforce Eames. There is a copy of Fiske's *Idea of God* in Japanese, given to the author by the translator. There are presentation copies of his own works to his mother. When Fiske got what he thought was a good bargain he was not reluctant to boast of it in the book; and in rarer works he would sometimes insert descriptions from Quaritch's and other dealers' catalogues. When a book was acquired under memorable conditions—and was a bargain to boot—then Fiske was moved to such an inscription as the one that appears in a 1784 edition of Cook's *Voyages*:

> A charming memento of one of the happiest days of my life—a good bargain too. The four volumes cost me one pound sterling. This beautiful copy of Cook's voyages, in this beautiful binding, just as it is, I bought in a queer little alley at Rochester, England, April 14, 1883—the ever memorable day when I first visited Rochester, with my dear friend, James Sime, and heard entrancing music at the cathedral, and told droll yarns at the Bull Inn.

Fiske's practice in critically annotating a book was to list on blank pages at the end the points and corresponding page numbers to which he could later refer. Occasionally he would write at the head of a blank page the word "Errors," and proceed under it to list page numbers. When more strongly moved he would inscribe "fallacious" or, as in Goldwin Smith's *The United States, an Outline*, 1893, set down frequent exclamation and interrogation marks throughout the book, coming to a climax at the last paragraphs with the remark, "a devil of a summary!" Books to which he gave no credit whatsoever had their title pages annotated by Fiske. On that of Belloy's *Christopher Columbus*, 1878, he wrote in his bold copperplate hand, with customary purple ink, "a trivial unscholarly book, crowded with blunders, but likely to please the mob of readers." In Gray's *History of Oregon*, 1870, Fiske wrote, "Gray is utterly untrustworthy in all that relates to Congregationalist missions and to the Hudson Bay Company. H. H. Bancroft (*N. W. Coast*, ii, 537) calls him 'Gray, the great untruthful,' and (*Oregon*, i, 96) 'that most mendacious missionary.' He hates and vilifies Episcopalians, Englishmen, Catholics, etc. The book fairly bristles with blunders." When the President of Whitman College in Oregon sent Fiske a copy of Nixon's *How Marcus Whitman Saved Oregon*, 1895, asking him to tell the Whitman story in his own distinguished style, Fiske dealt the book summary justice on its own title page: "This book is a romance, but it is not true. It is utterly worthless."

Today in that section of the UCLA library stacks where the *E* and *F* books on American history are shelved, one can walk along the aisles and, if one has come to know the Fiske books as well as I have, can pick them out from among their myriad fellows. Often it is the red morocco bindings, the marbled boards and end papers that give them a rich uniform likeness; and other times it is merely an intangible something that proclaims them to be his books.

I feel that John Fiske would be glad if he knew that his books were sheltered under one roof, even though it be in a corner of the continent far from his beloved Cambridge.

He once wrote: "There is a kind of human presence, all too rare in this world, which is in itself a stimulus and an education worth more than all the scholastic artifices that the wit of man has devised; for in the mere contact with it one's mind is trained and widened as if by enchantment." [53] Such a presence was John Fiske, and even to this day it endures in the books which he collected and read and loved.

[53] *Cambridge Fifty Years a City*, p. 43.

The Great Doctor R.

WHEREAS THE ROSTER of good booksellers is long, that of ones who might be called great is short; and by *great* is meant possessed of imagination, erudition, and energy to the degree whereby a lasting impact is made upon society.

Abraham Simon Wolf Rosenbach (1876–1952), B.S., Ph.D., D.A.E., H.L.D., D.H.L., was a bookseller good, great—and rich; and he had a powerful effect upon antiquarian bookselling, book collecting, librarianship, and scholarship. This massive biography explains Dr. Rosenbach's greatness; and at the same time portrays him as a sybarite, mother- and brother-dominated, imperious, lusty, latterly drunken, loyal to unfortunate old friends, devoted to a mistress yet never wedding her, a lifelong member of Philadelphia's Temple Mikveh Israel, trustee and benefactor of public institutions, a man in whom contradictory elements were mixed, world-famous and ultimately pitiful, and yet of such power and fortune in his prime as to immortalize himself as the greatest bookseller of all time.

Rosenbach has enjoyed the posthumous good fortune of having his biography written by two young men who worked for him— John Fleming, as a manager of his New York office; Edwin Wolf

A Review of *Rosenbach, a Biography,* by Edwin Wolf II and John Fleming.

II, as bibliographer in the Philadelphia store—and who loved him. With the firm's records at their disposal, uninhibited by surviving family (neither Abraham nor his elder brother Philip and their sisters married), determined to tell the whole story, and above all motivated by admiration and affection, the collaborators have written a book to match their master, scholarly and unpedantic, salted with bawdy anecdotes yet in good taste, a major chronicle of Anglo-American bookselling, a handbook for bookmen wherein no secrets remain unrevealed.

A great biography requires a great subject, authorship equal to it, and a publisher who recognizes it. Instead of reducing the text to omit the titles and prices of books and manuscripts bought and sold—a procedure suggested by one publisher— William Targ, bookman-editor, encouraged the authors to expand their text, knowing such data to be essential to those who will take this book as their bible.

A great bookseller is both born and made. Dr. Rosenbach's birth into a pioneer Pennsylvania Jewish family, the strong bonds between him and his mother, sisters, and brother; being the successor of his uncle, Moses Polock, a discriminating bookseller; and the business benefits that accrued from familiarity with neighboring families such as the Elkins, Wideners, and Wolfs—these are some of the factors of heritage and environment that made Abe Rosenbach eventually a great bookseller.

He made himself into a scholar by imaginative study at the University of Pennsylvania, with a doctoral thesis on "The Influence of Spanish Literature on Elizabethan-Stuart Drama." That he became a peerless salesman of Elizabethan literature was due in part to his reading knowledge of Shakespeare and his contemporaries. Learning, love, and belief, wedded to an innate pasion for buying and selling at a profit, also accounted for Rosenbach's enormous success.

"He was so sure of himself and his belief in books," Wolf writes, "that he set up a powerful magnetic field into which everything and everyone around him was drawn. . . . There was no one who could match Dr. Rosenbach's intellectual virtuosity when he set out to ingratiate himself. His manner was effortless;

the performance flawless. He had an endless supply of biblio-anecdotes which made the volumes he handled come alive, and he had the irresistible enthusiasm of a salesman convinced that what he was selling was better than anything else on the market."

Rosenbach was not only born of the right family in the right city; he was also born at the right time, enjoying his heyday before Depression, World War II, and taxes turned American book collecting from a personal to an institutional pursuit. He came on the scene when Huntington and Folger were spending millions in the creation of their libraries. Dr. Rosenbach had the wit and will, the flair and feel for books to match their bullion. By the time he died in 1927, Henry E. Huntington had spent $4,333,610 with Rosenbach.

The Doctor's prices bore no relation to his costs. They were outrageous, and with their bargain-basement odd figures, his prices were also amusing; in the catalogue called "Monuments of Wit and Learning," he priced Louis XIV's copy of a rare account of India at $267.50. Only two things mattered: what the buyer could pay for it and would pay for it. The Rosenbach catalogue came eventually to bear the epigraph, from *Proverbs:* "It is naught, it is naught, saith the buyer, but when he is gone his way then he boasteth." The Doctor made paying through the nose such an exquisite sensation that his "patients" sought it from him again and again and again.

And yet Rosenbach was not greedy. To impecunious bibliographer friends—and all the great bookmen of his time were his friends, including Wilberforce Eames, Clarence Brigham, Randolph G. Adams, Chauncey B. Tinker, and Lawrence C. Wroth —he gave bargains.

Dr. Rosenbach survived the Depression, and although there was never again another Widener, Harkness, Huntington, Folger, or Morgan, he nevertheless encouraged the development of Lessing Rosenwald, Arthur Houghton, Louis Silver, Philip Hofer, Donald and Mary Hyde, to cite some of today's leading book collectors.

Penguinlike in walk, slothful except when books were being

bought and sold, at once arrogant and gracious, bound by blood and tradition in partnership with a brother who was interested in food, women, silver, tapestries, picture frames—in anything but books—A. S. W. Rosenbach lives fully in these pages: testifying before Congress to defeat a tariff on rare books, lunching with President Coolidge, crisscrossing the continent from Philadelphia to San Marino, carrying books to Huntington, carrying checks to Philip, drinking a bottle of whisky a day, talking bawdily to clubwomen, fishing on the Jersey shore, and rowing out with his faithful Carrie Price to salvage cases of liquor jettisoned by rumrunners, emerging in the public consciousness as the supreme authority on rare and valuable books, and receiving as a result of his articles in the *Saturday Evening Post*—ghostwritten by Avery Strakosch Denham—three hundred letters a day, offering mostly junk. Hated by some, envied by many, feared by his competitors, Dr. Rosenbach was nevertheless able to exert his charm on all, no matter what their status in society.

Perhaps the lowest people in his scale were those librarians who worked for the titans whose agent he was, one of whom kept complaining about minor imperfections in hundred-dollar items the Doctor included in million-dollar packages. The lowest person in the authors' scale is Philip, the elder brother, who took their mother's place as the dominant figure in the Doctor's life. Philip is the villain of the book, Abe's financial scourge, on whom Wolf and Fleming pass scathing judgment.

Although Dr. Rosenbach's name will be remembered longest as a dealer in manuscripts, early printing, and Elizabethan literature, his interests were as wide as the world of books. He collected Melville and Western Americana before it was popular (and costly) to do so. Uncle Mo's collection of early American children's books was enlarged by the Doctor, described in a bibliography, and given to the Philadelphia Free Library. He also published an American Jewish bibliography. Bought and never sold were such great modern manuscripts as Wilde's *Salomé,* Joyce's *Ulysses,* and Douglas's *South Wind,* all of which are treasures of the Rosenbach Foundation in Philadelphia, directed by William H. McCarthy, to which the brothers left their home and its contents.

Although university-trained, Dr. Rosenbach had small respect for academic uncertainty. The Doctor didn't equivocate when he sold a book; it was invariably "the goddamndest copy you ever saw." He possessed that quality most lacking in academicians, and which they denigrate in those who have it: enthusiasm. As early as 1903 Dr. Rosenbach wrote, "Book collectors have done more to encourage the study of English and other literature than the college professors." Exceptions were recognized in Tinker of Yale, McDonald of Drexel, and J. Q. Adams, who became the Folger's first director.

Book collecting which is carried on for more than personal pleasure and has lasting results is usually the activity of a single person who enlists others in the cause. Professional timidity and orthodox library training are incompatible with bold and imaginative collecting. Many research libraries today are headed by "mavericks": Fred Adams of Morgan, Tom Adams of Brown, Pargellis of Newberry, Hammond of Bancroft, Peckham of Clements, Wright of Folger, Wyllie of Virginia, Buck and Jackson of Harvard, Babb of Yale, Dix of Princeton, Randall of Lilly—all are librarians *sans* certificate.

Actually, some of the most dynamic of institutional collectors today are not even librarians. President Harry H. Ransom of the University of Texas is spending money on a Rosenbach scale to give his state a great research library, and is being damned by his competitors, as was Dr. Rosenbach by his, for raising prices. Combine a bookish and acquisitive academic administrator and a head librarian; then watch the books fly through the air to that institution's stacks and vaults. Before joining the Guggenheim Foundation as associate secretary, Gordon Ray, the scholar-provost of the University of Illinois, and Librarian Robert B. Downs formed such a team. At Indiana, President Herman Wells and Lilly Librarian David A. Randall have made Bloomington a synonym for books, with support from librarians Robert D. Miller and Cecil Byrd, while recently in Kansas the combination of Chancellor Franklin D. Murphy and Librarian Robert Vosper wrought a bookish renaissance in Lawrence. Now the transfer of Murphy and Vosper to UCLA has the West Coast quaking; and if Texas and UCLA meet head on, the bibliographical fallout will be fabulous.

What do all these owe to Dr. Rosenbach? "To Dr. Rosenbach, more than to any other person," the authors answer, "the rare book libraries of the United States owe, if not their books, the philosophical concept of the importance of rare books, which has been the basis of their successful growth." It was Rosenbach who showed institutional collectors how to buy boldly, imaginatively, discriminatingly, and, above all, swiftly. To entrust book collecting to a committee is the surest way *not* to collect books.

There is today a growing *rapprochement* between librarians and booksellers, and efforts are being made by the library schools to recruit people who combine social idealism with bibliographical skill and courage to act. In his present post as librarian of the venerable Library Company of Philadelphia, Edwin Wolf is enriching librarianship with all he gained as Rosenbach's bibliographer, although he too is uncertificated.

I remember the Doctor toward the end of his life, at one of those times when books, not bottles, were on the table. We were in his home in DeLancey Place, which now houses the Foundation, the two macaws screaming for attention, while elegant old Philip poured the Lapsang Souchong tea he favored. From a packed bookcase the Doctor's plump hand plucked a tiny volume. He handed it to me, with a tender smile. "Ain't it the goddamndest copy you ever saw?" he murmured.

What was it? It was the only known copy of a volume printed in 1635, containing Robert Herrick's earliest work. At that exquisite moment when time had a stop, and in the presence of that refined passion for books, nothing else mattered. This sense of certainty and belief came from the heart of the man, a heart laid bare in this great biography.

The Reader, the Book,
and Christmas

ALTHOUGH the huge packing cases that came sliding down the ramp into the basement were *not* gift-wrapped, I recognized what they were from the time of year (it was the first week in November) and the size of the shipments. This was the way a bookstore's Christmas rush began. Every year I find myself drawn back to the milieu of my 1929 debut into the book world as shipping clerk in a similar metropolitan bookstore, when I had been armed with a B.A. and, more immediately useful, a nail-puller and a pry-bar.

Now I felt a bit envious as I watched the shipping clerk go into action with the same tools, minus the degree. From the freshly opened cases came that sweet smell of mint-fresh books, the blended fragrance of paper, ink, and pinewood. I love the basement atmosphere—piles of new books, bins made of packing cases, the dusty dark corners, and the sound of feet overhead. In another two weeks the sound would rise to thunder, as the store became a maelstrom.

I asked about trends in Christmas book giving. The proprietor laughed. "The longer I'm in the trade, the less I'm sure of it," he said. "The answer is yes and no. There are and there are not trends. Tastes do and do not change. The one thing I make sure to do each fall is to include a prayer with my Christmas order."

And to prove that tastes do not change, he showed me bins of Oz books, of Beatrix Potter titles, of *Little Women, Alice in Wonderland, The Secret Garden,* of Mother Goose and the Andrew Lang fairy tales, all of which are perennial Christmas favorites. To prove that tastes do change, he then showed me bins equally full of the brilliant lithographic books on horses, dogs, and cats, of travel and how-to-do-it books—all with one common factor: they were big.

We went out for coffee, and I recalled a recent experience which enabled me to see in retrospect the fixed and the changing tastes in books of the past fifty years. I had been told of a large private library which I might "cream" for the university before it was sold at auction. From causes unknown to me, the family line had come to an end, and the house which had been lived in by three generations was to be emptied of its contents and removed in the clearing for a freeway.

I approached the house with rising excitement. Your book hunter is an optimist, sustained through years of disappointment by the hope of finding gold in gravel—a Poe's *Tamerlane,* the Bay Psalm Book, a first edition of *The Pilgrim's Progress;* or, in California, a Zamorano imprint, one of those rare volumes crudely printed at Monterey in the 1830s by Don Agustín Vicente Zamorano, secretary to the governor of Alta California, who brought the first handpress to the frontier.

I wandered about the ground floor, sniffing for old books in calf bindings, whose fragrance will permeate a house. The only books I found were in the billiard room. They were quite a sight, albeit a disappointing one, for they were the choices of the subscription clubs, the popular and sometimes prefab publications of the past generation, all in their original dust wrappers. No sunlight had faded their colors, and the backs of the books made a rainbow spectrum. Although as separate works many had not fared well at the hands of time, they were totally interesting as an illustration of changing tastes. They could be removed en bloc and shelved together as a special collection, perhaps even read.

But they were not what I sought. After looking vainly upstairs, I went outdoors and found the watchman drinking coffee in his kiosk. "You didn't go high enough," he said, in reply to my query. "I'll show you where they are."

He led me to a concealed staircase, rising to an attic that stretched across the entire house. There they were—books, thousands of them, ranged around the room on redwood shelves, a sight more beautiful to a bookman's eyes than all the world's Aubussons.

"This was the old man's room," the watchman said. "After his wife died, he never came downstairs except to sleep. When the young folks redecorated, they said books didn't fit in with the color scheme, so they brought them all up here. That's his chair. Spent all his time reading. Matter of fact, he died there, with a book in his lap."

"*What* book?" was my silent question.

The watchman left, and I began to inspect the shelves, using all my equipment; nose, eyes, hands, and biblio-Geiger counter. Old books, yes, but not old enough. No gilded calf, no sober sheep. Mostly twentieth-century cloth, many with flyleaf inscriptions. They had been a book-giving family, at Christmas and on birthdays, the old folks each to the other and to their children and grandchildren, within conventional limits, guided in their giving by such arbiters as the clerks in bookstores, librarians, and book reviewers.

I felt at home in the setting, for it evoked my own early environment. The backs of books speak to one in the language of memory and association. It is wise, however, not to open them and try to reread the books of one's past. I recognized *The Rubáiyát,* illustrated by Willy Pogany, *Through the Grand Canyon from Wyoming to Mexico,* and Theodore Roosevelt's *Letters to His Children,* all of which I had received as boyhood Christmas gifts. I saw books my parents had owned: *The Garden of Allah, Mr. Britling Sees It Through, Love's*

Coming of Age, Trader Horn, alongside *Over the Top, Sorrel and Son, If Winter Comes,* and *Main Street.*

The books were higgledy-piggledy, and my librarian's instinct began to classify them. By the time I had made a round of the room, they were nicely arranged in my mind in a kind of chronological exhibition of changing tastes. From the turn of the century to the First World War, there stood the monumental sets of standard authors, printed on deckle-edged paper and bound in gold-stamped buckram or three-quarter morocco; the works of Hawthorne, Emerson, Stevenson, Mark Twain, Kipling, Conrad, Wells, and Galsworthy. Gift bindings by Sangorski on no matter what texts. Stoddard's *Lectures* on the coated paper beloved of silverfish. *Idylls of the King* in green and gold cloth. A bound set of *St. Nicholas.* Shelf-sagging *National Geographics.* Copies of the original *Life* magazine. *The Boy's Companion* with the beloved Mark Tidd stories.

Books of inspiration were shelved throughout. Elbert Hubbard's *Little Journeys to the Homes of the Great,* in the kind of binding David Magee calls "ooze"; Edward Carpenter, Ralph Waldo Trine, Henry Van Dyke, and Kahlil Gibran, rising (or descending) to the more practical gospels of the Abbé Dimnet, Bruce Barton, Walter B. Pitkin, Dale Carnegie, the Overstreets, and Dr. Peale.

There was evidence of old and new tastes in children's books. Is there a modern artist who has not illustrated *A Child's Garden of Verses?* Picasso perhaps, although he might have done it in secret. There they all were, from Jessie Wheeler Wilcox (my favorite) to Marie Laurencin. There was fantasy, from Peter Newell's *Hole* books to Dr. Seuss's unholy creations. Palmer Cox's *Brownie* books were sadly outnumbered by the productions of Walt Disney, Inc. With a surge of joy I saw the series of my boyhood: The Rover Boys, Dave Porter, Tom Swift, The Boy Allies.

Sight of the Oz books made me twinge. L. Frank Baum had been a friend of my father, and each time he came to dinner, he brought one of his books playfully inscribed to me. What would such a set be worth today if the books were in fine condition? Plenty. *Où sont mes livres d'antan?* Read to pieces and gone with the trash.

I spotted a title that had been my downfall in my bookstore year. It was a novel I had been reading intermittently in its serial appearance, and, when it appeared as a book and the store's Christmas order of a thousand copies arrived, I got only as far as to pry a copy out of the tightly packed case and settle down to read, when the boss came along and caught me in the act. "No reading on company time," he barked. It was then I decided to be a librarian.

I took *A Farewell to Arms* from the shelf and settled in the easy chair. I didn't open the book, no; just held it as a talisman and let the room's ambience envelop me. I felt utterly secure, for all was familiar. These were the books of our time, of my time, from childhood through the teens, twenties, thirties, forties, and fifties, illustrating the trend toward the bigger and brighter and better, the expression of Everyman's interest in the world. I saw nothing of unusual rarity or value, nothing that a research library would not already possess. It was the apotheosis of the familiar, and I relished it without feeling covetous.

Again I found myself wondering what the old man had been reading when the end came. I fancied that if I knew, I could retrace his life, following it back to birth from the single thread of that final book, in the way Orson Welles made a movie from Citizen Kane's dying word, *Rosebud.*

Reference books flanked the chair. Travel books too, especially on the South Seas, from *White Shadows* of Frederick O'Brien to Michener's *Tales of the South Pacific.* I didn't feel sorry for the exiled old man, that Prospero in his attic kingdom.

Then I saw among the books of fact and fancy a *Leaves of Grass,* in the Small, Maynard edition. On its flyleaf was the inscription, "To my beloved husband, Christmas 1904." Some of the poems were marked in pencil, whether by him or by her I would never know. Was *it* the one?

A revved-up bulldozer broke the spell. I rose to go. Books have their fates, the Roman wrote. The fate of that copy of Whitman was to go with me. The rest could make their own way in the world.

Around the World in
Sixty Books

COMPILING THIS LIST out of my head from remembered reading over nearly half a century has been great fun, and led me to reread old favorites. It is a very personal kind of list, made up of books that encouraged me to travel, books I read on my trip around the world, and books I read between my first trip around, in 1925, and the last one, in 1960.

It is of course highly selective, and could easily be increased to twice sixty or six hundred. I hope it will lead readers to chain-action reading—from *Moby Dick* to earlier Melvilles, from *Lord Jim* to the rest of Conrad, and so forth.

For those who wish to read these books, I suggest they take the list to their nearest public library and bookstore (new and secondhand) and ask for help from the book world's best helpers, librarians and booksellers.

Then fill the zipper bag with the best of all baggage, and take off around the world, either literally or imaginatively, and prove again what all readers know for gospel: there's no friend like a good book. (When no date is given after the publisher, the edition is a current paperback reprint.)

104

ROBERT LOUIS STEVENSON

A Child's Garden of Verses. Baltimore, Penguin Books.

I can trace my later wanderings to an early reading of these poems, especially "Travel."

FRANK G. CARPENTER

Carpenter's Geographical Reader: Asia. New York, American Book Company, 1911.

Carpenter's Geographical Reader: Europe. New York, American Book Company, 1902.

Schoolday reading of these little blue-gray volumes also whetted my yen to travel.

HOMER

Odyssey. New York, Mentor Books.

Read Rouse's translation. First and best of all travel books.

RICHARD HAKLUYT

Hakluyt's Voyages. New York, Dutton.

Classic collection of mariners' accounts, first edited in 1599, the immortal symbol of England as a sea power. The Everyman edition in eight volumes has a preface by John Masefield.

JULES VERNE

Around the World in 80 Days. New York, Dolphin Books.

I'll stick with the book and let those who will travel with the movie.

JOSHUA SLOCUM

Sailing Alone Around the World. New York, Dover.

In the seven-ton sloop *Spray,* Captain Slocum took three years to sail single-handedly 46,000 miles around the world, wrote the book himself; and finally, like Halliburton, was lost at sea.

MARK TWAIN

The Innocents Abroad. New York, Collins.

Nothing has changed, except the prices.

HERMAN MELVILLE

Moby Dick. New York, Dell.

This was luckily first read by me during a voyage by

freighter to France via the Panama Canal. Melville found language to match the majesty of the sea.

RICHARD HALLIBURTON

The Royal Road to Romance. New York, Grosset.

First published in the year I made my first global tour, Halliburton's dashing account of his two-year circumnavigation made me frankly envious of his vigor. Not to be envied was Halliburton's eventual fate to be lost at sea while crossing the Pacific in a Chinese junk.

ALDOUS HUXLEY

Jesting Pilate. London, Chatto and Windus, 1948.

This round-the-world book remains my favorite Huxley.

BROOKS ATKINSON

The Cingalese Prince. New York, Doubleday, 1934.

Travel book about a voyage around the world in the freighter of this name, by the cultivated drama critic of the New York *Times,* now retired.

JOHN LIVINGSTON LOWES

The Road to Xanadu. New York, Vintage Books.

This great study in the ways of Coleridge's imagination is particularly apt for travel reading because of its marine bias.

THOR HEYERDAHL

Kon-Tiki. New York, Permabooks.

During the sixteen-hour flight from Honolulu to Tokyo, I was sustained by this wonderful book. When the comics were all read and the GIs clamored for something to read, I gave them the paperbacks with which I had packed my zipper bag.

LAFCADIO HEARN

Japan, an Interpretation. Rutland, Vt., Tuttle.

Most celebrated of all American expatriates in Japan, Hearn's reactions to the country are sympathetic, penetrating, and essentially timeless.

ALLAN S. CLIFTON

Time of Fallen Blossoms. New York, Knopf, 1951.

An Australian soldier comes to Japan after the war and writes simply and movingly of his life there.

ROBERT PAYNE

Alexander the God. New York, Wyn, 1954.

I found this marvelous historical novel in an Air Force quonset library in Tokyo, and became so enthralled I got behind schedule.

The White Pony. New York, Mentor Books.

My favorite anthology of Chinese poetry in translation.

OSBERT SITWELL

Escape with Me. London, Macmillan, 1939.

This is an excellent travel notebook on the Far East.

HENRI FAUCONNIER

Malaisie. New York, Macmillan, 1931.

Romantic account of a French planter in Malaya.

W. SOMERSET MAUGHAM

The Gentleman in the Parlor. Garden City, Doubleday, 1936.

Travel book about Malaya which I prefer to Maugham's fictional books.

JOSEPH CONRAD

Lord Jim. New York, Bantam Books.

I have been rereading this romantic novel of Malaya for the past forty years, and I still think it one of the best ever written.

MARGARET LANDON

Anna and the King of Siam. New York, Pocket Books.

Acquired this one at the Bangkok airport, and can report the Siamese are still among the gentlest people on earth.

E. M. FORSTER

A Passage to India. New York, Harcourt, 1949.

Proves my thesis that a good work of fiction is a better guide to a country than a bad work of fact.

ZANE GREY

Tappan's Burro and Other Stories. New York, Grosset.

I bought this in paperback in Calcutta's Dum Dum Airport and read it between New Delhi and Karachi, with one eye on the page, the other on the arid landscape.

SIR RICHARD FRANCIS BURTON

Sindh, and the Races that Inhabit the Valley of the Indus.
London, Allen, 1851.
Classic work on the dry and wrinkled land now called
Pakistan, sight of which from the air, and on the ground
at Karachi, recalled our own arid Southwest.

CHARLES M. DOUGHTY

Travels in Arabia Deserta. London, Cape, 1936.
I was repelled by the barrenness of Arabia and the hardness
of its people, both of which Doughty was more than equal
to. Throughout the four-hour flight from Arabia to Egypt,
I saw only a single oasis.

ROBERT PAYNE

Journey to Persia. New York, Dutton, 1952.
His prose is as pictorial and rich as a Persian rug.

LAWRENCE DURRELL

The Alexandria Quartet: Justine (1957), *Balthazar* (1958),
Mount Olive (1959), *Clea* (1960). New York, Dutton.
A month after reading these novels of Egypt, I found myself
on the banks of the Nile at twilight, and all I saw and felt
was pure Durrell. In books such as these, literature truly
triumphs over life.

Reflections on a Marine Venus. London, Faber, 1953.
While flying from Cairo to Rome, I looked down on golden
islands in a blue sea, including Rhodes and Crete, described
in this sensuous book of poetical prose.

GERALD DURRELL

My Family and Other Animals. New York, Viking, 1957.
The younger brother of novelist Lawrence is the author of
a remarkable series of books about collecting exotic animals
and birds for zoos. In this hilarious book he writes about
prewar years on the island of Corfu.

HENRY MILLER

The Colossus of Maroussi. New York, New Directions.
A modern classic of travel through Greece.

NORMAN DOUGLAS
  Fountains in the Sand. London, Secker, 1936.
  Tunisia in North Africa is the subject of these brilliant travel essays.

PETER QUENNELL
  Spring in Sicily. London, Weidenfeld & Nicholson, 1952.
  Travel essays distinguished by vision both sharp and luminous.

NORMAN DOUGLAS
  Old Calabria. New York, Harcourt, 1956.
  The toe of the Italian boot has never been more lovingly polished.

D. H. LAWRENCE
  Sea and Sardinia. New York, Compass Books.
  A two-week walking trip through the mountainous island gave Lawrence rich material for one of my favorites among his many books.

MRS. CHARLES MCVEAGH
  Fountains of Papal Rome. New York, Scribner's, 1915.
  The first thing I do on revisiting Rome is to gaze at my favorite of them all—the Triton.

GILBERT HIGHET
  Poets in a Landscape. New York, Knopf, 1957.
  Vestiges of the great Roman poets move the author to beautiful descriptive writing of the Italian regions which they once inhabited.

ROBERT BROWNING
  Works. London, Oxford University Press.
  His poems of Italian places and people are miniature travel books, biographies, histories, novels, and have been among my favorite reading since youth.

JAMES JOYCE
  Collected Poems. New York, Compass Books.
  I reread this in Zurich for "Bahnhofstrasse," a lyric on the city's beautiful main street.

HAROLD LAMB

Charlemagne. New York, Bantam Books.

Bought this volume in a Zurich bookstore, and had it every morning in place of a pastry in an *espresso* bar.

MARCEL AUROUSSEAU

Highway into Spain. London, P. Davies, 1930.

A walking trip from Paris to Madrid, wonderfully savored and told, is the subject of this leisurely book by an Australian geologist.

LAURIE LEE

A Rose for Winter. New York, Morrow, 1956.

A poet's beautiful prose account of a season in Seville.

HENRY JAMES

A Little Tour in France. London, Home, 1949.

These are charming travel essays in the simple narrative style James eschewed in his novels.

ROBERT LOUIS STEVENSON

Travels with a Donkey in the Cévennes. New York, St. Martin's Press.

The perfect way to travel and to write, at leisure, thoughtfully and with deep regard for life and language.

GEORGE MILLAR

Isabel and the Sea. London, Heinemann, 1948.

A White Boat from England. London, Heinemann, 1951.

Two heroic books of husband-wife sailings from England to the Mediterranean, the first via French canals, the second by open sea and Gibraltar, in both of which life and language are in perfect register.

EUGENE DELACROIX

Journal. Garden City, Doubleday, 1952.

The perfect pocket book, on India paper, with 80 illustrations to accompany the painter's notes on life and art.

JOHN RUSSELL

Paris; with Photographs by Brassai. New York, Studio, 1960.

I read this aloud to myself every night in London, and had to restrain myself from backtracking to France.

ALEXANDER WATT

Paris Bistro Cookery. New York, Knopf, 1957.

Mmm.

L. RUSSELL MUIRHEAD, Editor

Blue Guide to England. London, Benn, 1957.

Indispensable.

R. J. CRUIKSHANK

The Moods of London. London, H. Hamilton, 1951.

Squares, parks, streets, houses, and history are evoked in these personal and nostalgic essays.

IRWIN BLACKER

Westering. Cleveland, World, 1958.

Leaving London Airport for New York on a TWA 707, I snatched the reprint of this novel of the Oregon Trail off the rack and read it at 29,000 feet above the Atlantic.

ANNE MORROW LINDBERGH

Listen! the Wind. New York, Harcourt, 1938.

Beautiful book about an Atlantic flight from Africa to South America.

AUSTIN T. WRIGHT

Islandia. New York, Rinehart, 1958.

This great utopian novel is also a travel book. Although my trip did not actually take me to Islandia, I was never far from it in spirit.

J. M. CORREDOR

Conversations with Casals. New York, Dutton.

This profound volume went all the way with me, and gave me courage to face the worries of travel on a tight schedule.

W. J. TURNER

Mozart, the Man and His Works. New York, Knopf, 1938.

This volume, based on the composer's letters, is packed with inspiration and nourishment for either wanderers or stay-at-homes.

RICHARD HENRY DANA

Two Years Before the Mast. New York, Pyramid Books.

First and best of all books of coastal California, this has been recurrent reading for me all through the years.

J. SMEATON CHASE

California Coast Trails. Boston, Houghton Mifflin, 1913.

Reading this personal account of a horseback ride from Mexico to Oregon by an Englishman in the vein of R. L. S. always reconfirms my love of the western shore. I'll never go it by horse as long as I can book my way.

Penguin Atlas of the World. Baltimore, Penguin Books.

Just in case you get lost.

Part III

BOOKS AND WRITERS

The Prolific Robert Payne

In this time of specialization the encyclopedist is a rare bird. A writer is supposed to know more about less. The surest way for a young university instructor not to climb the academic ladder is for him to spread his interests. Stick to your decade, or lustrum, or year, he is warned, or to the minute aspect of your minor writer. So if you seek an encyclopedist, don't look on campus.

Look in the research library—on campus to be sure, or in city —for if there is an encyclopedist today, he will not be apt to have his own working library. The late C. K. Ogden was an exception and, toward the end, even his working collection got out of house and he had to buy a six-story dwelling in London, throw out the furniture, and move his books in from half a dozen places. It was Ogden who reviewed the 13th edition of the *Encyclopaedia Britannica* in 1926, ranged through it, and found it wanting.

It was in a university library that I came to know another encyclopedist of our time. I refer to Robert Payne. When I asked him how many books he had written, he was at a loss to say. "A few more than forty," he guessed. "My mother is the only one who really knows. Sometimes I forget to tell her of my latest pseudonym and she loses count. We could look at the card catalogue."

We did, counting as we looked, and the entries added up to over sixty books—fiction, poetry, biography, travel, essays, and translations from Chinese, Russian, Danish, all published since 1938, when Payne's first novel, *The Mountain and the Stars,* which was about the Bolshevik revolution, came out under the pseudonym of Valentin Tikhonov. Two more novels, on other subjects, appeared in the same year under the name of Robert Young. Other Payne pseudonyms are Richard Cargoe, Howard Horne, and John Anthony Devon.

In 1939 Payne translated Kierkegaard's *Fear and Trembling* under his own name, and during the 1940s he swam into the public eye with a torrent of books about China—travel, politics, poetry, and biography, and Englishings of Chinese verse and prose. In 1945 he translated Pasternak's short stories, in 1946 coauthored a book about Sun Yat-sen, in 1948 a novel about the Buddha, in 1950 a biography of Mao Tse-tung. Few can match the unpredictable variety of Payne's biographies of Dostoevski, General Marshall, Charlie Chaplin, Albert Schweitzer, and the Rajahs of Sarawak, as well as novels about such disparate persons as Alexander the Great, Chief Joseph of the Nez Percé, Leonardo da Vinci, and Jesus.

"You should write a novel about Shakespeare," I once suggested to Payne. "I have," he replied laconically. I checked up. He had. In America it is called *The Roaring Boys,* in England *The Royal Players.* I not only checked up. I read it, and found it good, as I have read and found most of Payne's threescore books, including *The Wanton Nymph, a Study of Pride; Journey to Persia; The Roman Triumph; The Gold of Troy,* a biography of Heinrich Schliemann; *The Splendor of Greece;* and *The Splendor of France;* two books on the Church Fathers, one on canal building, another on Terrorism, a history of Islam, a book about Gardiner's Island, and one about Greta Garbo. You have only to name a subject and Robert Payne has either written or will write a book on it.

Born in Cornwall in 1911 of English-Irish-French ancestry, Pierre Stephen Robert Payne looks more like a Scandinavian than any of his ancestral types. Short and slight, with pale blue eyes, pink skin, and wispy blond hair, he meets people with his current turned off, is unassuming and gives no impression of being other than Mr. Everyman. He recalls Flaubert's dictum: Live like a lamb so you can write like a lion.

Although there is no reason why there should be a correlation between an author's appearance and his works, one is somehow reassured when one sees that Aldous Huxley looks and talks exactly as the author of his philosophical and witty books should, that Ernest Hemingway and his novels were of one piece, and that Edna St. Vincent Millay was an acted-out version of her own poetry. No such identification is possible when one meets Robert Payne. He doesn't resemble any of the writer-stereotypes, and his books are too varied to link him with any one or half dozen or dozen and a half of them.

Does this prodigious output mean that Payne's books are superficial and slovenly? No. Based on either research or travel, or both, his books are sound, competent, and sometimes eloquent in style.

Educated in France, England, Germany, South Africa, and China, in languages and mathematics, experienced as a Singapore shipwright (following his father's practice), as a cultural attaché and journalist in China and Spain, as a professor in an Alabama college, and finally as a resident of New York, Robert Payne is equally adept at social research or study in the stacks. His habit of living is geared to the mass production of books: sleep during the morning, see people late afternoon and evening, then study and write until daybreak. This was the way Balzac worked.

When Payne was living in Southern California, we met in the UCLA Library, always late in the day. He usually came in like a traveling salesman, in each hand a suitcase filled with books he had checked out. He would sit only long enough to smoke a cigarette—quiet, relaxed, only his eyes alive as he used them to photograph everything in sight. I once showed him a recent arrival—Thevenot's seventeenth-century account of India. Payne leafed through it, said nothing. A year or two later his novel *Blood Royal* was a brilliant re-creation of the Moguls, based on Thevenot and other sources. Nothing is lost on him.

Payne's problem has been to find publishers to keep up with his output, and this has led him to adopt pseudonyms in addition to the ones I have cited. Even he is not sure of all the names he has used. If his output keeps quickening and widening, he will also be giving libraries trouble. Even now he takes up more shelf space than most writers, or would if his books weren't in constant circulation. What better epitaph could a writer have than "His books were read"?

Voyages to the Moon

SEEN ON A CLEAR NIGHT, when at the full, earth's blond neighbor seems an inviting place. And so man has found it. For a long time he has been dreaming up ways of getting there, imagining outlandish contraptions, none of which is any more so than the machine we are now being shown as the most likely way of setting down our first landing party on the moon—a long-legged, insectlike vehicle not out of place among the strange devices imagined by antique lunarnauts.

It is not only at night that I have these bright thoughts. During the daytime at home, on the Pacific Coast northwest of Los Angeles, we have a far view into the skies above Point Mugu and Vandenberg Air Force Base, two points from which launchings are made; and sometimes when I am reading or weeding outdoors, I hear a distant rumble and see strange configurations of vapor in the sky, and I know that something's up.

Reading what? A paperback edition of *Voyages to the Moon*, that learned and lively book by Marjorie Hope Nicolson, first published in 1948, which in its dedication indicates the fruitful symbiosis that occurs when a great teacher has good students: "To the Smith College students in *Science and Imagination*,

1936–1941, from whose ingenious and amusing term papers their teacher learned more than she taught."

In this vastly readable book, Miss Nicolson's "launch pad" is based on classical antiquity, on Lucian and Plutarch, who imagined a world in the moon; on Galileo, who saw one; and on two English works published in 1638, one of which employed imagination, and the other science to elaborate on the lunar world.

Although not issued until five years after his death in 1633, Francis Godwin's *The Man in the Moone* was probably written in the century before, when the young man, destined to become Bishop of Hereford, was a divinity student at Christ Church, Oxford. For transportation his romance employed great swan-like birds called gansas to fly man to the moon. The book had an enormous and continuing vogue, being translated into many languages. The latest edition is as recent as 1959, published fittingly at Hereford, the seat of Godwin's bishopric.

The other moon book of 1638 was by the eminent mathematician, Dr. John Wilkins, F.R.S., who spun out his title in a characteristic academic qualification to read, *A Discourse Concerning a New World and Another Planet: the First Book, the Discovery of a New World; or, A Discourse Tending to Prove that 'tis Probable there may be another Habitable World in the Moone.*

In writing her *Voyages to the Moon,* which was originally the Alexander Lectures at the University of Toronto, Marjorie Nicolson took Dr. Wilkins's four possible means of flight as her basic outline. He maintained that if man is going to make it the 240,000 miles to the moon, it will be (1) by the aid of spirits or angels, (2) by means of birds, (3) by the use of artificial wings, and (4) by flying chariots.

Can we say that our Project Apollo, aimed to put a man on the moon by 1970 by means of rocket and lander, has added anything new to Dr. Wilkins's four means?

Among the valuable and corrective insights which characterize Miss Nicolson's book is the dismissal of modern claims to the invention of science fiction. She shows that Edgar Allan Poe,

Jules Verne, H. G. Wells, and C. S. Lewis all drew upon classical sources, Latin, English, and French, for their flights of fancy, and in turn have been used by our contemporaries such as Ray Bradbury. There is nothing new under the moon.

I met Marjorie Nicolson recently on a western college campus where she has been teaching and researching in the near-by Huntington Library, and I urged her to update her *Voyages to the Moon,* if only to show how the present is forever catching up with the past.

I couldn't keep from putting a typical librarian's question to her, asking, "If you were called upon, as I recently was, to choose a few basic books to go along in the first moon rocket, what would you select?"

"Bishop Godwin's, of course," she replied unhesitatingly. "After all, his feathered gansas are no weirder than our metallic landing bugs. And his three magic stones—Poleastis for heat, Mechrus for light, and Ebelus for reducing weight—are no more magical than our uranium and cobalt. Wilde was right: Life imitates Art."

Then she came right back at me and asked, "Well, what did you choose?" "Sorry," I replied. "I can't tell. My choices went into the committee's file of classified information."

Durrell in Dallas

WHILE IN TEXAS once on a library survey, I went on a spree. I was away from home, anonymous in a big hotel, and every night after the day's work I went wild. I could hardly wait to get out of the air-conditioned atmosphere of big rig-and-tool men. "What's your line?" one asked me, as we came down in the elevator. "Books," I replied. "Great!" he said. "I've been looking for someone to place a bet with." I was near the shakes when I pushed through the swinging doors of the resort next to the hotel, and reached for . . . a book.

Everything favored relaxation. Good light, easy chair, quiet people, friendly librarians, there in the Dallas Public Library, situated on the main street at sidewalk level, with only glass between people and books. Through the swinging doors, I found once again the security I have known all my life in the world of books. It was there my spree took place.

In the forest of literature, surrounded by stacks of books, all mine to have and to read, I drew back from the act of reading as the excitement rose in my veins. I experienced the paradox that the public library is one of our few remaining places of privacy, the refuge of the individual who wants to be let alone.

I sat there in anticipation for a long luxurious moment, the unread book in my hand, as with closed eyes I found myself transported backward in time to the Carnegie Library of my California boyhood, when a yea-saying librarian first set my foot on the bookish way I have followed ever since, a past evoked by the soft sounds of reading, by the sweet smell of paper and ink, as characteristic of libraries and bookstores as incense is of a cathedral.

What was the book I held unread in my hand? A boyhood bible for which I had instinctively gone to the shelf on entering the library, a book that had inspired my first writing, a grammar school serial called "The Quest of the Purple Dragon." It was *The Insidious Dr. Fu Manchu*.

I never did open it. Too risky. I had come a long way on the bookish road, and the prose that had excited boy would bore man. I slid the book back on the shelf, returned to my chair, and watched people come and go, with books in their arms and light in their eyes, free from pressure to read or not read this or that, there in the temple of our precious way of life, no one looking over one's shoulders, no reports being made to city fathers on who's reading what. I felt good.

What I finally settled down to read was another novel, one written from a vision and in a style more satisfying to my adult taste than Sax Rohmer. Here again however—Analyst, make of this what you will—the setting and subject of the book were exotic: diplomatic and romantic intrigue in Alexandria, the Egyptian city I had seen briefly as a youth while working on a round-the-world ship.

On the shelf of recent fiction I found Lawrence Durrell's *Mountolive,* the third volume in his Alexandrian tetralogy. I opened it at random and savored a prose each word of which was barbed to hook and to hold.

> It was the ancient city again; he felt its pervading melancholy under the rain as he crossed it on his way to the Summer Residence. The brilliant unfamiliar lighting of the thunder-storm re-created it, giving it a spectral story-book air—broken pavements made of tinfoil, snail-shells, cracked horn, mica; earth-brick buildings

turned to the colour of ox-blood; the lovers wandering in Mohammed Ali Square, disoriented by the unfamiliar rain, disconsolate as untuned instruments; the clicking of violet trams along the sea-front among the tatting of palm fronds. The desuetude of an ancient city whose streets were plastered with the wet blown dust of the surrounding desert.

I read the words with the mingled emotions of familiarity and freshness one gets only from an old love, a true love, words written by a man with the threefold power to sense, to see, and to say. In *Books in My Baggage* I told of my discovery of Lawrence Durrell as a poet, of collecting his earliest pamphlets and books, printed in or written about such a variety of places as London, Paris, Corfu, Cyprus, Rhodes, Greece, Egypt, Argentina, Ischia, Yugoslavia.

This was my first taste of his latest novel. Taste? Gulp. By closing time I was willing to relinquish the book, for I had absorbed it through all my senses by the magical act of reading; and I made no resistance to being put out on the street.

I returned to the hotel, convoyed by Cadillacs, and ascended to my chilly cell. Against all that threatened me, Durrell's prose was insulation, transfusion, reconciliation. Take your pill for allergy, your shot for virus. Give me a book, best of all specifics against illness or exile, against Dallas summer, Manhattan winter, even traffic in smog-veiled Queen of the Angels.

Roosevelt's Rough Riders

THEODORE ROOSEVELT might have said, paraphrasing Byron, "I woke one morning and found myself President." Rarely has a man gone over the falls quite as fast as did this first of the two Roosevelt Presidents; and rarely is a single book to be seen as so important a factor in the career of a public figure.

Such a book was *The Rough Riders,* first published in 1899, its dedication signed at the "Executive Mansion, Albany, New York," where the author was newly installed as Governor of New York, having literally rough ridden his way into office with a mounted escort of the men who had served under him in Cuba the year before.

Until the Spanish-American War, the ultimate career of Theodore Roosevelt was unpredictable. Born at New York in 1858, graduated from Harvard in 1880, elected to the State Assembly the next year, a health-seeking rancher and hunter in Dakota Territory for four years, defeated in the mayoralty election of New York in 1886, later to serve on the city's civil service and police commissions, and through all these years steadily writing books of history, and biographies, and narratives of his western life—who could have predicted Roosevelt's future role as na-

tional leader, reformer, conservationist, and exponent of the
Strenuous Life?

No one in America was hotter than Roosevelt for war with
Spain. "Have you and Wood declared war yet?" was President
McKinley's joking daily query of Roosevelt, who was serving
then as Assistant Secretary of the Navy. "No, sir," was the reply.
"We are waiting for you to do it."

In the meantime Roosevelt had readied the Navy to strike,
had alerted Dewey to seize the Philippines, and was in such
a compulsive lather of impatience that when the sinking of the
Maine in Havana harbor finally triggered the declaration,
Roosevelt resigned from the Navy secretariat, and set about
with Leonard Wood, an army medical officer, to organize the
volunteer regiment of mounted infantry which came to be
known as the Rough Riders.

Seen from today's viewpoint of mechanized and missile war-
fare, the idea of a band of horsemen sweeping through the
Cuban jungles is preposterously romantic. Roosevelt had no
inhibiting restraints. With all the fervor of a Crusader of the
Middle Ages sworn to liberate Jerusalem from the infidels, he
set about to drive the Spaniard from the New World. He was
fanatically imperialistic, bloodthirsty, and righteous.

The Rough Riders trained at San Antonio, Texas, in the lee
of the Alamo, sacred to the memory of Bowie, Crockett, and
Travis. In their make-up we encounter the twin strains of
Roosevelt's hero worship. From the East came his own breed of
the aristocratic Harvard-Yale athletic type who lived (and died)
by the sportsman's code of fair play. From the four territories
of the West, which had given Roosevelt health and adventure,
he recruited cowboys, hunters, and prospectors, some with Indian blood.

The muster-out rolls of the volunteers, included in appen-
dices to early editions of *The Rough Riders,* give the home
towns of the men, and we find many of them from such places
as Prescott and Safford in Arizona, from Santa Fe and Raton
in New Mexico, and with native names like Luna, Catron, and
Armijo.

From Arizona came Bucky O'Neill, famed frontier marshall and mayor, who endeared himself to Roosevelt as a poetry-quoting philosopher, and who was killed in Roosevelt's presence at Santiago. Today in front of the Yavapai County courthouse in Prescott there stands a Remingtonesque equestrian statue of Bucky O'Neill by Solon Borglum.

It was on the dusty wind-swept San Antonio plain that Roosevelt first demonstrated on a large scale the administrative skill and ability to inspire and to lead men which made him such a dynamic chief executive. In a month the volunteers were organized, disciplined, and trained, horses were bought and broken, mule teams procured.

With the transshipment of a thousand men, animals, and equipment by rail from Texas to Tampa, port of embarkation, Roosevelt came into frustrating contact with the bureaucratic inefficiency against which he fought so stubbornly. At Tampa the confusion was compounded. The railhead was inadequate, unassigned transports were insufficient, no single person was in command—all was chaos.

The supreme irony of the entire adventure occurred in Florida. The men were embarked for Cuba, their mounts were left behind. The few horses that were taken were thrown overboard off Cuba to swim ashore. It was here that Roosevelt lost one of his two horses. The Rough Riders' mounted exploits took place only in Texas training and at mustering out at Montauk. This was a bitter disappointment to Colonel Roosevelt, for he had had fond hopes, in the best Crusader's style, of direct encounters between his mounted men and the Spanish cavalry, in which he had no doubt that the rugged Southwestern range horses would outshoulder and rout the Spanish ponies and their riders.

Actually there was little hand-to-hand fighting between Americans and Spaniards. Rifle and cannon dueling went on; casualties came from both random firing and sharpshooting. Roosevelt gallantly led the famous charge at San Juan Hill which preceded the surrender of Santiago. It is a miracle he was not killed.

What would have defeated the Americans, if the Spaniards had been able to hold out, was disease—malaria—and it was Roosevelt who, as a volunteer and not a regular, subject to court-martial, forced the War Department to repatriate the troops before they died of fever. The round-robin letter he wrote to Washington was given to the newspaper correspondents in Cuba, an example of the press agentry which Roosevelt practiced throughout his career.

As a Navy man, Roosevelt was severe in his strictures on Army bungling in the Cuban campaign. *The Rough Riders* pulled no punches. His private letters from Cuba were even more out-spoken in his condemnation of General Shafter and Secretary Alger. It was fortunate that we were at war with a fourth-rate power.

It was inevitable that Colonel Roosevelt came galloping home, with toothy grin, glasses, and sombrero, straight into the hearts of the American voters. He quickly became Governor of New York, Vice-President of the United States, and, with the assassi-nation of McKinley, the twenty-sixth President of the United States, taking the oath of office in Buffalo on September 14, 1901.

The Rough Riders is a book unique in American history, poli-tics, and literature in the role it played in making its author President. When I say the book, I mean also the experience it recounted and the philosophy it represented. There is no di-chotomy between the book and the man.

Theodore Roosevelt could write. He was a writer before he was anything else. He had a natural gift for narrative prose, and his master was Francis Parkman. *The Winning of the West*, the multivolume work which led to Roosevelt's presidency of the American Historical Association, was a continuation of Parkman. Van Wyck Brooks called it "a history only pedants could disparage, a fine, flowing, scholarly narrative."

The Rough Riders is written in unadorned prose whose sole aim is to tell the story. This characteristic is evident in the opening paragraph:

During the year preceding the outbreak of the Spanish War I was Assistant Secretary of the Navy. While my party was in opposition, I had preached, with all the fervor and zeal I possessed, our duty to intervene in Cuba, and to take this opportunity of driving the Spaniard from the Western World. Now that my party had come to power, I felt it incumbent on me, by word and deed, to do all I could to secure the carrying out of the policy in which I so heartily believed; and from the beginning I had determined that, if a war came, somehow or other, I was going to the front.

There is a classic simplicity and straightforwardness about *The Rough Riders,* and also a sense of dramatic urgency which carries the reader forward through the month of preparation, attainment of the Cuban front, the brief and bloody engagements, the retreat before malaria vanquished the victor, and finally the more relaxed mustering out at Montauk.

Much action is packed into small space. The pressure of public life kept Roosevelt from any tendency he might have had to wax expansive. *The Rough Riders* was written while he was governor of New York. However, he always had the ability to do a dozen things at once. While in training at San Antonio, he wrote letters in rapid succession to President William McKinley, the poet Robert Bridges, Senator Henry Cabot Lodge, and to his family; and even the feverish fighting at Santiago, when he slept in sweat-drenched clothes and swatted mosquitoes, did not stop the flow of Roosevelt's prose. He was a born writer, and writing for him was a natural function, like breathing out and breathing in.

Another characteristic of *The Rough Riders* is its sympathy with the people with whom Roosevelt was associated, the Spaniards excepted, at least one of whom he personally killed with a revolver. The book is a gallery of personal portraits—Bucky O'Neill, dying with a Spanish bullet through his head; McGlinty, the little bronco buster who could keep in step only when on horseback; college men and half-breeds. All are sketched with the sure sympathy that was one reason for Roosevelt's popularity.

For years after the war, Roosevelt kept in touch with the Rough Riders, holding reunions, making speeches, helping the distressed, even keeping miscreants among them out of jail.

The Rough Riders is spartan in its celebration of duty and devotion to cause. Roosevelt had no patience with the introspective approach to war reporting. *The Red Badge of Courage* had appeared in 1895 and made its author famous. Stephen Crane was a newspaper correspondent in Cuba, but Roosevelt does not mention him, preferring to praise Richard Harding Davis and John Fox, Jr. The following seems to be a reference to Crane's novel: "I did not see any sign among the fighting men, whether wounded or unwounded, of the very complicated emotions assigned to their kind by some of the realistic modern novelists who have written about battles."

It should not be concluded that Roosevelt was not realistic. His battle book is fluently and sometimes gruesomely so, as when it described the huge land crabs that hungrily ringed the wounded.

Natural history was indeed one of Roosevelt's major interests, birds being his especial concern, and he had published papers on "Summer Birds of the Adirondacks" and "Revealing and Concealing Coloration in Birds." His criticism of John Muir as a naturalist, made after the two of them had camped together in the Yosemite, was that Muir had no eye for or knowledge of birds other than the water ouzel.

Roosevelt brought to his prose the same exuberant vitality that Browning put into his poetry. "How good is man's life, the mere living," the poet cried, "how fit to employ all the heart and the soul and the senses forever in joy!" "The Strenuous Life" was the doctrine Roosevelt preached for the national welfare, and it would pain him today to see the decline of physical fitness in Americans which has led to our yielding Olympic supremacy to the Russians.

Roosevelt practiced what he preached: riding, swimming, boxing, kicking and tackling, and tramping. Leonard Wood, his commanding officer in the Rough Riders, tells a story about the latter:

A tramp with the President usually meant that the invited ones would arrive rather smartly turned out. They usually departed, however, more or less complete wrecks. I remember one day the remark of the delightful representative of France, who had been taken across and up and down the creek, and up and down the banks, until only a portion of his clothing was left, but he still had on his gloves. The Colonel asked him why he was wearing gloves. He answered with Gallic quickness: "Oh, you know we might meet the ladies."

The direct descendant of Roosevelt as a writer is Ernest Hemingway, who lived and wrote the "Strenuous Life," glorifying physical fitness, bravery, sports, and deploring bureaucratic inefficiency and confusion; and I have no doubt that if the two had been contemporaries, they would have been cronies.

"Like Jefferson, and no other President in all the years between," wrote Van Wyck Brooks, "Roosevelt fraternized with naturalists and storytellers, novelists and poets. First, last, and always a literary statesman . . . a list of Theodore Roosevelt's friends would virtually amount to a literary history of the epoch."

The door of the White House was open to the ones he liked. He was one of the first to recognize Edwin Arlington Robinson, Edgar Lee Masters, and Vachel Lindsay. Ambrose Bierce was at the White House. Owen Wister was an intimate. Booth Tarkington, Ernest Thompson Seton, Joel Chandler Harris, Frederic Remington, and Hamlin Garland were among his favorites. Roosevelt's swift reaction to *The Jungle* (1906) led to the correction of the stockyards and packing house conditions whose muck Upton Sinclair raked over with such zeal. "He is a wonder," St. Gaudens said to a friend (Roosevelt had the sculptor redesign our coinage). "He knows us all . . . knows our work and our rank. It is amazing."

Roosevelt had his dislikes, however, and chief among them was Henry James. The realism of Zola and his American disciple Frank Norris was also unacceptable. Henry Adams's *Democracy* was "mean and foolish." Macbeth was a hero, Hamlet a mollycoddle. Sex was anathema. Dreiser and Lawrence would never have dined at the White House or Oyster Bay. Nationalism, manliness, and morality were qualities Roosevelt valued in literature as in life.

After *The Rough Riders* Roosevelt became a national and international figure, and henceforth he unfortunately wrote, as Van Wyck Brooks remarks, "with his foot as it were on the loud pedal, and the charm of his books on the Old West had vanished with it."

From 1900 until his death in 1919 at the age of sixty-two, Roosevelt was mostly a journalist, writing speeches, addresses, editorials, reviews; most of his output too hasty to have lasting literary value. Among his later books, *African Game Trails* is the freshest and the best, opening up the old vein of his ranching books of the 1880s. "History as Literature," his presidential address to the American Historical Association in 1912, is an eloquent statement of his Parkmanesque philosophy, ranging far and wide over his reading span. An essay on "Books for a Holiday in the Open" is a fine essay on Roosevelt's reading habits, and might well be placed in every room in the White House as a reminder that Literature does not begin with mysteries and end with westerns, as some of the incumbents since Theodore Roosevelt would seem to believe.

Several essays of Western Americana are memorable—on a cougar hunt at the Grand Canyon, on the Navajo country, and on the Hopi snake dance, all marked by gusto, precise observation, and flowing style.

He was a man, Theodore Roosevelt, a statesman, a literary man, a great American in heroic mold; and *The Rough Riders* is a book in which his best qualities are present. For it and a few other books, he is remembered. In the American West Roosevelt's name is revered because of his securing for the people their natural heritage, through the extension of forest reserves and the establishment of national parks and monuments. The Big Stick, the Square Deal, and the Strenuous Life are the phrases of his epitaph. *The Rough Riders* embodies them all.

Dr. Krutch's Southwest

I HAVE LONG BEEN INTERESTED in the relationship of a writer to a region, which results in "bookscapes," and sometimes literature. Searching through history one can find examples to prove various things about what causes this fruitful fusion. To be born and remain in a place sometimes does it: Thoreau. To be born in a place and leave it also does it: Joyce. Balzac's Paris, Dickens's London, Dos Passos's Manhattan—all prove what? Would the birth of Robinson Jeffers in Pittsburgh and of T. S. Eliot in St. Louis have led one to predict that the former would become famous for celebrating the California coast and the latter the "wasteland" of London?

Likewise unpredictable were two of the lasting books of Californiana, both written by transients through the Golden State —*Two Years Before the Mast* and *The Silverado Squatters*. One-book Dana! Not only could he never reach the heights again, but no one else of any time or place has succeeded in writing a more truthful, felicitous, and lasting book of Californiana which is also American literature. Thousands of books have been written about the state, and by those with greater knowledge of it than Dana. They remain merely Californiana, while this early example of narration and description endures as a masterpiece of imaginative journalism. I use the latter word advisedly, for the book was written from a journal of the voyage.

As one who lives on the same coast, I can verify that wind and weather, beach and bluff remain essentially as Dana described them. There have been a few changes back from the shore. I have seen icebergs and albatrosses and ships under sail, and I know of no writer who brings them into sharper focus than did the young Yankee seaman.

"Coastal fog spreading inland" says the weather report, and on his brief honeymoon in the Napa Valley above San Francisco, Robert Louis Stevenson saw it happen, and wrote *The Silverado Squatters*, a work of California which bids fair to live long as English literature. His native Edinburgh and Dana's Cambridge do not live in their books as do the remote environments which they inhabited for a brief time.

It is always a delight to come upon the right man in the right place at the right time, which produces fusion or fission or whatever we call that process whereby a book is created. And there can be no generalizing, no rules or laws, no way of foreseeing or ordering it to happen. The artesian well of prose may start to flow even in the midst of the dry academic landscape, as in the case of Austin T. Wright, professor of admiralty law in a university, who secretly wrote that life-giving work of the imagination called *Islandia*.

As appreciative as I am of the books written by Joseph Wood Krutch when he inhabited New York and Connecticut, taught at Columbia and was a Broadway critic—his *The Modern Temper* promises to be as pertinent to the 1960s as it was to the decades since 1929—I believe that the books he has written since emigrating to Arizona may prove to be the crown of his literary work. Thirty years ago who would have predicted that urbane Professor Krutch would eventually retire to the desert city of Tucson and there become a conscience-voice for those who would preserve the balance of nature and conserve a beautiful region against unbridled commercialism?

Perhaps the excesses and splendors of the California coast and the Arizona desert require as correctives the sober prose of "foreigners" such as Dana and Krutch. Long experience in seeing and sensing nature, and in saying what he saw and felt, had prepared Joseph Wood Krutch for what has wrecked many a lesser writer. The enormous landscape, the extremes of weather, the proliferation of a wanton populace are stunning, confusing, and depressing phenomena. It is hard to keep prose under control when writing, for example, about the Grand Canyon. One either goes purple like Zane Grey or lapses into a Mark Twainism such as, "Great place to throw your old razor blades!"

In his three books about the most colorful state in the Union —*Grand Canyon, The Voice of the Desert,* and *The Desert Year* —Krutch blends biology, ecology, and philosophy in pleas for the retention of wilderness areas. Among its native boosters Arizona has no spokesman to equal Krutch. He speaks for the desert as John Muir did for the mountains.

Now Krutch has written *Forgotten Peninsula,* a book about Baja California, the last frontier of the Spanish-American Southwest. This long, dry peninsula is no place for tourists. South of the border there are no roads for low-down finny cars. Water is found only in occasional holes. There is in fact no civilization. But there is life and, as described by Joseph Wood Krutch, it appears in perfect focus, a thing to wonder at, and read about.

What was it in this writer's destiny that led him from Morningside Heights to Scammon's Lagoon, where the gray whales migrate to breed three thousand miles from the Bering Sea? Krutch's autobiographical *More Lives Than One* holds the answer.

Fig Tree John

Who can say precisely where it begins? Rolling down U.S. 54 to junction with U.S. 66 at Tucumcari, I saw the Southwest gradually appear, as the land grew more barren and beautiful; and by the time I had entered New Mexico and was climbing into the Upper Sonoran life zone, to piñon and juniper, and even higher to ponderosa pine at Flagstaff, I sensed around me that vast complex of mineral mountains, saguaro and mesquite desert, and those mostly subterranean rivers—the Gila, the San Juan, and the Bill Williams—all seeking union with *the* watercourse of all the Southwest, that old canyon-carving, silt-laden, turbine-turning, crop-nurturing, gulf-bound Rio Colorado. The Mesa Verde, Shiprock, and the Grand Canyon were to the north; the descent to Lower Sonoran in the south, the abandoned smelter at Clarkdale, the open pit mine at Morenci, its copper-tailings pistachio-colored, Piños Altos and Cochise's Stronghold; and before me, in the west, my homeland on the coastal plain.

One need not be a native of a place to write truly of it. Perceptive power, absorptive capacity, and creative strength are the qualities which when brought to bear upon a region result in literature. D. H. Lawrence was born in Nottingham and spent only four months in Australia, yet his novel *Kangaroo* is a classic expression of the little continent. Pittsburgh-born Robinson Jeffers did not come to the Carmel coast until he was grown to manhood; the poetry he wrote thereafter is more golden than any thus far produced by native sons and/or daughters of the Golden West. Willa Cather's *Death Comes for the Archbishop* rose from her Nebraska roots to become a Southwest classic.

Back in 1920 a fourteen-year-old New Jersey boy came west for the first time and, through a Pullman window on the Sunset Limited, gazed on the Salton Sea, a body of water created in the year of the boy's birth when the Colorado broke channel and raged where man intended to raise crops. Thanks to the Southern Pacific Railway the river was restrained, but the overflow remains to this day.

This was Edwin Corle's introduction to a region which gradually came to dominate his imagination between the ages of seventeen and nineteen, as he drove back and forth between a home in Hollywood and a ranch near El Centro. From the beginning he wanted to be a writer. Before graduating from UCLA in 1928 he had the good fortune to study English composition with the late Herbert F. Allen, a modest professor who had a greater influence on Corle than any other single teacher.

Graduate work at Yale and travel abroad did not seduce Corle from eventual union with the Southwest. Once loved, this land can never be left. Its spell is ineluctable. Exiled from it in Europe or doomed to dwell on the wrong side of the Hudson, a Southwesterner sickens for his dry and wrinkled land where "sky determines." During the Depression Corle returned to Hollywood and had no difficulty in earning a living as a radio writer. Whenever time permitted he drove far out into the desert country, funneling through San Gorgonio Pass or Cajon Pass, to that "mystic mid-region" between the mountains and the river. Here he talked and listened and made mental notes, holding his fire until he returned to his typewriter in Hollywood with stories of the people he met, absorbing the sun-and-sage essences of the land.

The story of *Fig Tree John* was suggested by the name itself.

Names on signs and maps have always interested Corle, and his impulse to see a locality is often due to the lure of the name—note in his work the use of Garlic Spring, Bicycle Lake, Twenty-Three Skidoo, the Dirty Devil, and the Bright Angel.

Corle first saw the name Fig Tree John on an Automobile Club of Southern California road sign near the Salton Sea, pointing to the water hole where the Indian by this name once had a dwelling place.

By 1933 Corle had enough desert stories for a book. The only one which would not reduce itself to proper length was the story of Fig Tree John, and so Corle omitted it and published the others a year later as *Mojave, a Book of Stories*.

Then Corle set to work on his first novel—the story of Fig Tree John, which had moved into his mind and moved everything else out. He found that the old Indian was dead and his son gone away. He drifted up and down the desert, from Yuma to Mecca, questioning, recording, staying for a while with rancher Edward P. Carr, whose land was next to that claimed by Fig Tree. Carr was a man of erudition and Corle believed him when he declared that the character was not a California Indian but an Apache. From this rancher he also got the story of Fig Tree John's son, Johnny Mack, and his Mexican wife—a woman shared, in Apache tradition, by father and son.

Then the theme became clear: every time the irresistible body of white civilization hits the immovable object of Apache culture, it is the Indian who breaks. The old generation is destroyed, and the next generation goes white. Fig Tree John became to Corle a symbol of Southwestern Indian culture, religious and ritualistic, uncompromising, moral, and doomed to extinction at the hands of the white race which it could not comprehend, and which, in turn, was too materially busy and nervously impatient to try to understand it.

The very first novel about Southern California had the same theme. In 1884 Helen Hunt Jackson's *Ramona* damned the whites for what they did to the Indians, although in her romantic indignation Mrs. Jackson turned the squalid Californios into technicolored Castilians.

Corle boldly transplanted his Apache theme to the desert country he knew best. For information about the Apache people he traveled to all their reservations in Arizona and New Mexico. Back from the field he studied further in the Southwest Museum at Los Angeles—a great collection of books and artifacts founded by Charles F. Lummis, enriched by the Munk collection of Arizoniana, and headed then by the great ethnologist Frederick Webb Hodge. Of all the tributes Corle subsequently received for his writings on the Southwest, he values none higher than the presentation inscription in Hodge's *History of Hawikuh*: "To Edwin Corle who knows the soul of the Indian, with sincere appreciation."

Corle made Fig Tree John into a White Mountain Apache from the White River country of central Arizona, the most wild and warlike of the Athapascan people. There is no preaching in the book. Corle stays out of it. The characters are the book— they and the desert and Salton Sea—and the novel proceeds inevitably to its denouement, strong, sad, and honest.

It was in every way a compulsive book, as indeed all good and great books are and, once the story, theme, and research were fused, the writing (done in a small apartment in the heart of Hollywood) proceeded at white heat, from September 3 to December 23, 1934. No editing was required by Liveright's T. R. Smith, and the book appeared in September, 1935, followed by an English edition in the next year. A selection from the novel was published in *Continent's End*, a collection of western writing, edited by Joseph Henry Jackson, in 1944. In 1952 an abridged version was published in a paperbound edition by Pyramid Books, with the usual lurid cover and inflammatory title, *Apache Devil*.

Edwin Corle went on from this first novel to write many good books about the Southwest, including two about the Navajos called *People on the Earth* and *In Winter Light*, but in my opinion none surpasses *Fig Tree John*. Many strong, good forces found union in it.

Erna Fergusson: First Lady of New Mexican Letters

PEOPLE ARE what interest Erna Fergusson the most, and people are drawn to her because of the interest she takes in them. The screened porch of the old Armijo house on North Rio Grande Boulevard in Albuquerque, which she inhabited with a housekeeper until recently, was a kind of river road salon. Here Miss Fergusson relaxed in a chaise longue, with books, magazines, and newspapers around her, the telephone at her elbow, and received calls and callers of a fascinating variety.

On my last visit there I found her happily recalling a tea party she had given the day before. "Among the guests were five young men," she exclaimed, "every last one of them just twenty years old and a second- or third-generation Albuquerquean!"

"What did you talk about?" I asked her, who was then seventy-four years old.

"The draft," she said, ruefully, "and the hair styles of their girl friends. Those seemed to be their chief concerns."

She also recalled another party she had given the week before in honor of her niece and nephew-in-law from New Jersey —her brother Francis lectures on the theater at Rutgers University—when she took the young couple east of the Sandias to Cerrillos.

"We saw a ghost town, lunched at the Tiffany Saloon, and called on my old friend Father Chavez."

"Tiffany, the jeweler?" I asked, half joking.

"Of course. Tiffany's famous turquoise mine was near-by."

"Do you share your brother Harvey's distress at Albuquerque's urban sprawl?" I asked, remarking that this other famous literary brother, who lives in California, hasn't been back to their native town for a dozen years.

"I'm reconciled to so-called progress," she smiled. "It's not the first time this crossroads has been invaded—Spaniards, Yankees, health-seekers, tourists, and now the scientists and industrialists and their employees." She paused, and the smile vanished. "My own concern is for the intolerance some of the newcomers are bringing with them from border states."

"You mean discrimination against the Spanish Americans, such as Joseph Foster wrote about in his novel *Stephana?*"

"I do, and I don't approve. I hope this element will move on. Part of the charm of Albuquerque has always been its polyglot character. Look at me, with German grandfather, French–Scottish–southern U.S. father, I made my living first by taking dude parties to the Indian dances. Half of my best friends in New Mexico are of Spanish heritage."

Among other distinctions held by Erna Fergusson is that of being New Mexico's first woman dude wrangler, having managed her own Koshare Tours until Fred Harvey took over. During World War I she came to know every county and corner of her native state as a field worker for the Red Cross.

Her father, Harvey B. Fergusson, studied law at Washington College in Virginia, whose president was General Robert E. Lee. He came to White Oaks, New Mexico, in 1883. There he "batched" with several other young men, all destined for political careers—William C. McDonald, who in 1911 became the first Governor of the State of New Mexico, Albert B. Fall, the first Senator, and Fergusson himself, the first territorial delegate to Congress.

A fourth young pioneer who shared the housekeeping and cooking was Emerson Hough, who later recalled their experiences in his *Land of Heart's Desire*.

Fergusson went on to settle in Albuquerque and marry the beauteous Clara Huning. Erna was born in Castle Huning, a beautiful and unique structure, built in 1883 and torn down by later owners in 1955, leaving a dusty vacant lot. Harvey, Lina (Mrs. Spencer C. Browne), and Francis were born in the old Spanish-style house which Franz Huning had bought in 1850, and gave to his daughter on her marriage in 1887.

Although Erna Fergusson followed her B.A. from the University of New Mexico with an M.A. from Columbia University, and has lived in and written books about Mexico, Cuba, Guatemala, Venezuela, Chile, and Hawaii, her first and last love is New Mexico. Her books about it and the wider Southwest are among the best written about the region, for they are blended of knowledge, love, and understanding. The deep attachment she feels for New Mexico, and her ability to reconcile herself to the social changes it is experiencing, as well as the tempered affection with which she expresses herself, have earned for Erna Fergusson the title of New Mexico's First Lady of Letters.

When one visits her, sharing tea and talk of the wide world, one never knows who will come or call next—Witter Bynner of Santa Fe, Paul Horgan of Roswell, Frank Dobie of Austin, to name three of her closest literary friends; or Lawyer Will Keleher, University President Tom Popejoy, Roland Dickey of the University of New Mexico Press, Robert Oppenheimer once of Los Alamos; an occasional Indian, or a neighbor girl on horseback, who reins up, leans down, and calls hello.

Her sympathies are simple and human, which is why people of all ages and cultures feel at home with her. During one of my visits she was called in turn by a high school teacher, a priest, the editor of a new "little magazine," a local bookseller, and a young Democrat who wanted advice of a woman who, if she had chosen politics instead of writing, could have ably represented her state on the highest level, for she has the qualities of politician and diplomat: liking for people tempered with shrewd judgment, tolerance, persuasiveness, energy, and a sense of humor.

We moved into her adjoining study where she sat at her worktable to autograph a copy of her *Mexican Cookbook* in its charming new paperback format. Part of one wall is given over to pin-ups, the central place of honor being occupied by photographs of President and Mrs. Kennedy.

"I had my money on that young man," she said. "ever since I read his *Profiles in Courage*. Any man who admired the Senators he wrote about in that book was a man to watch."

She went on to tell of her meeting with John F. Kennedy when he was campaigning in New Mexico. The Albuquerque Democrats chose Miss Fergusson to be first in line to greet him when he came off the plane. She presented him with a specially inscribed copy of her *New Mexico, A Pageant of Three Peoples*, then moved slowly off on her crutches (she had just had a corrective operation on a lame hip), her role having been played, when she realized someone had followed her and was tapping on her shoulder. It was Kennedy.

"I just wanted you to know," he said, "I like what you wrote in your book."

The atmosphere in Erna Fergusson's home is one of books, pictures, old furniture, and a rainbow quilt that belonged to her mother, and is pervaded by a sense of lived-in comfort. She is not a book collector in the way of first editions and fine bindings, nor is she an introverted writer who broods about form and style. Her writing is straightforward, clear, and simple, intended to say what she means and to mean what she says.

"What started you out as a writer?" I asked.

"It was Kyle Crichton," she replied, "who encouraged me first to write some sketches of Old Town for the *Albuquerque Herald*. This led to an interest in the Indians and my first book, *Dancing Gods*."

"Did your brother Harvey encourage you to be a writer?"

"In a way," she laughed. "He said any fool can write a book. And so I proved him right."

Those early local sketches were published by Merle Armitage

in 1947 under the title of *Albuquerque*. In 1931, Alfred A. Knopf had brought out *Dancing Gods* (the title was supplied by Witter Bynner), reissued in 1957 by the University of New Mexico Press. It is the best of all books on the Indian ceremonials.

A deep and genuine interest in people is the most valuable quality an author can have who wishes to write about other lands. It is the secret of Erna Fergusson's success as a travel writer. Her first book on Mexico was called *Fiesta in Mexico* (1934), and twenty-one years later she followed it with *Mexico Revisited*. They are penetrating and illuminating studies of that country.

Such a book also is *Our Southwest* (1940), by far the best general introduction to the region. Much needed is a new and up-to-date edition of this work.

"Too late," she confessed. "It would take much traveling and talking, and with my bad hip I am just not up to it. Still, if I get help, perhaps I can do it."

The charm and value of Miss Fergusson's books is that they are on a satisfying middle ground between the extremes of academic treatise and uninspired journalism. She is a combination of scholar, reporter, and able prose writer. Her style is clear and simple, her emotions cool. Every now and then, however, they light up, and we get passages of transcendent writing.

Her love for New Mexico earth and sky is deep and abiding, and along with her passion for people, it is why she, of all the Fergussons, has remained rooted in her native soil.

"I like it here in the river valley," she said, "living among people who do what they like to do, and know how to do it."

She is thus drawn the closest to people who are deeply involved in what they do, whether it be the gardener, the county agriculture agent, or the bookmobile librarian with whom Miss Fergusson once spent a day, on her rounds. In 1955 she attended a meeting of librarians in Los Angeles, and held six hundred of them in thrall as she traced the origins of library service in her native state, properly crediting the pioneer achievements, then and now, to the ladies, God bless them!

Her favorite New Mexican characters are all women; no Billy the Kids for her. They include Sister Blandina, Susan Magoffin, and Susan Wallace, the three of whom were the subject of Miss Fergusson's last Lecture under the Stars in the University's famed summer series.

"I quit while I was still a success," she laughed, confessing that now an hour's lecture was too tiring.

We were talking about Old Town. "Let's go see it," she said. "I'll at least show you where I grew up, if not where I was born."

We coasted down the river road with the leisurely Sunday traffic, and threaded our way through the changing street pattern to the old twenty-room Fergusson adobe, now the Manzano Day School. If there is a master plan for the preservation and development of Old Town, it is not readily apparent. The area is marked by uncertainty, the Plaza disfigured by garish billboards.

After a visit to Albuquerque, her sister Lina wrote from Berkeley, "Whatever the changes in town, it is a comfort to know that Albuquerque is still entirely surrounded by New Mexico!"

"Nothing changes this view," Miss Fergusson said, when we had returned at sundown to the screened porch and saw the last golden light on the Sandias. "I shall be happy to end my days here in sight of the mountains."

The time was late summer, and the great cottonwood in front of the house was beginning to feel the cold nights.

"You must come back and see it in fall and winter and spring," she said, as I left. "Cottonwoods and Albuquerque are synonymous for me."

As for me, New Mexico and Erna Fergusson are synonymous —most beautifully and meaningfully so.

Part IV

MUSIC AND TRAVEL

Music into Silence

WHEN I WAS A BOY our cook was a Russian woman, not well educated but passionate about music; and so whenever a Russian musician came to town my mother bought her a concert ticket and one for me too, because Cook and I were friends and every night before dinner she let me scrape the dish and lick the cake frosting from the wooden spoon.

Thus it was that one night we went to hear Rachmaninoff. I must have been about twelve and had just succeeded in mastering the C-sharp Minor Prelude in recital. We had keyboard seats in the orchestra, and Cook was so excited that she kept talking to herself in Russian, somewhat to my embarrassment, for the genteel folk around us showed their breeding by turning to stare, arch brows, and titter into hankies.

When Rachmaninoff came on stage, bowed once from the waist like a soldier, then swept up his tails and began to play, I forgot my embarrassment. I had never heard anything like it, nor ever seen a man's hands move so fast. Even more than the music, I remember Cook's rapture throughout the recital. Her lips moved soundlessly and tears welled from her eyes. Through her I heard the music; from her I learned for the first time the emotional power of great music greatly played.

Sight of the program kept all these years reminds me of the evening's main morsels: Moussorgsky's *Pictures* and Liszt's *B Minor Sonata*—monuments of piano rhetoric, subsequently wrecked by Rubenstein and Horowitz, those muscle-men whose flagrant *rubati* should have won them long sentences.

It was one of the unlisted encores—not the Prelude—played by Rachmaninoff that night which became a part of my subconscious assets, forgotten for the next fifteen years, as was indeed the recital itself, until I heard him play it again, far from home, alone in a foreign country; and the simple melody and rhythm of his own Serenade affected me then in the way Lawrence writes in the poem called "Piano":

> . . . the glamour
> of childish days is upon me, my manhood is cast
> Down in the flood of remembrance. I weep like a child for the past.

Rachmaninoff played that night in the Casino at Nice. I went by bus four miles from the fishing village, wearing a blue corduroy suit and espadrilles on my calloused feet; and I bought the cheapest of all tickets, which entitled me to standing room at the back of the hall. He was older, thinner, grayer, but once again he bowed from the waist, tossed tails over the stool, and cast his spell over a cosmopolitan audience. He played Schumann, Chopin, and Liszt's *Sonnetto del Petrarca*; and last, the Serenade. Cook was long dead. My thermometer of love low. The economic barometer equally so. Music comes alive, Nietzsche said, when for the first time we hear in it the voice of our past; and that night I knew what he meant.

What did the future hold for me, composer *manqué*, poetaster, unpublished prosateur? I walked home, guided by the flashing light on Cape Antibes, fell into bed, emotionally spent, physically exhausted. And woke purged and refreshed. For, by great art we live and die and are born again.

Years passed.

Rachmaninoff died in Beverly Hills during the war. I never

knew he was living there until the news of his death was in the paper. A week later there was a memorial concert on the radio. A mezzo-soprano sang songs he was said to have composed for her long ago in Russia when they were lovers—"The Nightingale" and "O Cease Thy Singing, Maiden Fair." And as she sang, Yeats's lines echoed in my mind:

> That we descant and yet again descant
> Upon the supreme theme of Art and Song
> Bodily decrepitude is wisdom; young
> We loved each other and were ignorant.

II

Looking back from the plateau of middle age I can see the stages of my musical development, from childhood delight in the new Victrola to learning to play the piano and then the woodwinds, followed by the feverish years of dance music for college proms, on shipboard, in mountain lodge, and night club; and then an emotional wakening to symphonic music, study of pipe organ; and finally concerts heard in the musical centers of Europe and America.

It was during my last year in college that I first became aware of the depths and heights of my own emotional response to life. Perhaps it was because I had met the girl I was eventually to marry; or it was the stimulation of two college professors, C. F. MacIntyre and B. F. Stelter, who first made poetry live for me; or the flowering of friendship with Gordon Newell and Ward Ritchie. My personal renaissance came as I broached my twenties.

I wanted to play music, hear music, read music, and read about its composers. I gulped Rolland's three-volume *Jean-Christophe*. Beethoven was my god, and I wrote bad poetry in his praise. I read Weingartner's treatise on his symphonies. The great odd-numbered symphonies—Third, Fifth, Seventh, and Ninth—I acquired on records and wore them scratchy. I formed the conviction then, which has never left me, that of all man's creations music is the most nearly divine.

The climax of my symphonic experience of Beethoven—I did

not arrive at his quartets until I was in my thirties—was a concert in Paris, at which the Ninth Symphony was preceded by Mozart's Requiem. It was my first winter in Europe. I was alone. To be alone in Paris, after having been there with a beloved, was also a passionate experience. The great river-souled city of stone and light was still humming with the echoes of desire.

Libraries in the mornings and early afternoons, pilgrimages to the monuments for César Franck and Claude Debussy, cafés until dinner, concerts in the evening, followed by exalted walks home alone amidst the crowds—what a regime!

It culminated the night Weingartner conducted a Mozart-Beethoven double bill in the Théatre Sarah Bernhardt. For once I had a good seat: first row in the balcony where I could pillow head on arms. It was my first symphony concert outside the western provinces. Back home I had hated the "subscription series" audiences, composed of dowagers and old maids, whispery and bored, or timidly responsive.

The Parisian audience was the musical elite of the world's capital, and I was thrilled as much by its glitter and beauty and intentness, as I was by the playing of the huge orchestra under Weingartner. It was my first hearing of the Requiem, that swan song from the composer's deathbed.

At the intermission I sat bemused. My eyes roved the theater, imagining rendezvous with the beautiful women I saw there. All of this from the exalted, yet impersonal state to which Mozart had transported me.

Then the musicians and the singers returned to the stage and Weingartner launched the Ninth. I thought I knew it by heart, had heard it out. I was wrong. The German conductor made it new for me. By the end of the choral movement I was crying from the joy of it.

I had never heard such an ovation. At home only the gallery cried, Bravo! Here the entire house roared its approval, and I experienced union with them, with the performers, with Beethoven. In a trance I left the Théatre and drifted with the throng, coming finally to rest at a sidewalk café table, beside a charcoal brazier. From an old *vendeuse* I bought a cornucopia of roasted chestnuts, shelled and munched the rich meats, and sipped a glass of tawny port.

Toward midnight I was back on the Left Bank for a snack of bread and Gruyère. I had never been so long in such a state of serenity, wherein all was clear, calm, and reconciled. *Wem sich mein Musik verständlich macht, er ist allen Jammer der Welt erhaben,* Beethoven once said to a disciple; and on that winter night in Paris, alone but not lonely, I knew what he meant: *He to whom my music makes itself understood is uplifted above all the sorrows of the world.*

III

The Weingartner concert was neither my first nor last musical experience in Paris. Soon after arriving on the banks of the Seine I went to the Opéra Comique to hear *Carmen*. So unconfident was I of my spoken French that when my place in the long line brought me to the ticket window I pushed a slip of paper on which I had written *"un billet pour ce soir s'il vous plait."* With no expression on his face the man pushed a ticket toward me and muttered what later I understood was *"quat' fr'."*

"What?" I said automatically in English. *"Comment? Combien?"*

The man held up four fingers. I paid, grabbed my change, and rushed into the theater. I might have known that I was going to "peanut heaven" on a sixteen-cent ticket, and after a perilous odyssey I arrived in the topmost row of the highest gallery, so close to the ceiling that I had to sit hunched over and stare down through smoke-blue air at the tiny stage. I was among the roughest kind of workmen, corduroy-garbed, sabot-shod, with berets topping their villainous heads, all smoking the vilest tobacco, and accompanying the stage action by what I *thought* were obscene comments and what I *knew* were lewd gestures.

But the music, ah the music! What Nietzsche called the "pure yellow" music of Bizet flowed out of the pit in all its flamencan wit, passion, and despair. And the *ouvriers* responded to it by humming and whistling and making castanets with their snapped fingers. What a rowdy, good-humored crew! Although I could not understand or say a word to them, I was just as much with them as I was with a chamber music audience at a concert two years later in the Salle Pleyel.

This time I was not alone. I was well dressed, understood and spoke French (albeit with an accent that placed me as an Alsatian), and could hold my own in any milieu.

The Lener Quartet played the Franck and the Debussy quartets, followed by the Brahms Clarinet Quintet, and to an ideal audience—men and women of many races and colors, all drawn together by love for the quintessence of music; and as the strings wove their spell they became relaxed, bemused, and transfixed in a variety of positions, like a painting.

From where we sat in the balcony's side we could survey the entire audience. Some looked straight ahead, some sat with eyes closed. Others leaned back their heads or bent over and covered their faces with their hands. In the balcony's first row some leaned on their elbows and stared at the stage, or pillowed their heads on their arms and slept.

Sound of the music and sight of the people worked on us like magic; and my friend and I hardly breathed so perfect was our response, so deep our communion with sight and sound. And when the final notes of the Brahms had sounded there was no ovation. Only a slow awakening from the spell, a stirring to life again, a subdued exit from the hall.

We walked to the near-by Place de l'Opéra and found sidewalk seats at the Café de la Paix. It was a mild summer night. We sat over our drinks, bemused by the music, staring at the passing world, and not talking. Sometime after midnight two-wheeled vegetable carts lumbered by, horse-drawn to Les Halles; great wheeled high carts, heaped higher with luminous cauliflowers, radiant cabbages, golden carrots, like a dawn vision of freshness and plenty.

The last time I heard music in Paris it was a year later. On my last night in the city, a moon-bright May night, I went alone to the Opéra to hear *Le Crépuscule des Dieux*—as the French translate *Der Götterdämmerung*—and I found myself in the back row of a loge from where I could see the opposite loges but not the stage. No matter. The music was what I had come to hear, not to see the Wagnerians bend the boards with their heavy tread. The chair was uncomfortable, and so I stretched out on the floor with my back to the wall, to the apparent horror of the French family who occupied the front of the loge—the daughter excepted, a sweet thing who turned her head again and again and smiled. I beckoned her to join me and she pretended to be outraged. What a delightful flirtation we had!

And how relaxed I was, stretched out on the carpeted floor, musing and smoking, glancing at the girl and, beyond her, at the dark red silk-trimmed loges across, all but darkened, and to the glitter of the great candelabraed ceiling; while over and above all rose the ocean of Wagner's music, swelling to climax in the immolation scene, followed by the apotheosis of the closing theme which sounded in me for years after—and still does.

I walked home to my hotel, stopping on the Pont des Arts to look up and down the river. It was my last night in Paris; I was transported by that realization and by the music to an emotional stratosphere in which I was perfectly reconciled to what had been and what was to be. Apollinaire's haunting bridge poem was in my mind, its refrain flowing with the river:

> *Vienne la nuit sonne l'heure*
> *Les jours s'en vont je demeure. . . .*

IV

I must confess never to having heard grand opera in Italy. How I regret now that I did not experience Verdi at La Scala. I did not even go to Milan. So effectively did the lily town of Florence enchant me that I left her only briefly during the four months I was in Italy. Genoa, Pisa, and Naples knew me in passing, and I spent all of a week in Rome. There I bicycled into the Campagna, placed wild violets on the graves of Keats and Shelley, fell in love with the Cyrene Venus in the National Museum, feared the fleet buses which hunted the streets like predators—and heard Toscanini conduct.

The orchestra played the *Roman Carnival Overture* of Berlioz, Respighi's *Pines* and *Fountains of Rome,* and the Haydn 102nd in B-flat Major. The concert was played in the hall called the Augusteo, a circular building said to have been erected on the site of Augustus Caesar's tomb.

I had the good fortune to get an overflow seat in back of the orchestra, so that I faced Toscanini. Not only did I see the *maestro* as his musicians saw him, his disciplined gestures, his face alternately mobile and masklike, but I heard him exhort the players by singing and shouting; to all of which I responded kinetically, as if I were a musician once again.

Rome held nothing for me after that concert, and I quit the city on the following day, returning to Florence where the window of my room on the Arno overlooked rosy-tiled roofs, the Duomo and the Campanile, to the hills of Fiesole beyond. The intimacy of Florence was charming and irresistible. The concentration of its treasures surrounded one with sculpture, painting, architecture, bridges, and gardens—all accessible in short walks. Even the Duce himself had not been able to keep Florentines from walking in the streets rather than on the narrow sidewalks.

One rainy afternoon I heard Sabata conduct a symphony concert in the municipal theater with its blood-red décor. More than the music I remember the beauty of the Florentine women, and how elegantly they were gowned. Another time I heard an evening concert of chamber music by candlelight in the Sala Bianca of the Palazzo Pitti. A string quartet played Schubert and Brahms; and the great Ottorino Respighi himself rendered his own piano compositions, and accompanied his wife in Brazilian songs by Villa-Lobos.

Signora Respighi was a magnificent woman, her black hair impeccably coiffed, and her large, well-proportioned body molded in a white gown. The music, the white room, my awareness of the paintings by Botticelli, Raphael, and Michelangelo housed in other rooms under the same roof, the performers, and the sophisticated audience—all blended in one of the rarest musical experiences I have ever had.

All that was lacking to make it perfect was the beloved companion. Or was it her absence that made it perfect? I sensed that inseparable mingling of joy and sorrow, that bittersweetness, in which pleasure and pain are inseparable, and what Yeats had in mind perhaps when he wrote:

> O chestnut tree, great-rooted blossomer,
> Are you the leaf, the blossom or the bole?
> O body swayed to music, O brightening glance,
> How can we know the dancer from the dance?

V

My European base was the old Burgundian ducal capital of Dijon. The town's chief claim to musical fame was. antiquarian, Jean-Philippe Rameau having been born there in 1683. There was little current music worth listening to, except for occasional concerts by the boys' choir of the Cathedral. When they sang Palestrina in their sexless voices, the great stone temple echoed like a sea shell.

It was my radio—called T.S.F. by the French—that solaced me musically during the years of self-imposed exile in Dijon, a city which Victor Hugo called *délicieuse ville, mélancolique et douce.* I bought an old-fashioned set with so many dials, batteries, and antennae that it took me a week to master its combinations. When I did, there opened for me an international world of music, from London to Warsaw, in which most of the broadcasting was by advertising-free state monopolies. Over the Prague and Bratislava stations I heard lyrical hours of Smetana and Dvořák, while Budapest broadcast Dohnányi, Bartók, Kodály, and gypsy café music. Vienna played Mozart. Warsaw ranged the repertoire of Chopin. From Radio Berlin I absorbed programs of Bach, Beethoven, Brahms, and Wagner. La Scala broadcast opera every night. The B.B.C. taught me to love Vaughan Williams, Elgar, and Delius.

My apartment was high above a square in the working

quarter, and I wore headphones, which enabled me to shut out the noise of wheels and shoes on cobbles, the ring of bicycle bells, bloot of auto horns, and the drunken quarrels of my proletarian neighbors.

One summer night I heard an uninterrupted broadcast of *Tristan und Isolde* from Bayreuth. Instead of between-the-acts spell-breaking commentators, the Stuttgart radio broadcast the ticking of a metronome in order that listeners might know the station was still on the air. So exalted was I by that five-hour program that I went for a long walk through the quiet town, ending up toward dawn at the Buffet de la Gare, which was open all night.

My choice of programs was not always highbrow. *Le jazz hot* was becoming a cult in France, and I listened weekly to a *disque* broadcast from Paris. Once the announcer's remarks about American jazz were so mistaken that I wrote him a letter about some of my own experiences as a dance musician.

The next week I heard it read over the air, and then I began to get letters from *aficionados* all over western Europe. One even came to see me—a young French saxophonist who prevailed upon me to spend a weekend at his home in Chaumont, fifty miles to the north in the province of Champagne.

Quel weekend! He was the only child of a wine merchant, and lived with his parents in a château on the edge of town. He had recruited an orchestra among the musicians of the district, and they were gathered to greet me in the music room of the château. None of them could play "in the groove," but I didn't care. I took off my coat, rolled up my sleeves, loosened my belt and shoelaces, and went to work on a period grand, painted in the manner of Fragonard and Boucher. Then I seized my friend's saxophone and blew the kinks out of it, smote the string bass, and ran amuck on the traps. We were deliriously happy.

The session lasted all day, all night, and on until noon of the next day. Sustenance and stimulation were provided by servants who kept the ice buckets filled with champagne and the buffet fat with *patés*, poultry, *écrevisse*, bread, and sweet butter. One by one the players dropped out, until only my host and I were left. After a twelve-hour sleep I was driven back to Dijon by a chauffeur and footman. My friend went to a sanitarium for a rest cure.

Since then my musical debauches have been confined to chamber music.

The Way It Sounds

I WRITE ABOUT the way it sounds. Not the way it is. The way it sounds. Music, that is. And I write not to instruct but to entertain, and, I hope, delight, the way music delights, by a mingling of sound and sense. When young, I wanted to be a composer, but I had no talent for composition. I was merely a good performer. Before marijuana, I got the same effects, and merely from music itself. I was musically well brought up by a piano teacher, a woman who weighed 250 pounds. I was afraid of her, for she made me practice. Once she picked me off the stool and shook me, then slammed me down and snarled, "Now will you play it the way it reads?" I was always sneaking in bits of my own, corrupting the text, perverting the dynamics—a precocious little Stokowski.

Years passed, and by the time I reached my twenties I admitted the truth, that I was not and never would be a composer. So I burned my woodwinds, dynamited my piano, and left music for language. More years have passed, and I have persisted in learning how to write, to be a writer. Always though with music in my mind, in my blood, and, I hope, in my words.

I write about two things: playing music and hearing music.

Fortunate is he who can do both. Man has a need to participate. He is not meant to stand alone. Making music together with other men and women is one of the most satisfying things a man can do. We have all seen how music transforms those who are making it.

I was up in Montana once, to speak at the dedication of a library, and the ceremonies opened with the inevitable singing by the high school glee club. I've seen a lot of homely kids, but when that group of robed country boys and girls filed in and lined up, it seemed to me a new low in homely awkwardness. Then they began to sing; and I saw them transformed by the alchemy of music from brats to cherubs, rapt and transfigured.

Once upon a time I was a student in France. It was not long after I had abandoned music for literature, and I had occasional moments of weakness and doubt. I missed playing ensemble. I was lonely. And then I had a wonderful experience.

One day I was walking down the Rue de la Liberté in Dijon. Though the main street, it is narrow and crooked, and often the sidewalk shrinks and dumps one into the street. I was passing the town's music store, when I heard a violin being played. It was *what* was being played that transfixed me—the opening phrases of César Franck's Violin Sonata. Has any other sonata an opening to match it? Tender and grave, at once questioning and assertive, a restrained dialogue between violin and piano, asking, telling, leading slowly to marriage and union, all sounds resolved in mutual fulfillment.

I stood in front of the shop, while the sidewalk crowd flowed around me, and listened to the violin. Someone was just fiddling around, as the saying goes; trying out an instrument, perhaps; starting, stopping, tuning, but always the same phrases, always the César Franck, and without the answering piano.

It was a sibylline summons to me, for only the year before I had played the piano part of the Franck sonata in a student recital. I entered the store. The music was coming from the rear. It was a young woman playing. Though her back was turned to me, I recognized her as the violinist in a string ensemble that played gypsy music in the town's leading café. I sat down at a

piano and played the first notes of the sonata, softly, question-
ingly. She turned around, her eyes flashing. I stopped. "No!"
she cried. "Don't stop! Play!"

I did. She did. We did. It was a ragged performance, but we
never ceased until we had played it through. By the time we
had finished, an audience had gathered. It was France, where
people have time for spontaneous things. And when we were
through, hot, sweaty, and happy, the proprietor closed the
store and set everyone up for *vin blanc-cassis* in the nearest café.

II

Once in San Diego I heard music that sounded good to me,
coming when it did, and that evoked memories of my years of
music-making. I had flown in from the east. We had crossed
the Colorado at Yuma, and in the late afternoon light the river
was meandering and relaxed, its long course nearly ended, the
waters of its final tributary, the Gila, gathered in its flow. Unlike
my illustrious namesake, who first descended the Colorado in a
boat, I have made only aerial surveys of the river. It is a beautiful
watercourse from the air, accepting tributaries in junction after
junction: the Gunnison, the Green, the San Juan, the Virgin,
the Little Colorado—confluent waters, heavy with silt until they
drop their burden in Lake Mead, then spin the turbines at
Hoover Dam to bring the electric power that has ruined Los
Angeles's climate—and finally make their crystalline getaway to
the Gulf, dividing Arizona and California in more ways than
one.

In San Diego I registered at the U. S. Grant Hotel, relished a
sea-food dinner, then went for a walk. A Marine band was
tuning up on the Broadway bandstand—a band of eager beavers
ready to blow every kink out of horn, trumpet, and woodwind.
I didn't think I could take it, and so I returned to the hotel,
undressed, and stretched out peacefully on the bed. I was still
hearing the music of Bach that had been playing earlier—the
Goldberg Variations, with the theme which says *found, loved,
lost*, or in greater terms of life, *born, lived, died*; and the best

of all music was still pulsing in my veins with soundless eloquence.

Then the band began to play, with such violence and volume as to be heard all the way back to Pima County. I got up and uselessly closed the window. The music was coming through the walls. And gradually it seduced me. The way those kids were playing Sousa, even a cigar-store Indian would have begun to beat time and to march. Perhaps they were just home from Korea or just leaving for there; in any case, they were playing with all their hearts and other organs. I got up and opened the window and began to march around the room, ready for anything, to go anywhere, which is of course what the composer intended.

And then the music changed, as they played a band arrangement of "Porgy and Bess," best of all American music since MacDowell. Again I collapsed on the bed, completely undone; and when a single trumpet played "Bess, Yo' Is My Woman Now," the way it sounded was heavenly. It took me back twenty-five years to the last time I had heard music in San Diego—trumpet music, too, playing Bach, up on the boat deck of a ship in the harbor. It was the S.S. *Yale*, coastwise steamer between San Diego, San Pedro, and San Francisco, and I was the saxophone player in the ship's orchestra.

It was the summer of 1928. After school was out, I had been persuaded by well-meaning, obnoxious friends to give up music and get a so-called healthy outdoor job that would build me up from a busy year of classes by day and dance music by night. I have never believed in exercise, and after two weeks of wheeling cement on the college campus I was ready for a breakdown. Those barrows of sloppy stuff weighed more than I did, and every time I poured one into the conduit ditch I nearly went in with it.

The only thing that made the job endurable was the friend I was working with. During our lunch hour and in the short evening before we turned in early, we read aloud Meredith's "Modern Love," and also the poetry of Rossetti, Hardy, and Robinson Jeffers. And we drank a lot . . . milk.

One day I returned to the fraternity house after work and found a telegram from San Diego. It was from a musician I had once played with—a pianist who directed the orchestra on the *Yale*—offering me the tenor saxophone job, starting the next morning when the ship called at San Pedro en route north.

"You're not going to take it, are you?" my friend asked.

I hit him as hard as I could, and ducked, for he was twice my size—an ideal type for wheeling cement. Then I rushed to my room and made sure my reeds were good ones. I always used Vandoren reeds, and an ebony mouthpiece inlaid with silver.

I was dockside in San Pedro the next morning when the *Yale* arrived—a slim white vessel with thin black stacks; Lord how she pitched and rolled when she rounded Point Conception and met those northwest swells in from Alaska!

The first morning was spent in rehearsing. The piano player was a little tyrant and a first-class musician, and we played everything from his manuscript arrangements. He was like my old piano teacher—a classicist, intolerant of improvisation—and his Bible was Bach. He was one of the earliest jazz musicians to discover the gold mine in the *Well-Tempered Clavichord*. His arrangements were full of ingenuity and high spirits—good music for the time and the place.

The *Yale* was at sea four nights a week, in harbor three; and in the wrong harbor—San Diego. Our sister ship, the *Harvard*, was the lucky one, berthed three nights in San Francisco. The *Yale* docked in San Francisco at ten in the morning, and sailed south again midafternoon of the same day, not allowing much time to do the things youth likes to do, yet we managed to do them anyway.

What about the trumpet music of Bach that I thought of when I heard the Marine bandsmen playing Gershwin? Our pianist on the *Yale* doubled in brass. He could play piano with his left hand, the trumpet with his right, and the crowd loved it. Off duty he would sit hunched up in his bunk and play a Bach partita for unaccompanied instrument until he made you cry; or he would set off the pyrotechnics of a Bach fugue until you saw the rockets burst.

We had returned to the ship one night from our broadcast over a local radio station, just as the bugler on one of the Navy ships in harbor was playing taps.

"I'll show that s—— of a b—— how to play taps!" cried our little hero in a frenzy, as he unpacked his trumpet and rushed up to the boat deck of the *Yale*. He was high in every sense. We had made one stop, between the station and the ship, and our whistles were still wet, especially his.

Then came the fieriest exhibition of virtuosity I have ever heard. He not only played taps and variations on it, but also every other bugle call in the armed forces of all the nations, and then Bach, until the entire inner harbor of San Diego, thronged with anchored vessels, was ringing with music.

Then signal lights began to wink from ship to ship, as commanding officers grew confused. What was happening? Was it war or peace, taps, or reveille?

A Navy launch came alongside and we were hailed. "Who's doing that?" was the cry. "An enlisted man?"

"Hell, no," was the answer. "It's Gabriel!"

III

In these my middle years, at once more stormy and more peaceful than those of my youth, I have come to love the poetry of Yeats, and I find myself reading again and again the letter he wrote in his early seventies to his younger friend Dorothy Wellesley. It was after he had been ill and was convalescent that he wrote to her, "Part of my sense of solitude was that I felt I would never know that supreme experience of life—that I think possible to the young—to share profound thought and then to touch."

Is there anything as thrilling as to hear great music—share profound thought—with a beloved? Yes, of course, or nearly so. To hear it alone. Sometimes I escape from campus on a Friday afternoon and go by myself to the Philharmonic Concert. Once a cellist was to play the Dvořák Concerto—music almost too rich for my blood—and was seated restlessly on stage, with instrument between his knees and bow in hand, waiting through the orchestral opening for his entrance, when he saw a small piece of white paper on the platform in front of him. It bothered him, and he reached toward it as if his bow were a stick with a nail on its end, and tried to spear the paper.

The audience tittered, and the conductor turned around and felt to see if his clothes were in order. The audience laughed. The cellist pointed at the piece of white paper. The conductor looked puzzled, then grinned. The orchestra kept playing, of course, and finally the soloist reached out his bow and scraped the paper along the floor to where he could bend over, pick it up, and pocket it, barely in time to make his somber entry in the solo part.

Music is all around us; above, below, in, and out, almost as universal and beautiful as love itself, from which all music comes; and one hears it wherever he goes. Take the music of the penny whistle I once heard in the streets of Chartres. I had gone to see the cathedral for the first time; and all morning I had drifted in and out and around the gemlike building. Then I ate lunch in a workers' restaurant and was having a *café* on the sidewalk, when I heard the music approach.

It was a street air, played on a penny whistle at regular intervals, monotonous and haunting. As it came nearer, I saw its maker: a middle-aged peasant, lean and brown, with grape leaves in his leather hat, and wearing leather pants and jacket; a peddler of goat cheeses—probably a Basque—carried in a wicker basket on his back. In his hand was a wooden whistle, a pipe with stops, and every few moments he put it to his lips and played his tune, which meant of course, Buy my cheese, come buy my cheese.

And I did, hypnotized by the music to do his will. Somehow I managed to accost him and buy a cheese—God knows why, for I don't like cheese, goat cheese least of all. And I saw his face, his yellow-brown-green eyes—but he never saw me. He looked through and beyond me, his mind on distant things. And this is remarkable: his breath smelled fresh, like a cow's. That man had been eating grass. Man? The Great God Pan.

IV

The final episode in this suite of musical tales is about the most unmusical of all music—the sounds made by the bagpipe. The hero is a Scot of course. He was a big man, built like a bulldozer, and silenter. Throughout the ten-day voyage on a freighter from London to New York, he paid no attention to the rest of the passengers. There were only half a dozen of us, including my wife and me, an English nurse from Nyasaland, an older Englishwoman from Bedford—an exuberant woman who had borne twelve children and was en route to visit one of them in what she was certain was the Indian-infested wilderness of Iowa—an extroverted American theatrical agent, caged like a tiger on the recreation-free freighter, and finally the dour Scot, whose name was John Douglas.

He was not rude. He said the necessary minimum of social phrases but no more. I thought at first he was just big and dumb and bored, with no inner life and not much of an outer one, and I christened him somewhat contemptuously, "Johnny Scot." Midway across the Atlantic I witnessed something which was a clue to the real man, but it was I who was too dumb at the time to know it.

I had arisen at daybreak and started up from the boat deck, where the few passenger cabins were, to the hurricane deck above the bridge. As I mounted the ladder and peered over the top, I saw Johnny Scot with his back to me. I stopped and stared, for he was dancing, a solo Highland fling, that intricate one in and out of imaginary crossed swords, and with such delicacy of movement as to make his two-hundred pounds seem feather-weight. He was dancing to music of his own making, whistling a bagpipe tune—a two-part tune, with droning bass and squealing treble. I watched, and listened, in awe, unbeknownst for a long minute, before I backed silently down the ladder.

Then it came to be the last night before New York. We were about fifty miles off coast, a moonless June night, the Milky Way banding heaven clear across, from Scorpio in the south to

Stella Polaris in the north. We were running through a fleet of becalmed sailing boats—little ones, *R* boats, perhaps, like tired butterflies—in regatta from Providence to Newport. They had the right of way, and our freighter, its outspoken captain from Flatbush on the bridge, was having artfully to steer among them.

All of us passengers were up on the hurricane deck—even Johnny Scot—and the theatrical agent, seeing everyone peaceful, had to stir things up by proposing that we play that old parlor game of going round the circle and each telling the story of the most moving incident in his or her life.

Johnny's turn came last. I thought he would pass, with the Scottish equivalent of "no comment." I was wrong. I was never more wrong. He told a story, a most wonderful story, in an expressionless voice, with an accent as thick as the porridge in his native land.

"I was an officer with His Majesty's Forces," he said, "and after the war I was in Vienna, in charge of military police in the British zone. We had many civilian employees from several countries. One was an Italian girl from a hill town named Terradoro. Her name was Giulia. She was young and beautiful, with dark hair and dark eyes. She was small too. Came hardly to my shoulder. I called her my Italian friend.

"Time came for her to return to Italy, and on the last day in the office she came to me and said she wanted a souvenir. What do you want? I asked. She opened a drawer in my desk. It was full of confiscated firearms. She picked out a small gold-handled revolver—a beautiful little killer—and said she wanted it to take home as a souvenir.

"I told her no. It was against the rules. The weapons were inventoried, and besides, it meant the death penalty for any civilian caught with arms of any kind.

"She kept begging for the gun, and I finally gave in. First, though, I did two things. I removed the cartridge chamber and kept it, and then I made her take a vow never to reveal to anyone under any circumstances where she had obtained the gun. Then she returned to Italy."

He paused and lit a cigarette, and in the match flare I saw his rugged face, wearing no expression. We were quiet, waiting for him to resume.

"Six months passed," he said at last. "And I got a long furlough. I had never been to Italy and I had a strong desire to see Giulia again. She had stopped writing. So I took a jeep and went over the Brenner Pass. Nice scenery too, those Alps—if I hadn't seen the Highlands first.

"I arrived at the village, near Florence, toward evening, parked the jeep, and entered the local tavern. When I asked for her, the place fell silent. Perhaps it was my accent. I had learned only bits of Italian from her—those few necessary words a man learns from a woman—but they knew who it was I wanted.

"After a few rounds of wine, on me, I persuaded the tavernkeeper's wife to talk. I learned that Giulia was in prison. For life. The charge? Illegal possession of firearms. She had shown her souvenir to a supposed friend and had been denounced to the American soldiery as a Communist agent.

"They told me that she had been offered her freedom if she would tell who gave her the revolver. She wouldn't tell. They even tortured her. Still she wouldn't talk. She never talked.

"And so because the revolver was incapable of being fired, she got a life sentence, instead of the death penalty which would otherwise have been hers."

Again he stopped and smoked in silence. It was probably the most talking he had done in a long while, and he was out of breath. Then he spoke again.

"I went to the American military headquarters early next morning, and because I was a high-ranking officer, I got through to the Colonel in charge. I told him where Giulia had obtained the gun. The Colonel sent for the transcript of the trial. It was brief. He read it through, then wrote out a summary order for her release."

The Scot looked at me then and said, "You Americans can get things done in a hurry when you want to." I warmed to the compliment, then cooled when he added, "Most of the time they're the wrong things."

"I took the order for her release," he continued, "and drove to the women's prison in the outskirts of Florence. It was still early, and when they led me to the ward where Giulia was confined, I saw her through the bars, sitting with her back to me, combing her hair. Ah but the lass had beautiful hair."

At that point I thought I detected a rising half degree of warmth in his voice, but I couldn't be sure. It might have been merely his accent.

"Then she put on her stockings," he said. "Still with her back to me. I waited for her to hold them up and look for runs, the way women do, before I called her name.

"She jumped up as if she had been shot in the back and turned around, and her face was terrible to see—terrible and wonderful and beautiful all at once.

" 'Oh Johnny!' she said, and sat down again. 'You've come to visit me. How good of you.'

" 'No, lass,' I said, 'I've come to take you out.' And the warden, who'd come with me, held up the Colonel's order and nodded yes.

"She got up again then, and came toward the door like a sleepwalker, and at that moment the turnkey opened the door, and she walked on through, and she put her arm through my arm and her cheek against my cheek—and 'Oh Johnny' was all she could say, over and over and over."

He stopped then, and it was a long while before anything was said. Then the woman from Bedford asked, in that matter-of-fact way the English have.

"Then what happened, Mr. Douglas?"

I thought the Scot never would rouse himself and answer, but at last he did, almost inaudibly.

"Then what happened? Not very much. I had never seen Venice, and so I put her in the jeep, and we drove as far as we could, and then I hired a gondola, and we went all the way."

With that he got up and descended the ladder to the cabin deck, and we heard his door close. It was the next morning when I saw him again, and again he was his old solitary silent self. We were off Ambrose Lightship waiting for the pilot, then approaching the most beautiful landfall in the world for a homesick American, all of us at the landward rail—all but Johnny Scot; he was at the rail, yes, at the seaward rail, the rail that looked back to the Old World.

By midafternoon we had cleared quarantine and were docked on the Hudson side of Manhattan, along about 26th Street. The Scot didn't more than nod good-by to any of us, and the last I saw of him he was walking off the pier alone, making his sure and delicate way like a dancer among the obstacles of freight and baggage, carrying his worldly goods in the form of two large duffel bags. And he was whistling that darned bagpipe tune.

Talismans for Travelers

THE CONSTANT TRAVELER carries talismans to ward off evil—
a medal, or coin, or pocket Bible. On my flying trip around the
world, I had two. One I kept in my pocket and fingered when
the going was rough: an iridescent fragment of wave-worn
abalone shell, smooth and cool to the touch. The other I kept
in my head and hummed when trouble was near: a few bars of
music by Mozart, from the final movement of his Divertimento,
K. 334. Both were associated with the security of home in
Malibu. I had found the shell fragment during my last walk on
the beach the day before leaving for Travis Air Force Base near
Sacramento, where the MATS flight originated that was to take
me across the Pacific to Japan. The music was the last recording
I played on the morning of my departure; it sounded almost
too beautiful to leave.

Why does one leave home? There have been various reasons:
the Golden Fleece, the Apples of the Hesperides, a woman's
face, uranium, to reach the moon. None of these applied to me.
I left home to make speeches in Asia and to buy books in Europe, and I was strongly motivated to do both. Only on that
final morning before leaving Malibu, my motivation was low,
and it took a mighty effort to shove off for Travis.

172

No talismans were needed all the way across the Pacific. A weekend in Honolulu was idyllic. I hired a blue jeep with a fringed top, and with a bag of papayas at my side dawdled around Oahu, stopping here to watch surfers daring enormous waves, and there to witness a ceremonial dance by a hundred Japanese men and women of all ages, led by a caller with a microphone, all clapping hands and dancing a dreamy shuffle-step back and forth in slow rhythm.

Back at Waikiki I parked near the Diamond Head Light and waited for darkness to bring on the flashing signal. Later I sat in an easy chair on the beach in front of the Moana Hotel and listened to the orchestra. Thirty-five years had passed since I had been one of that hotel orchestra, playing my way around the world as a college musician. I liked being older. That "youth's a stuff will not endure" suits me fine.

Four A.M. departure from Hickam Field, on the shore of Pearl Harbor, in a MATS *C-121G,* a Navy-flown Constellation loaded to capacity with armed forces personnel and miscellaneous cargo including Embassy pouches, found me fingering the abalone fragment for a moment when, after a long run and no take-off, the commander cut power and taxied back to the head of the runway. The delay was momentary. Soon we were airborne, and eight hours later we landed on Wake Island to refuel plane and passengers. Another eight-hour flight and then a rainy twilight arrival at Tachikawa Air Base, near Tokyo, and after a romantic ride along a narrow lantern-lit shop-lined street, I was billeted at Washington Heights, on the edge of tree-filled Meiji Park.

No talismans were needed in Japan. The weather was fair, and each morning I had the good omen of seeing Fuji in the sky. I even heard Mozart being played at a wedding reception at International House—chamber music by a Japanese quartet, wearing tuxedos. The bride and bridesmaids were dolls in colored silks.

One morning I made my way on foot to the Imperial Hotel and found it reminiscent of Aztec or Pueblo buildings, strange, dark, brooding, and beautiful.

My last night in Tokyo I ate with Air Force librarians at a French restaurant in the mazy heart of the jumbled city—a meal *à la mode française,* featuring shrimps, filet of beef, lettuce, and strawberries and cream prepared by a drunken chef with a knife between his teeth, a good man to call "friend."

A side trip to Osaka and Kyoto called for no talisman's powers. All went beautifully and I would happily have bogged down at the Tarawaya Inn, where I was tenderly cared for by Naoko, a gray-haired woman who spoke the international language of smiling eyes.

My luck began to run out after I left Japan. Predawn arrival at Clark Field, sixty miles from Manila, saw a critical health officer delaying me because of an alleged deficiency in my "shot card." Additional inoculation for yellow fever, required for the imminent transit of India, was administered by an obliging pharmacist's mate; and finally I was billeted, as exotic bird-calls announced the dawn, sinister sounds inharmonious with Mozart.

I was glad to leave the Philippines the next day, aboard another *C-121,* the so-called Embassy Run, which had originated at Travis and come via Honolulu and Guam, and would take me via Saigon, Bangkok, Calcutta, New Delhi, and Karachi, to Dhahran and Tripoli, where I would leave MATS for an Al-italia connection to Rome. I hated the contrast of plenty within the fenced compound of Clark Field and poverty without, the stinking squalor, the corruption of black marketing.

We took off and climbed over the naval base at Subic Bay, and thence above fantastic cumulus clouds, blinding white over blue water, flying smoothly at eighteen thousand feet to landfall on the Indochinese coast, the dark blue sea shading to green, a honey-colored surfless beach leading to dunes and tea-planted terraces.

During a two-hour layover in Saigon to unload pouches and personnel, I observed lingual vestiges of the French, eau de Cologne for sale, and, utterly un-French, the delicate beauty of the Indochinese women with slender legs and flower-petal faces. Over a *citron pressé* made with Evian water, I unpacked my paperbacks and sought in vain to make sense out of Alan Watts on Zen. Everywhere I was struck by the rudeness of Americans with cameras, equaled later by their dullness in the slide stage.

For eight hundred miles northwest to Bangkok we flew over unbroken jungle, and through cumulus towers with a bump and a roll. Then it was sixteen miles to town from the airport, past gilded temples and open sewage, with ugly sights of modern farm and road equipment standing broken and idle. Technical training must accompany our largess of materiel; otherwise its fate is to rust to death.

In the lobby of the Grand Hotel I fingered the abalone when no reservation awaited me. The MATS protocol officer got on the phone, however; and on a swift and daring ride through the teeming streets, all the people out of doors in the humid weather, I went by pedicab to the "Rat," short for the Ratanako-sindr Hotel on Rajadamneon Avenue. Settled in a tennis-court-size room, I went down to the bar and bought a liter of ice-cold Evian water for my room, then sat in the vast lobby over another *citron pressé*.

When I looked for a cab to return to the Grand for dinner I found my pedicab man. "I wait you," he said, with an angelic smile. Back he drove like a devil, and I went up to the roof-garden restaurant, as the sun was setting over smoky Bangkok. Filet mignon somewhat reconciled me. I was entertained by eavesdropping on a reception being given by the University of Maryland's delegation to the University of Bangkok, realizing anew the folly of cocktail talk.

Downstairs I found my pedicab parked at the curb, the little driver sound asleep. I shook him gently. He opened one eye and smiled. "I wait you," he said, and away he went. This time we took a circuitous route back to the Rat through the twilight swarm of people, people, people. I conversed with my driver in mutually unspeakable pidgin English. "I wait you" seemed to be his total vocabulary, but he could sure pedal, steer, and end at the Rat.

I slept poorly with bad dreams. The room was hot save for a stream of cold air shot at me by a blower. Five thirty breakfast, six o'clock bus departure, eight o'clock take-off. More jungles, cloudy mountains, a glimpse of Rangoon through a rift in the overcast, and then descent to Calcutta over the delta of the Ganges.

Dumdum Airport: uniformed officials each with a minutely specialized role, screened lobby, overhead fans, reed and brasswork, and the *Kama Sutra* for sale. It was all right out of Kipling, except for a B.O.A.C. Comet on the tarmac. Even though I was in transit through India, immigration and health formalities were imposed, and a team of Indian officials sought flaws in my papers. I kept humming the Mozart and fingering the abalone. All was in order, including the yellow fever shot. It seemed miraculous.

Back on the plane, seated in reverse as all MATS flights are, I belted up in relief and awaited the next ordeal at New Delhi. The plane was nearly empty now, save for the fourteen-man crew that flew and maintained the *C-121* throughout its two-week round trip between Travis and Dhahran. They include the commander-pilot, copilot, two navigators, two radio men, an engineer, two mechanics, an electrician, a metal worker, a medical doctor, and two cabin boys. We were flying over a semiarid brown land that resembled eastern New Mexico. No green, no green at all. Occasional dry watercourses and mud villages, and heat haze. It was apparent why famine has always plagued India.

Overnight in New Delhi, at the Imperial Hotel, I was billeted with three young Air Force officers, on leave from Japan to visit Agra and the Taj Mahal, 140 miles away. They had a car engaged and invited me to go with them and be their librarian. We talked late, long, and earnestly over our rich country's role in impoverished Asia. They had learned Japanese and were sensitive to the needs of people with standards different from ours of Cadillac, chrome, and cellophane. I was proud of these young spokesmen and hoped they were not an impotent minority in our armed legions.

I spent another poor night in a bed directly beneath a fan

that squeaked and flashed blue on each slow turn. The suite was hot. One of the sleepers snored.

The morrow's flight to Karachi again found the plane nearly empty. Against a head wind of twenty-nine knots we made a ground speed of 225 mph. The earth was obscured by a dusty heat haze through which I saw dry river courses, occasional cultivated fields, but no trees, no green. After a lunch of dry toast, apple, and tea, I dozed, then went forward to the cockpit and gazed ahead on the monotonous course. The automatic pilot was on duty.

On the ground two hours in Karachi, desert capital of Pakistan, in the ancient land of Sind, about which R. F. Burton wrote two books, we took on cargo and a planeload of GIs returning home after a year's tour of duty at Peshawar, on the Afghanistan frontier. A communications relay station, my seatmate told me, between snatches of his *Lolita* and my *Tappan's Burro*, on a frontier of tribesmen, transversed by the Khyber Pass, like our Wild West of a century ago.

It was not until a few days later, when our *U-2* was brought down by the Soviets, that I learned what "communications relay station" meant. Peshawar was our base for the flights over Russia from Pakistan to Norway.

The Arabian landfall was fabulous—as we came in across the British oil concession of Bahrein, fifteen tankers huddled like waterbugs—descending over swirling patterns of salt lagoons in shades of yellow and green, like shot silk or peacock's tail, over sandy shoals in emerald water like a great jellyfish.

On the ground at our Dhahran air base trouble met me. I had no visa for Saudi Arabia. I had been assured that transiting passengers did not require a visa. Wrong. The plane emptied, and I was left on board alone, fingering the abalone, humming K. 334. The MATS officer came aboard and briefed me. There had been incidents. Americans were barely tolerated. Keep quiet, he said, perhaps they will relent. I did, and they did—finally, four hours later; and I was allowed to go to officers' billets on an overnight visa.

It was a fair desert night, under Vega and Antares, as I walked between white oleanders in flower to the mess hall for a ten o'clock supper, feeling more homesickness than hunger; then slept till I was alerted at four thirty for six o'clock departure.

We were hardly air-borne on the eight-hour leg to Tripoli when the cabin board flashed and the commander's voice announced a power loss and a return to base after dumping gasoline. A four-hour delay and away again, successfully, high above Arabia Deserta, in all the transit sight of only a single oasis, a black escarpment with a green orchard in its water-bearing lee. I would henceforth read Doughty and Bell and Stark with new understanding. The ground from eighteen thousand feet was like a crinkled molasses cookie, and then the Gulf of Aqaba, blue jewel between golden beaches and brown malpais.

After all the trouble I went to in Tokyo to get a visa from the British Embassy for the United Kingdom of Libya, it was never needed. High over Egypt the plane had another power failure, and we made an emergency landing at Cairo. "I could fly this baby on one engine," the commander apologized, "but MATS won't let me."

And so it was I found myself dining that night at Shepheard's Hotel on grilled *loup de mer estragon,* chicory salad, and *poire flambé.* My waiter was Austrian, a native of Salzburg, a Mozartian no less, and recognized K. 334 when I hummed a bar and told him how it and the abalone shell had brought me safely into Egypt—and would take me out again in the morning, I hoped.

After dinner I walked along the banks of the Nile in the mauve twilight, smelled the bitter smoke of cooking fires, saw the bats stitching up the darkness; and it was pure Lawrence Durrell, with life and literature in perfect register.

I felt good, very good, for I had secured the last unbooked seat on a KLM flight to Rome in the morning, MATS having announced an indefinite delay while a replacement was flown in from Dhahran. After a deep seven-hour sleep I was up at six and had villainous *café au lait* at the high window, swatting flies as I watched sunrise over waking Cairo. En route to the airport I felt no affection for the Arab world, its belled goats, donkeys, and camels, and people, shouting and stinking. I preferred it as transubstantiated by Durrell's wizardry in the Alexandria Quartet.

Let us praise all Dutchmen and their airplanes, I said, when Flight 858, a Super Constellation, arrived from Bangkok and Karachi, precisely on schedule. My passport was handed back, and I boarded and collapsed with relief, as we were air-borne nonstop on the way to Italy.

In spite of loyalty to MATS and our brave boys abroad, I was glad to be flying first class on KLM, nibbling hors d'oeuvres and devouring filet mignon, as we passed the southern sea face of Crete, golden loaf on a blue plate, its mountains frosted with snow. I was glad to be leaving the East, all of it, Far, Middle, and Near, with its flies and filth and unbearable contrasts of poverty and plenty, camels and Cadillacs competing incongruously, convinced that the American image we are offering in export version to the Eastern world is the wrong image.

Rome in the rainy spring was idyllic, all soft shades of green and yellow, trees and stucco, seen from the Janiculum at twilight. After supper with old friends at a family restaurant in the Campo de Fiore, I strolled through history, relaxed, secure, glad to be home again in Europe, a mere five thousand miles from Malibu.

Later, as talisman, I had Mozart to the life, played by Lilli Kraus in Paris and by Denis Mathews in London, more K. numbers than I could ever count, all beautiful, the abalone unfingered in my pocket. And a million books to buy.

The Road to Salzburg

As a book collector gains experience he seeks to expand his operations. Too recent or unprolific authors are no fun. Collecting A. E. Housman or A. E. Coppard is begun and over too soon. Not everyone can hook leviathan, as Wilmarth Lewis did Horace Walpole, and thence be scornful of minnows. If the prolific author is also vast, embodying history, geography, and the ambience of his time, then is the collector set for life.

Now in my middle age I find that I have hooked a big one, after years of smaller fry and some not so small. D. H. Lawrence kept me occupied for twenty years, starting with the Modern Library edition of *The Rainbow* and culminating with the *rarissima* second edition of *Lady Chatterley's Lover*. It took me fifteen years to accumulate all of Lawrence Durrell, lacking only his first novel, *The Pied Piper of Lovers*. Perhaps it will be my exit-door-prize; it would be nice to go out with book in hand.*

Thirty years ago I began to collect books about Wolfgang Amadeus Mozart (1756–1791) and recorded music by him. Then I had no inkling of his size. The proportion of his music that was played was like that part of an iceberg above water. I was

* Didn't have to wait. I found a copy in a London bookshop, May, 1963.

still bemused by Beethoven, awed by the way he hammered on the door; I had to learn infiltration rather than frontal attack, to appreciate iridescence rather than primaries, Rembrandt to Van Gogh.

The first time I heard the Salzburger clear was when Weingartner conducted the Requiem at the Théatre Sarah Bernhardt in Paris, and at a later concert the "Jupiter" Symphony. What before then had been mincing music was newly heard as pantherswift, subtle, and strong. Then the mind sought to understand what had moved the emotions, and I began to read, and made a simple beginning that knew not its end; I read Sacheverell Sitwell's monograph on Mozart, newly published in 1932.

In a secondhand bookshop in Florence I found a translation of Mozart's letters into French, and also Ghéon's idolatrous *Promenades avec Mozart*. His was a sad life, bittersweet, chromatic, ambivalent, prodigious, and pitiful, and also enormously productive and climaxed repeatedly by soaring fulfillments, such as the openings of *Figaro* and the *Magic Flute* in Vienna and of *Don Giovanni* in Prague.

With the publication in 1938 of Emily Anderson's translation of Mozart's letters, we had for the first time in English the whole man, full-blooded, coarse, tender, sensual, sensitive, industrious, gregarious, joyful, and lovable. Leading from Miss Anderson's footnotes were new paths of reading and collecting.

By then I owned an eighteenth-century road atlas of Europe, so that I could follow Mozart's journeys in search of recognition and security. There began to grow in my mind the thought that someday I would attempt to write about Mozart and the new life he had given me. Not a biography. There are many good ones. Not a critique. Einstein has said it all to suit me. Not a bibliography, although one is needed in English. There is also a new iconography, *Mozart and his World in Contemporary Pictures* by Otto Eric Deutsch, as well as his recent *Mozart, Die Dokumente seines Lebens*.

What then? Something that would involve literature and music and the world, fed by my own collection of scores of books and hundreds of LP recordings. The essence of it all. The distillation of thirty years of collecting, reading, traveling, hearing, dreaming.

I remembered Mörike's *Mozart aus der Reise nach Prague,* through which we drudged in college German. Too labored and sentimental. I read G. Lowes Dickinson's *The Magic Flute.* The earthy man and his heavenly music were not therein.

It was while riding on the railroad, the New Haven, en route to a conference at Yale, that I found the road for me. I was reading the current book in my baggage, *Mozart in Retrospect* by A. Hyatt King, a gathering of essays by the curator of music in the British Museum, when I came on a reference to *A Mozart Pilgrimage.*

The next day in the Yale Music Library I took that book to a quiet corner, dog with bone, growled figuratively at neighboring readers, and began to read.

In the summer of 1829, thirty-eight years after Mozart's death, Vincent and Mary Novello made a pilgrimage to Salzburg in order to present to Mozart's sister, Nannerl, then living in straitened circumstances, a sum of money subscribed by various people. Both kept journals. For years their two diaries were among the Novello memorabilia preserved forgotten in a Genoese villa. The story of their chance discovery during World War II by Edward Croft-Murray, a member of the British Museum staff, quartered as a soldier at the Villa Novello, was highly romantic. They were edited for publication by Nerina Medici di Marignano, a Novello descendant, and Rosemary Hughes, and are a primary source of information about Mozart's sister and widow, who survived him by half a century.

Here then was a project for my later years—to go over Mozart's European itineraries, to see what he saw of landscape and architecture, to hear his music wherever possible, and to be alert for Mozartiana which might have escaped the fine combs of Jahn, Abert, Einstein, and Deutsch. For example, the lost letters to Nancy Storace, the first Susanna. There in the stillness of the Yale Music Library, on a winter's day, I heard the inner voice say, Seek and you will find him.

And so one fine day, after retirement, will find me on the road to Salzburg and beyond, my Mozart collection transferred to my own built-in retrieval system and the 626 Köchel-numbered compositions readily hearable on my mobile components.

Books That Weren't
in My Baggage

"Aren't you taking any books?" my wife asked, as I began to pack my suitcase for our trip abroad. "Hundreds," I replied, and went on putting in shirts and socks. "They're all in my head."

I had remembered an encounter during the war with the late Isaac Foot, Lord Mayor of Plymouth, who had come on a mission to America with six suitcases of books and one dispatch case of clothes. He told me the selection of the books had upset him for a week, even then he lacked the ones he really wanted. "Next time," he had said, "I'll keep it to two books—the Bible and *Lorna Doone*."

Yet early the next morning, as we were descending through overcast for the landing at Zurich and had a vision of snowy fields and villages and shining Alps, I found myself wanting a certain book—John Russell's *Switzerland*, in the Batsford series, a civilized view of a civilized country I had read by chance the year before. And it occurred to me that airlines on the international runs might well arrange for paperback printings of characteristic books, to give their passengers more lasting fare than the ephemera they now dispense so lavishly: newspapers and magazines, toiletries and toys, food and liquor.

What would we offer on flights to the United States?

At a concert in the Tonhalle, pleased with the early hour and the exclusion of late-comers, I recalled another good book by John Russell—his monograph on Erich Kleiber, the conductor, who died at Zurich on the two-hundredth anniversary of Mozart's birth, a model work of biographical criticism by the art critic of the London *Sunday Times*.

And then there were the works of James Joyce, of course, there in the city where he toiled on *Ulysses* and where he died and is buried—the great novel and the single poem, "Bahnhofstrasse," and Frank Budgen's *James Joyce and the Making of Ulysses*, a Zuricher's reminiscence of those years before fame. In a bookshop in the Bahnhofstrasse, I admired their stock of Joyce and Joyceana, but I didn't need to open a single book; I had them all in mind.

In Salzburg at last, on all too brief a stay, I found Mozartiana new to me and sent home several parcels of books for later reading. There and in Zurich I was impressed by the knowledge and taste of the employees, even the youngest ones, accounted for by the apprentice system followed in the European book trade whereby to be a bookseller calls for a course of work and study similar to that required of librarians.

I did weaken and bought one book for my baggage: a paperback translation of Annette Kolb's *Mozart*, an impassioned biography with scathing judgments on those who failed Mozart the most, including the Archbishop Colloredo, Baron Grimm, Mozart's wife, Constanze, and the Viennese public.

It was March in Salzburg, and we were ahead of the festival throngs. The museum of Mozart's birthplace was nearly deserted, and it was also unlighted and unheated, which seemed to me exactly right. Wrong, however, is the statue of him in the Mozartplatz, a travesty of his likeness which should be pulled down and melted up. The near-by Papageno statue, and the Mozartbrunnen in St. Gilgen, depicting the boy Mozart with his violin, are beautiful.

Entering Austria over the Arlberg Pass, on the one day the ribbon road was open without chains being imperative, was less harrowing than leaving Austria over the Brenner Pass. Although the latter is lower and more of a plateau route through the Alps to Italy, it carries enormous trucking traffic, is two-lane, and it was snowing all the way.

The Brenner was the very route Mozart and his father followed on their first trip to Italy in 1770—Innsbruck, Brennero, Bolzano, Trento, Verona, Mantova, Bologna, and Firenze; and it was also the way Goethe went, when he first felt Italy's hot breath.

> *Kennst du das Land, wo die Zitronen*
> *bluhen,*
> *Im dunkeln Laub die Gold-Orangen*
> *gluhen,*
> *Ein sanfter Wind vom blauen Himmel*
> *weht,*
> *Die Myrte still und hoch der Lorbeer*
> *steht?*

No lemons or oranges were to be seen in the snowy Dolomites as we funneled down to the Lombardy plain; only a million fruit and nut trees in bloom, and the stuccoed-over stone houses painted in pastels proved we were on the sunny southern side of the Alpine wall. After a crossing of the flood-stage Po on a temporary bridge made of planks on boats lashed together, we got onto the Autostrada del Sole, Europe's finest expressway, and stayed there all the way through the Apennines into Tuscany.

Robert Browning remains my favorite "Italian" poet, and I found myself wanting my volume of his collected poems, if only to recall the correct text of "De Gustibus," whose only remembered lines were:

> What I like best in all the world
> Is a castle precipice-encurled
> In a gash of the wind-grieved
> Apennine.

In Florence for the first time in thirty years, I found myself pleased with the reconstruction of the Ponte Santa Trinità. We stood outside the Casa Guidi and paid homage to the Brownings.

The Mediterranean shore, from Pisa to Valencia, was like a library of remembered readings—Trelawney's *Last Days of Shelley and Byron*, Ezra Pound's *Pisan Cantos,* and, in Genoa, Richard Altick's *The Cowden Clarkes.*

Traveling without guidebooks and without cameras to fuss with and to come between eyes and the world, makes for a fresh vision of all that passes, in which landscape is seen for what it is and not for what someone has said it is. The time to read is later. Besides, driving on today's continental roads requires unbookish attention; and bedded down at night the newspaper is best for unwinding the nerve ends.

So I bought no books in San Remo, Nice, Arles, or Montpellier. In the latter town I did recall, however, that it was here that Rabelais took his M.D.; and that made me wish I had with me my copy of Albert Jay Nock's *A Journey into Rabelais's France,* to my taste one of the best travel books ever written, in which Nock went over Rabelais's trail from Chinon to Montpellier and the Isles of Hyères, to Paris and Metz, relating literature and history to landscape and lore. I wish that Nock, one of our most civilized writers, had done a series of such philosophical travel books on, for example, Petrarch and Erasmus, on Casanova and Goethe, Europeans who transcended frontiers.

Rolling toward the Spanish border below Perpignan, the road led through Sète, and I was struck by the town's welcoming sign with a quotation from Paul Valéry—"île singulière"; and then I realized that it was the Sailors' Cemetery that inspired Valéry's most famous poem, "Le Cimetière Marin." And there it was, on the hill above the sea.

On our first visit to Spain, a whole library of books avalanched over me, and I reeled under the impact of Cervantes, Borrow, Ortega y Gasset, Unamuno, Somerset Maugham, and Roy Campbell. The latter's *Portugal* is in the Nock vein—philosophical, opinionated, crusty, passionate. I had read it only recently, and it was fresh in mind. True, it is about Portugal, not Spain, but

I discovered the great fact of life which determines the nature and character of the entire Iberian peninsula and is common to both countries: the Pyrenees.

I intend to reread *Highway into Spain,* an account by the Australian geographer Marcel Aurousseau, of a walking trip from Paris to Madrid. As much as I appreciate Sacheverell Sitwell's *Spain* and his other travel books, I miss in them what is present in Aurousseau—a sense of landscape, of those physical features of earth which have determined character, art, literature.

Northbound from Madrid—Zaragoza to Huesca to Jaca—threading foothills, following river courses and encountering only sheep, shepherds, and dogs, a sudden sight of the Pyrenees across the valley of the Río Aragón was perhaps the noblest moment of the entire trip. High over the white battlements, I saw the figure of the medieval hero Roland, and heard the dying fall of his horn.

Earlier, at Toledo on Good Friday, in the cathedral jammed with worshipers and refugees from the cold rain, we had seen a roomful of El Grecos canceled out by a single Goya in their midst: "Christ Taken Prisoner," a heartbreaking revelation that made Goya and Rembrandt blood brothers. I would like to have reread Max White's novel *In the Blazing Light,* which I remembered as deeply understanding of Goya.

Sheep are the dominant animals of Castile and Aragón, and I shall never forget the sight of one great flock, as we switchbacked down *cuestas de contreras* to a crossing of the Río Cabriel and saw a thousand sheep flowing through rocky underbrush consisting entirely of rosemary in bloom and heard the din of their bells. French, not Spanish, is a book I read before we left home: Marcel Moyal's *On the Road to Pastures New,* the account of a sheep trek from Arles, two hundred miles northeast, to the summer uplands of the Savoy Alps.

Following the Garonne from Pau to Toulouse, and then the Tarn to Albi, and finally keeping a rendezvous with my old Dijon professor, Georges Connes, high in the chestnut forest of the Rouergue, we found ourselves in the river country so beautifully described by Freda White in *Three Rivers of France,* the Tarn, the Lot, and the Dordogne.

We were planning to go up the west side of the Massif Central, France's volcanic backbone, when a chance note in *Figaro Littéraire* changed our route: Lascaux had been closed the day after Easter. Green organisms were appearing on the walls, threatening to obliterate the paintings. André Malraux was coming with a team of parasitologists to see if the invaders could be repelled.

So we went due north into the wintry Haute-Auvergne, to Rodez, Saint-Flour, Aigues-Chaudes, Clermont-Ferrand; and I admitted to wanting a copy of Robert Louis Stevenson's *Travels with a Donkey in the Cévennes,* the country to the east, and of Philip Oyler's *The Generous Earth,* a book about the farm life of the river people to the west beyond Mont-Doré, the source of the Dordogne.

Destination Vézelay, the hill village in northwestern Burgundy, site of the Basilique de la Madeleine, the Romanesque church from whence St. Bernard preached two crusades, and the place to which Romain Rolland returned from Swiss exile. I had seen him once, years before, reading in his garden, an old man *au-dessus de la mêlée.*

A pity Henry Adams did not also do for Vézelay what he did for Mont-Saint-Michel and Chartres. There are still a few books to be written. All that's needed is leisure, learning, love.

If I found myself wanting a single book in Paris, it was John Russell's *Paris,* published four years ago. I did buy Jean-Victor Hocquard's *Mozart,* cast in the form of a dialogue between "Le Mozartien Fervent" and "L'Amateur Éclairé," an admirable potpourri of words and pictures.

In Paris I saw another of my old teachers, C. F. MacIntyre, poet and translator, bedridden since a stroke several years ago. His are among the best translations ever made of Baudelaire, Verlaine, Mallarmé, Corbière, Rilke, and Stefan George. And a book of his own poems, *Cafés and Cathedrals,* published by Oxford in 1940, remains a model of European travel poetry. Belonging to no clique and having no claque, MacIntyre is the perennial maverick. I wished for *Cafés and Cathedrals* in my baggage; it weighs so little, reads so well.

After six weeks on the road in search of spring, it was a great moment when we wheeled onto the wharf at the *gare maritime* in Boulogne, albeit in a cold rain, drove onto the Channel ship *Maid of Kent,* and had our first cups of strong English tea with bread and butter. We slept that night in Dover, at the foot of the white cliffs, to the sounds of gulls and foghorns. Only one thing was lacking, and neither the hotel library nor my memory could supply it: the text of Matthew Arnold's "Dover Beach," a poem to give the lie to those who say the Victorians were incapable of passionate utterance. As I lay awake trying to get its lines in order, I decided that a copy of the *Oxford Book of English Verse* would not have overloaded my baggage.

Part V

BOOKMAN IN THE SOUTHWEST

The Sense of the Past

I HAVE BEEN TRYING to recall when it was that I first got the sense of Southern California's past. Not while I was a boy. I grew up in South Pasadena, on the sunny side of the Raymond Hill, and my time was divided between reading books in the library and raising hell in school. I was an imaginative boy, and my reading led me to people the landscape with characters I was reading about. There was a Kentucky scout named Henry Ware, and miscellaneous Texans in the boys' books of Joseph Altsheler. When I came to Zane Grey, my hero was Lassiter of the Purple Sage. All through grammar school and high school I was unaware that Southern California had a past. My immediate environment, with the Las Flores adobe, the Old Mill, and the Frémont Oak on the bank of the Arroyo Seco, were taken for granted as part of the present. In back of our house on Marengo Avenue the concrete ditch in which we played Texan Scout or Mormon Villain was known as the Sanky. It wasn't until years later that I learned the word was a Yankee corruption of *zanja*.

Address, Seventy-fifth Anniversary of the Historical Society of Southern California, Los Angeles, 1958.

As lovingly good as my father and mother were, they gave me no sense of Southern California's past. My father was a horticultural scientist whose collecting embraced the records of Caruso, the rugs of Armenia, and the chairs of Windsor. Although my mother and her people were Hudson River Valley Quakers from way back, she spent most of her life here in Southern California, until her death at eighty-seven, being homesick for England; and when she went there for the first time in her middle age, she never wanted to leave. And so she was always filling our shelves with books of English literature and lore. The only thing she liked about Southern California was the climate. She had not the least interest in local history before 1900, the year she first came to Southern California. Nor was my education at Occidental College any help, even though I took history from Robert Glass Cleland, English history.

And so, paradoxically, it was not until I went to France to study in the University of Dijon that I began to get some sense of Southern California's past—and then it was by way of literature and landscape, not history. I lived a romantic student life, studying the poetry of Byron and Shelley, Whitman and Robinson Jeffers, and writing a book about the Carmel poet.

And then, on my way home, I discovered Dana—a grubby copy of *Two Years Before the Mast* bought in a London bookstall, which made me homesick, reading it in a boardinghouse in the lee of Primrose Hill, looking out on the rainy slope of London's only hilly park.

Dana was a lengthwise Californian, observing the harbors and the hills from San Diego, and the point which bears his name, to San Pedro, Santa Barbara, Monterey, and Yerba Buena, and he described it in transparent prose of an enduring toughness. This is the gift all writers seek—to write language that incandesces yet does not melt. There have been thousands of books about California, only a handful of which can stand with Dana. Why is this? Because the power to see, to sense, and to say is rarely united in a single writer in perfect proportions. It happened only once to Dana in this book of his springtime. He lived a long and useful life, but never again wrote anything to approach his California book.

When after three years' absence I returned to California in the Depression, poor in purse and rich in spirit, I saw the landscape with new vision, both clearer and sharper. There was only one difficulty: when I was little, the big houses had dwarfed the newly planted neighborhood trees. Now that I was grown to manhood, the trees too had grown, and now they made the houses seem small. Today Southern California has kept a few great immemorial trees—the Ellwood Queen in Goleta, the Moreton Bay fig at the Southern Pacific Station in Santa Barbara, the Santa Rosa deodars in Altadena, the cathedral camphor in Pomona—which are veritable shrines. In general, however, trees are having a hard time these days—trees and pedestrians, those vestiges of a vanishing way of life.

In 1933 distance and reading had combined to lend enchantment to California's past, of which I had grown up in ignorance. As a boy I had worked two summers on the vast Di Giorgio Ranch southeast of Bakersfield, unaware that the shades of Garcés and of Beals were at my side. Then in Europe I read *The Flock* by Mary Austin, and thenceforth the mountains of Tehachapi and the southern plain of the San Joaquin merged in my imagination, with no time barrier between the *entrada* of Francisco Garcés, the camels at the fort in the time of General Beals, and my own rabbit-hunting boyhood in the Weed Patch.

Now I came downstate through the passes of Newhall and Cahuenga with Frémont; and it was the same throughout Southern California. No more Kentuckians and Texans. I had found that my own land had pioneers and heroes. Drake and Cabrillo had sailed its shores. Portolá and Anza, Garcés and Serra had been lost in its mustard fields and suffered its chaparral. And everywhere I went, from the dunes at Yuma, near the site of Garcés' martyrdom, to the dunes at Oceano and landmarks named by Portolá, across the fertile landscape where the foliage of pepper and olive trees streamed like smoke in the wind, in the sunlit valleys and the blue shadow of the Sierra Madre—

everywhere I sensed their presences at my side. Through a reading of history and literature, I had gained a sense of the past, and now this past made sense to me. This was the land of my childhood and youth, this was the land I loved, and my roots sought the nourishment in its soil.

The Depression was a bad time, and yet good came of it. Prepared to teach, I found no teaching jobs, and so I went to work in a bookshop on West Sixth Street in downtown Los Angeles. This move determined my future. The knowledge and experience I gained and the people I met led inevitably to the work I now do as a librarian, teacher, and writer.

This was the cultural heart of Los Angeles—public library, clubs, cafeterias, a park, the Philharmonic Auditorium, and the bookshops. What more could one ask? (Well, perhaps a river, a harbor, a body of water which gives soul to a city.) I came to know C. C. Parker and Ernest Dawson, Bishop W. Bertrand Stevens, Elmer Belt, Bruce McCallister, Homer Crotty, and Will Clary, Althea Warren, Phil Townsend Hanna, Ernest Carroll Moore, Henry R. Wagner, Robert Ernest Cowan, Frederick W. Hodge, Carl Wheat, J. Gregg Layne, W. W. Robinson, Paul Jordan-Smith, and my boss, Jake Zeitlin—all of whom, and many more, haunted the bookshops of that locale.

The two years I spent on Sixth Street, and the earlier year on Colorado Street in Vroman's Bookstore of Pasadena, I count fully as important educationally as the years in college and university.

Chamber of Commerce literature often measures the cultural level of a community by its churches, schools, libraries, and museums. Add bookshops. No city is civilized that does not support a variety of bookshops. The number and quality of bookshops in and around Los Angeles, as compared with those in the San Francisco Bay region, indicates to me that Los Angeles now equals San Francisco as a center of civilization in California. One needs more strength to survive our centrifugal life here in Southern California, but from those strong survivors will come the children who will make the future. From our pres-

ent dispersal of cultural centers—Santa Barbara and Ojai, Riverside, Claremont, Pasadena, San Diego, La Jolla, Laguna, Long
Beach—will come eventual unification into one metropolis. Call
it "urban sprawl," if you will. My imagination sees it as a kind
of spiral nebula on earth, a vortex of actual power and potential
beauty. Materially all we need will be abundant water and pure
air. Spiritually we will need the inspired leadership of churches,
schools, and civic groups.

And this is where I come at last to the Historical Society,
whose seventy-fifth anniversary we are celebrating tonight. What
has the Society done in the region's growth to cultural maturity?
What should it do in the years ahead? The first question can be
answered by looking at the record; the second by looking at the
radar screen of the future.

The "record" is a row of bound volumes which take up only
a few feet on a library shelf. These in turn could be reduced to
an inch of microfilm. The founders of the Society, who met
together for the first time on November 1, 1883, are long since
departed this life. Much of what they and others wrote about—
the landmarks of Southern California—have disappeared, bulldozed into oblivion, and those that are left will soon be gone.
The Prudential Building and the Park La Brea Towers are the
look of the future. To survive at all, the remaining landmarks
of wood and adobe will need loving care.

I have lived with this short shelf of books, representing the
Annuals and the Quarterlies of this Society, published continuously since 1884, handling one or two before I went to work,
and doing the same at night when I came home; sometimes just
looking, skimming, sketching; other times reading an article
clear through, and then leaning back and reflecting on what
I read.

A strange, wonderful, rewarding experience it has been, as
gradually my own life in Southern California since childhood
was extended and enlarged to include all that the writers for
our Society knew and were.

The history of these seventy-five years can be reduced to

biography, to the biographies of a comparatively few thoughtful, persistent, dedicated men who believed the work of the Society was worth doing.

No one of this great lineage is more heroic than the Society's first president, Colonel Jonathan Trumbull Warner, whose first two names were troublesome for the Spaniards to pronounce, whereupon he changed them to Juan José. Colonel Warner stood six feet three, and his Spanish nickname was Juan Largo— Long John.

President Warner's inaugural address appears in the Society's first publication, which also includes the Constitution, Standing Rules, and List of Officers and Members. One of the primary purposes of the Society, seventy-five years ago, has pregnant meaning for us in this later age. These are President Warner's words:

> Just as we now eagerly prize the records of the early Colonial life and growth of our State and people, so will our successors prize the records which we shall preserve for them. . . . This is the underlying principle to which we owe our origin. . . . Here is a new and unoccupied field. It has been the home of the white man for more than a century, and now, in the midst of the inrushing flood of immigrants, old landmarks are rapidly disappearing. Things which are now common, in a few years will be rare; and, after a few years more, will cease to be.

Colonel Warner wrote this in the boom of the eighties. How would he have expressed his emotion during the boom of the twenties, or of the postwar forties and fifties?

Time can be stopped by a watch, can be measured by a gauge, say those who would have it so; and these include Shakespeare, for did he not say:

> And time, that takes survey of all the world,
> must have a stop.

This should make it easy for the historian in search of the past, if history were only the past. How much time separates the future from the present, and the present from the past? The rhythm of history is the beating heart, and time is the interval between each heartbeat. Our past history here in Southern California, in the few years since man has kept records, has been preserved largely by the efforts of this Society, by the foresighted hindsight of its founders and chroniclers. Up to 1900 much is known. Since 1900, and particularly during the booms of the twenties and forties, history has been happening too fast to be handled. It has been piling up data too numerous for any single agency to accumulate.

No library has all the telephone directories of all the towns in Southern California since the telephone was introduced in 1902. There is not even one complete file of the Los Angeles *Times*. Where can one find all the colored post cards of Southern California scenes since the beginning? Or the books and pamphlets, circulars, handbills, tickets, and other printing ephemera. The Huntington Library has the best collection before 1900. About ten years ago the UCLA Library began to collect anything and everything printed in Southern California since 1900, regardless of what form it is in or what subject it is on. Standing orders were placed with book scouts to "bring 'em in alive" and in bulk—and in these years have been amassed ten thousand pieces of printed Southern Californiana which are kept in chronological order. This is the cultural humus that will fertilize studies in history and literature.

This is good, but it is not good enough. We need to divide the responsibility for local newspapers, directories, documents, and other printed records, not to speak of manuscripts and business papers, among the local institutions. It is too enormous a job for any one.

And then we need to focus our historical studies on this more recent past, for with every heartbeat of time it recedes from us, buried deeper and deeper beneath the records of the vanishing present. We need more studies such as the recent ones by Donald Duke of the Pacific Electric and the Angel's Flight. Of Green and Green Pasadena bungalow architecture. Sunkist packing houses. The little red Santa Fe stations, the burnt ochre buildings of the Southern Pacific. The resort hotels, of which only the beautiful Coronado is left. Movie-house stucco and studios. The

Venice canals. Wooden oil derricks. Going, going, gone. We should employ a photographer to do nothing but photograph the local scene, day after day, up one street, down another, recording the present before it is lost to view. Southern California still has many beautiful backwaters, unknown to or disregarded by the Chamber of Commerce. Dare I speak of Bunker Hill?

Much *is* being done. Centers of study and publishing exist in colleges and universities and museums. There are historical societies in the several counties. Magazines such as *Westways*. Newspapers.

The teaching of history in the primary and secondary schools should begin with the bright interval called the present, rather than with the distant past, work back and then come forward. By the first method, there is no break in the time stream; one slips off the bank of the now and swims upstream against the gentle current. A very few swimmers, called mystics—and we are said to have more of them, at least self-styled, in Southern California than anywhere outside of India—a true mystic can swim either way in the time stream, which is without beginning or end.

The sense of the past must be part of a culture's common sense if a culture is to call itself civilized; and not merely the distant past which the popular mind tends to make more romantic than real. The earliest heroes of Southern California— Portolá, Anza, Serra, and the first Yankees—have served us well. Let us come down the years and assemble a hall of later ones.

It is not enough to write and talk about history, or to make and show pictures of it. Needed to excite the imagination are symbols of beauty and truth. Monuments such as the one in limestone of Garcés which is Bakersfield's noblest sight; or the ones in obsidian by Donal Hord in San Diego, to Montezuma and to Water; or the Pioneer Memorial Wall and Waterfall at Fort Moore Hill.

Here in this semiarid land, whose lifeblood is the water we have and have not, every town should rear a monumental fountain to the water gods. One of them was William Mulholland, and we have honored him with a fountain on Riverside Drive.

This is only a start. We should be inspired by St. Louis, which commissioned Carl Milles to create the monumental fountain called "The Meeting of the Waters," to symbolize the river union which takes place there, where the Missouri and the Mississippi flow together.

In the years to come this Society should assume the role of conscience of the community, of the region's self-respect, of spokesman for survival. What other group is there without self-interest? We have few or no material possessions. In the eternity of future-present-past we have the stability of mobility. As a group we are timeless, unhampered, unhindered, free. All the land we can claim as ours, all of nature's beauty, and man's ambivalent struggle to build and to destroy. I do not despair of the troubles that presently beset us because of industrialized overexpansion. We have the drive to catch up with ourselves, and when we find ways of curbing our aggressive vitality, then will we flower and produce fruit with great works.

In addition to preserving the missions, we should not neglect the few remaining old California ranches, taking as our model the Rancho Los Cerritos, so beautifully restored by the City of Long Beach and operated as a cultural center by the Public Library. The Casa de Adobe at the Southwest Museum is likewise an oasis in the urban wilderness. When form follows function, as it did in the missions and the ranchos, then a truly native architecture results.

From the farthest southeastern corner where the Colorado drops the last load of silt into the Gulf, to that wavering boundary line where wind and weather, landscape and flora tell us that Southern California ends—all of this changed and changing region is our responsibility, to observe and report on man's transforming acts, to preserve the records, to fend off ruination and oblivion, and to imbue the people with *the sense of the past* in every meaning of the phrase. Only in this way will we keep faith with our founders.

Fountains in the Sand

FROM WHERE I LIVE on the edge of that vast body of undrink-
able water, to the subterranean rivers of Arizona, ours is a water-
dependent culture. Since childhood, my emotions and thoughts
—and now that I am grown to manhood and have become a
writer, my verbal imagery—all have been determined by water
or the lack of it. I have been through fire and have known
thirst; my dreams are of rain forests, my prayers to the river gods.
I am no irrigation engineer, however, no dowser; and if I had
to choose between water and books, I would take the latter; and
at least have a book in hand, as I grew dirty and died of thirst.

I am not a typical Angeleno. I am an old-timer in the land
south of the Tehachapis, one who grew up in the citrus groves
and the mustard thickets. I have been in the heart of the lemon
country on a moonlight night when a hundred thousand trees
were in bloom, and the Great God Pan was enthroned. Now the
trees are being snaked out by the roots, grove by grove, and
the TV aerials that surmount the tract houses all suck down
the same nonsense.

As an irrigation boy, I saw my first fountain in the sands of

Address to Arizona History Conference, Tucson, 1960.

Kern County, on the southern edge of the San Joaquin Valley. There was no sculpture on it. It was a concrete irrigation stand-pipe—a tall one, requiring a ladder to look in at the top. It was a beautiful sight when one did, of crystal water brimming over, like a tear in an eyeball. When the cantaloupe trucks went by on their way to the packing shed, the swampers tossed fruit to me, and I stashed the melons to cool in the standpipe.

I learned about water's behavior from having to fight it with a shovel. Sand swallows water, unless it is channeled and stored in catch basins. Subdued water has made that part of Kern County a garden. In our society today, marked by absorptive elements that swallow our energy and leave no trace, I see institutions which I liken to fountains, channels, and reservoirs, which nourish, direct, and conserve our cultural forces against the sands of oblivion.

These institutions are present in Arizona, as they are in Southern California, though fewer in number and therefore more precious. I mean universities and colleges, historical societies, museums, galleries, parks and monuments, libraries and book-stores—institutions whose concern it is to educate, to transmit, to conserve, and to civilize. Their role is to educate the young and the old in a sense of values, to preserve the records of our time, and to collect and cherish the artifacts of times past. They help civilize the primitive strain in us which is childish, cruel, wasteful, and given to self-indulgence and entertainment as the main object of existence.

I have worked all my life in such institutions, in a land which has been washed over by waves of immigration, afloat on a rising sea of stucco. Only the hardy and tenacious have survived this saturating, scouring process. Landmarks of wood and adobe have been mostly lost. That a few have survived is because a few people cared, believed, spoke, and acted—people who have what I call the sense of the past.

To live only in the present is not enough. We need the past for its intellectual and spiritual nourishment, and we are at-tached to it by the umbilical of tangibles, by the sight of old buildings, in the shade of old trees, wherein and under our present was determined—places of decision where our destinies were decided.

I traversed the Papago Reservation once in spring when the desert was a garden, and saw "the men with long eyes"—the Indians' way of describing astronomers—creeping up Kitt Peak; and when I came upon the city of Tucson, it was in some ways like coming upon a desert. Many American cities are deserts. Some of them have oases, however, that make the sterile urbanization bearable. The Alamo in the heart of San Antonio, the Plaza in Santa Fe, Balboa Park in San Diego, the Hugo Reid Adobe and County Arboretum in Los Angeles—green places of growing things and running water, and monuments to our heroes.

When a city has bulldozed its historic sites into oblivion and wishes to regain its soul, it needs memorials to the past, either replicas of old buildings or symbolic representations—monuments, shrines, and fountains. It is sinister that the only museum in Yuma is the Territorial Prison; at least the courtyard is ennobled by a statue of Father Garcés. The Governor's House in Prescott is a more fitting memorial. The restoration of old Tubac enriches all of Arizona.

The imagination is stirred by reminders of history, even when they are as simple as a sign. I was driving into London once on the Great Southwest Road—a freeway known as a dual carriageway—when I saw a sign that read, "Here in this meadow, in the year 1215, King John signed the Magna Carta." Although I dared not stop, or even slow down in the flow of traffic, my imagination was arrested. I had passed the Meadow of Runnymede, cradle of our civil liberty, surrounded today by factories and filling stations; and lusted after, no doubt, by subdividers.

In my student years in Dijon, that old city famed for its wine, mustard, snails, and gingerbread, I learned that Dijon was once a walled camp, a *castrum,* on the Gallo-Roman frontier. Today no Roman vestiges remain, but the French have made a memorial to those who brought law and order to the western world. The progress of the original wall around Dijon is marked by marble tablets sunk at intervals in the walls of present buildings.

Each day as I walked to the university from the *pension* where I lived, I passed one of these memorial tablets, headed "Dijon Gallo Roman, Plan of the Castrum, showing the Location of the Fortified Wall erected against the Barbarian Invasions in the year 273 of our Era." And though I was an adopted Dijonnais, as I am an adopted Californian, I always felt intense local pride and the thrill of remembered history when I read that stone inscription.

Is there a point to my story? There is. Tucson was once a walled camp, founded in the year 1776, protected like Dijon against the barbarian invasions. Where are the walls today? Who will show me where the walls once ran?

Here in Tucson, place of the Dark Spring at the Foot of the Mountain, the cool old-timers, the ardent immigrants, the historians in deed or thought all know what I am talking about. It is happening here, as in London and Los Angeles, this bulldozing of the past that will obliterate it, if someone does not stand up and say, *No.* In olden times the dragon that ravaged the countryside was called Grendel, the hero Beowulf. Today the monster is called City, and who is the hero?

Arizona has no Alamo. No Magna Carta was signed here. Those modern Romans, the Spaniards, came and went, and left few memorials. Anglos came trapping down the Gila, or trooping through to California. Some stopped to trade and to dispossess the Apaches, or arrived later in search of health or, still later, to divert the dude dollar into the reservoirs of guest ranch and motel. The tree-planting Mormons came and stayed.

What survives longest on earth is spirit, not form. The idea of Christ's sacrifice outlives a million crosses. When the Parthenon finally falls, the Greek ideal will be fresh. China's wall crumbles; China's poetry lasts. The Alamo will outlive Tombstone, and for the reason that the Texans died for liberty, while those who sleep in Boot Hill merely died. The difference between the monument to Tom Mix and his horse Tony, which stands by the highway north of Tucson, and the monument to Robin Hood on the outskirts of Nottingham, is the difference between ephemeral entertainment and lasting legend.

Arizona is mostly landscape. The beauty of Phoenix lies not in the business district, but in the colored fields which surround the city and call for a Cézanne to paint them. Up in Coconino County, where the Museum of Northern Arizona is a kind of cathedral in the pinewood, one's eyes lift to the Sacred Peaks, as one inhales the incense of sawmill. In Yuma, the mind is possessed by the sundering Colorado and the drama of the river crossing.

From the air, Tucson is the red roofs of the University, is the Dove of the Desert; or at closer range from the ground, Tucson is the Arizona-Sonora Desert Museum of Arthur Pack, the Arizona State Museum directed by Emil Haury, the simply beautiful building of the Arizona Pioneers' Historical Society, or De Grazia's Mission in the Catalina foothills, his primitive shrine to Our Lady of Guadalupe.

The downtown district, the neon speedways, the proliferating tract houses, the plants and air base, and Old Tucson, are the economic base, essential to the economy and standard of living, yet identical with the same things in a thousand boom towns across America, synthetic, standardized, spiritually sterile. We have them all in Southern California: faster freeways, gaudier neons, huger plants, and also competing morticians, movie studios, and Disneyland. Let who will praise them. When materialism, phony religion, and entertainment become the highest good of an era, the end may be nearer than we know. By the sands of the Arroyo Seco, I lay me down and wept.

It was not a quest for entertainment that brought Kino to Pimería Alta. Garcés did not go to Oraibi to see the Hopis dance. The bricks of San Xavier were not fired, the adobe of Guadalupe was not molded, by a lust for amusement. It was not for fun that the Udalls made the weary trek to St. Johns. Likewise, the founders of the University of Arizona were not motivated by shallow things. Historical societies do not revere the past because it was a time of amusing entertainment.

These fountains in the sand were built, and are flowing today, because their founders were strong and faithful, believed in truth as a course of action, and loved their fellow men. In the origins of Disneyland, Old Tucson, and Scottsdale, in the present exploitation of Tombstone, and in the manufacture of weapons, however necessary the motives involved, I do not perceive the forces of faith, truth, love, and service; and I say that if we build not on these foundations, then are we building on sand, and will perish.

I prefer stone to stucco, I want Grimms' Fairy Tales in the original black and white, rather than in Technicolor. Against those who would build a cocktail lounge on top of Mt. San Jacinto, the wildest mountain in Southern California, against the barbarians wearing dark glasses, I take my stand with the Sierra Club and the Desert Protective League.

We need to sort out and to name things, and to choose among them what is good and true, what is fair and strong, then to take a stand on their behalf. It is our duty to speak out in meeting. We have noble examples in our history. We have Franklin, Jefferson, and Lincoln, Theodore Roosevelt, John Muir, Charles F. Lummis, and the Old Curmudgeon, Harold Ickes. Thanks to them and their kind, we have union and liberty, we have parks and landmarks. And we have a national conscience that will not let us sleep when the people are dancing in the streets.

In the United States Senate, it was Arizona's Henry Fountain Ashurst, the Silver Tongued Clarion from Coconino County, who alone had the courage, and the eloquence, to harpoon the Kingfish and haul Huey Long up short.

The role of a university in our society is a major one. Regents, administrators, teachers, scientists, librarians, students, joined as they are in the search for truth as it serves society, all have an obligation to stand firm and to speak out. Man has an eternal need to believe in something. A university exists partly to provide good and true things for the common belief.

Here in this oasis in the desert, goldened by orange, greened by palm, and pacified by olive, are fountains that flow with teaching, research, and publications, and other forms of public service. Contrary to what some of the alumni believe, athletic victories bring a university no true prestige. If the University of Arizona is famed beyond the borders of this state, it is because of the work of such men as Homer Shantz and A. E. Douglass, Frank Lockwood and Byron Cummings. The *Arizona Quarterly,* and the newer *Arizona and the West,* give the university a name that is wider than a region.

No atomic pile stores more potential energy than a university library, and no university is greater than its library, witness Oxford and Harvard. When Benjamin Ide Wheeler came to Berkeley in 1899 as president of the then undistinguished state university of California, these were his words: "Give me a library and I will build a university around it." They did. He did.

The collection, preservation, and careful use of the records of a society are signs of cultural maturity and responsibility. Arizona's distinguished Senators—Carl Hayden and Barry Goldwater—are leaders in the preservation of Arizona's pioneer heritage. Mulford Winsor and his successor, Alice B. Good, insured the survival of the state's early newspapers. In the Historical Society, the devotion of Eleanor Sloan and Mrs. George Kitt was matched by the generosity of W. J. Holliday. They have good successors in Yndia Moore and Ray Brandes. In the university library, the new Special Collections division, headed by the perceptive Phyllis Ball, is the result of the dedicated work of one woman, Patricia Paylore.

And finally, I pay tribute to what was here before the Hohokam, and will be here after the last Papago has gone to his beany heaven; I mean the landscape, the Arizona landscape, which both overwhelms and restores us, glorifies even as it humbles us. From cloud and mountain comes the element which makes the desert flower. Never should we end our praise of water—blue water of Havasu, red water of the Little Colorado, hidden water of the Gila, sandy water of the desert spring which begins to flow again when the rain comes "with love in its touches." Of the four elements all are fair, all are essential, but in the Southwest who would deny that water is the fairest? From childhood, we should be taught to revere water. Each community in this arid land should dedicate a fountain to the water gods.

I have walked among the pines on the crest of the Catalinas, and looked down on the city of Tucson and its widening stain, and beyond to Baboquivari, and eastward to a blueness in the sky that was Mt. Graham; and though I had a book in my hand and a friend at my side, I read not; neither did we speak; for in this land, the mountain, sky, and desert are of an unspeakable beauty, of a majesty beyond tribute, beside which the works of man, and man himself, are trivial and transitory, as ephemeral as this year's stand of grama grass.

If we pray, let it be for perspective; let us ask that, as Southwesterners, we be more worthy of the beauty that surrounds us, and will survive us, that we learn better to cherish our natural heritage and our human traditions, our history. Amidst the sand which is oblivion, may we keep our fountains clean and full of the water which is life. And may they brim and flow over, make us flower and be fruitful.

Vanished Arizona

And so, in the delicious quiet of the Autumn days at Nantucket, when the summer winds had ceased to blow and the frogs had ceased their pipings in the salt meadows, and the sea was wondering whether it should keep its summer blue or change into its winter grey, I sat down at my desk and began to write my story.

SUCH WAS THE BEGINNING, more than half a century ago, of *Vanished Arizona,* the unpretentious book by Martha Summerhayes which has come to be the classic account of army life on the Arizona frontier in the 1870s, as seen through a woman's eyes, and which has been republished, for the fourth time, by George Chambers' Arizona Silhouettes in Tucson, with historical notes by Ray Brandes, curator of the Arizona Pioneers' Historical Society.

Last winter I went over the trail of Martha Summerhayes, from Snowflake to Yuma, from Fort Apache to Ehrenberg, and from Fort Whipple to Fort Lowell and Mission San Xavier del Bac, to see for myself how much of her Arizona has really vanished and how much remains the same.

Why has *Vanished Arizona* become a classic? Because it was thoughtfully written by a person with feeling, perception, and

a corresponding gift of language; by a woman civilized, courageous, and compassionate, whose words go straight to the heart.
There are thousands of books on the West, only a few of which
meet these standards.

My intention was to follow Martha Summerhayes' trail as
faithfully as possible, going where she went, from her first
entry into Arizona, at Yuma, in 1874, to her last visit to the
Territory fifteen years later, at Tucson; and though some of
today's highways do not follow the old routes of the army
wagons, most of the roads remain the same, albeit smoother, and
not as much of Arizona has vanished as Mrs. Summerhayes
feared it had.

It was really the way of life, not the landscape, that she referred to in her title. Writing in 1908, she observed, "Railroad
and automobile have annihilated distance, the army life of those
years is past and gone, and Arizona, as we knew it, has vanished
from the face of the earth."

If I had been completely faithful to her route, I would have
chartered a ship in San Francisco and come around Cape San
Lucas and up the Gulf of California to the mouth of the Colorado River, and made my way (not in a stern-wheel steamboat,
as she did, but rather by flat-bottomed skiff) to Yuma, Ehrenberg, and Fort Mohave above Needles; thence overland to Fort
Apache in the White River Mountains, and back to Fort
Whipple at Prescott, Fort McDowell near Phoenix, to Ehrenberg
again and back to McDowell, to Florence, Fort Lowell at
Tucson, and thence to posts in the eastern United States.

Weather forced me to be unfaithful to Martha Summerhayes.
A fine Christmas spell was drawing to a close. The forecaster
warned of an influx of arctic air moving southward, with snow
imminent from the Mogollon Rim north. So in Tucson I rented
a car, and headed for the tall timber, hoping to make it to Fort
Apache before the snow did.

And I practiced what I have preached: I took books in my
baggage—a few basic Arizona books for this particular journey,
stacked on the seat beside me, and a road map. The books included the new edition of *Vanished Arizona*, of course, Byrd

Granger's revision of Will C. Barnes's *Arizona Place Names,* the *Arizona State Guide,* and Ray Brandes' *Frontier Military Posts of Arizona,* published by Dale Stuart King in Six Shooter Canyon at Globe.

Before I had gone a hundred miles, I found myself wishing I had brought John G. Bourke's *On the Border with Crook;* and passing through Florence, another Arizona classic set up a clamor in my mind. While staying overnight in Florence, Mrs. Summerhayes had met the writer of that other book I wanted with me— the famous Charles D. Poston, author of *Apacheland* (1878), an extraordinary poem about the history and geography of Arizona. "A very agreeable and cultivated gentleman," Mrs. Summerhayes described Mr. Poston.

Not all of the Florence of her time has vanished. A few stuccoed-over adobes remain, and an olive grove at least a century old, the trees badly in need of pruning. Dated 1891, the courthouse is definitely post-Summerhayes.

If I had taken the left turn at Apache Junction and gone on to Phoenix and up the Verde to Fort McDowell (now an Indian school), I would have seen enormous changes. The basic elements of Phoenix's fame, however, have not changed. "I was hearing a good deal about Phoenix," she wrote, "for even then in 1878, its gardens, its orchards, and its climate were becoming famous."

Instead I turned right toward Globe and the Salt River Canyon crossing, climbing toward the White River Mountains under the approaching weather front. The car heater was purring, the windows were rolled up, for snow lay on the ground, beautiful against the red rocks and green pines.

The turnoff at Carrizo on State Route 73 took me back to an unvanished Arizona. That this is the White River Apache Reservation was confirmed by sight of a pink-blanketed Apache squaw, leading a purple-trousered boy, and carrying a blue-hooded papoose in a cradleboard. Among the pine trees along the road, Indian families were gathering wood in pickup trucks to meet their eternal needs of cooking and heating. From wickiups thatched and patchwork-quilted against the cold, and from cabins with TV aerials, wood smoke flattened out under the low sky, filling the air with its fragrance. In the White River Valley I turned off at Fort Apache, now the Theodore Roosevelt Indian School.

It still preserves the appearance of the army post where Lieutenant John Summerhayes and his wife Martha were first stationed, in the winter and spring of 1874, and where their first child, Harry, was born. The old parade ground is now the playing field. There is a log building that could have been Major Worth's headquarters. The long stable still stands. Later buildings are of the rose-colored Coconino sandstone.

I stood on the edge of the White River ravine and looked down on the skeleton cottonwoods and elms, and gathered some of the little yellow berries on bushes among the dry grass. It was in this ravine that Martha Summerhayes attended an Apache Devil Dance, which she described with dramatic power. She frankly admired the good looks of Chief Diablo, and forgave the sins of adulterous squaws whose noses had been cut off by their vengeful spouses.

"Poor creatures," she wrote, "they had my pity, for they were only children of Nature, after all, living close to the earth, close to the pulse of their mother." She was truly compassionate in her view of the Apaches, who were regarded then as the cruelest of all tribes.

It was here at Fort Apache that her lifelong loyalty to the army was forged. Let her tell it in her own words: "I was getting to learn about the indomitable pluck of our soldiers. They did not seem to be afraid of anything. At Camp Apache my opinion of the American soldier was formed, and it has never changed."

Her opinion of Indian Agents was also formed here, and it was not a good one. Unfortunately, Mrs. Summerhayes never met John P. Clum, Indian Agent at the San Carlos Apache Reservation to the south of the White River, or her opinion would have been different, for Clum shared her humane outlook.

In the spring of 1874 Lieutenant Summerhayes was assigned to a company at Fort McDowell. The baby was only nine weeks old when they made what Mrs. Summerhayes describes as "A Memorable Journey."

"I heard them say," she wrote, "that we were not to cross the Mogollon Range, but were to go to the north of it, ford the Colorado Chiquito at Sunset Crossing, and so on to Camp Verde and Whipple Barracks by the Stoneman Lake Road."

I followed her trail through Show Low to Snowflake under a lowering sky that threatened snow at any moment, not risking the turnoff she took to Heber. Beyond there, no roads show on the map even today, which enables us to understand the roughness of that journey in 1874—six cavalrymen, two ambulances, two army wagons, and a Mexican guide—during which an Apache cradleboard was all that saved little Harry from death by shaking. At the rocky ford over the Little Colorado, all of their baggage was soaked. Books were in her baggage—editions of the classic German authors—and later at Ehrenberg she unpacked and sought to dry them out in the ovenlike air.

It was in this part of Arizona, on the earlier journey to Fort Apache, that Mrs. Summerhayes encountered the most famous of all the soldiers on the Apache frontier.

> One day a party of horsemen tore past us at a gallop. Some of them raised their hats to us as they rushed past, and our officers recognized General Crook, but we could not, in the cloud of dust, distinguish officers from scouts. All wore the flannel shirt, handkerchief tied about the neck, and broad campaign hat.

I pressed on northward to Holbrook and turned west on U.S. 66, through Winslow to Flagstaff, gradually distinguishing the Sacred Peaks from the clouds on the horizon. Snow fell in the night, calling for an oatmeal breakfast before I ventured down U.S. 89A, the newly opened road which connects with the Black Canyon route to Phoenix. I drove cautiously on the skiddy surface, prepared to put on chains I had in the trunk if a fall in temperature iced the road.

Then came the dramatic drop off the Mogollon Rim, as ponderosa yielded to juniper. Earlier in Flagstaff I had overheard a native assuring a frostbitten dude, who had come west in search of sunshine, that all he had to do was to go thirty miles due south and there he would find sun, flowers, and birds. I proved him right.

The red cliffs of Oak Creek and Sedona, and snow-covered Mingus Mountain, were lures in the west. My compass pointed eastward, however, to Stoneman's Lake. Alas, the sticky red clay road leading up to it called for a four-wheel drive vehicle. I didn't risk it. Besides, the lake is not as Martha Summerhayes saw it. For years it has been virtually dry, and any water in it last winter would have been frozen over. Here is how she described it:

> Toward sunset of the next day, which was May Day, our cavalcade reached Stoneman's Lake. We had had another rough march, and had reached the limit of endurance, or thought we had, when we emerged from a mountain pass and drew rein upon the high green mesa overlooking Stoneman's Lake, a beautiful blue sheet of water lying there away below us.
>
> It was good to our tired eyes, which had gazed upon nothing but burnt rocks and alkali plains for so many days. Our camp was beautiful beyond description, and lay near the edge of the mesa, whence we could look down upon the lovely lake. It was a complete surprise to us, as points of scenery were not much known or talked about then in Arizona. Ponds and lakes were unheard of. They did not seem to exist in that drear land of arid wastes. We never heard of water except that of the Colorado or the Gila, or the tanks and basins and irrigation ditches of the settlers. But here was a real Italian lake, a lake as blue as the sky above us. We feasted our eyes and our very souls on it. Stoneman's Lake remains a joy in the memory, and far and away the most beautiful spot I ever saw in Arizona.

At Camp Verde some of the old-time Arizona has been kept from vanishing in the beautiful little museum, housed in one of the four surviving post buildings. There may be seen army relics, women's gowns, letters and documents, and Apache and Yavapai basket- and beadwork. The natural setting beneath the Mogollon Rim, in the broad and fertile Verde Valley, is of a beauty time does not alter. Incense of burning juniper sweetened the cold clear air.

The road over Mingus Mountain, to Lonesome Valley and Prescott, was icy, so I more nearly followed the way around the mountains taken by Martha Summerhayes from Camp Verde to Whipple Barracks, doing in an hour and a half a journey that took her a long day. Fort Whipple is now a Veterans Administration Hospital Facility, with a properly antiseptic air. I do not believe any of the handsome buildings are much older than 1900.

Although I had left the bad weather when I dropped off the Rim, the north itself remained curtained in cloud. Not a glimpse did I get of the San Francisco Peaks beyond Flagstaff, or of Bill Williams Mountain. On her original trek across from the Colorado River at Fort Mohave (the Fort was completely obliterated in 1942 and so I did not follow her trail there), Mrs. Summerhayes was enthralled by the way Bill Williams Mountain dominated the landscape.

"It seemed to pervade the entire country, and took on such wonderful pink colors at sunset," she wrote.

> Bill Williams held me in thrall, until the hills and valleys in the vicinity of Fort Whipple shut him out from my sight. But he seemed to have come into my life somehow, and in spite of his name, I loved him for the companionship he had given me during those long, hot, weary, and interminable days.

From Fort Whipple, the Summerhayes family was assigned to the river post at Ehrenberg. Ehrenberg! the place she had recoiled from when they had stopped there briefly en route up river from Fort Yuma to Fort Mohave. "I did not go ashore. Of all dreary, miserable-looking settlements that one could possibly imagine, that was the worst."

Being stationed there all through the summer of 1875 did not raise her opinion of Ehrenberg; and if she returned today, I am sure that it would remain low, for it is a ghost town.

I explored Ehrenberg's lone surviving feature of the 1870s—the graveyard. In her time, it filled Mrs. Summerhayes with horror, for the coyotes used it as a feeding ground. Today it is a huddle of nameless rock cairns, over which highway workers have erected a crude monument, with pioneer relics cemented in its base. Across the river in California, on the lower lands to which water is accessible, Blythe flourishes.

Her revulsion at Ehrenberg's heat and squalor evoked some of Martha Summerhayes' most vivid descriptions of desert life, when a newly killed snake's rattlers were her baby's favorite toy. Air conditioning and refrigeration have made life bearable today on the Colorado Desert, and dams on the river and diverted water have tamed and reduced the savage Colorado of which she wrote with awe and respect.

I took the road on the Arizona side a hundred miles down-river to Yuma, passing through the Signal Corps installation known as the Yuma Test Station, and I can testify to the fact that the United States Army has *not* vanished from Arizona. I was also content that the season was winter.

The best vantage point at Yuma is from the hill on which the Territorial Prison Museum stands. From there one can look far up the lazy river, lined with yellow willows in December, and, if the wind is right, get the pungent smell of arrowweed noted by Martha Summerhayes. Fort Yuma was the first army installation in Arizona, established in 1849. Today only Fort Huachuca remains active.

In 1877 Mrs. Summerhayes returned to Arizona, after recuperating from Ehrenberg at her ancestral home in Nantucket; and in Chapter Twenty-four of *Vanished Arizona,* called "Up the Valley of the Gila," she waxed lyrical.

The December sun was shining brightly down as only the Arizona sun can shine at high noon in winter, when we crossed the Colorado on the primitive ferry-boat drawn by ropes, clambered up into the great thorough-brace wagon (or ambulance) with its dusty white canvas covers all rolled up at the sides, said good-bye to our kind hosts of Fort Yuma, and started, rattling along the sandy main street of Yuma City, for old Camp McDowell.

I wondered if I had really grown to love the desert. I had read somewhere that people did . . . I did not stop to question the subtle fascination which I felt steal over me as we rolled along the smooth hard roads that followed the winding of the Gila River. I was back again in the Army. I had cast my lot with a soldier, and where he was, was home to me.

Eighty-three years later to the month, I took the Gila Trail from Yuma to Gila Bend, and experienced the same joyous feelings described by Martha Summerhayes. To breathe that clear sun-warmed winter air of southern Arizona is even more precious today to a smog-bedeviled Southern Californian. In her time, emigrants offered prayers of thanksgiving when they crossed the river from Arizona into California. Today the reverse is true.

Time pressed, and at Gila Bend instead of following her trail into the Valley of the Salt to Phoenix and Fort McDowell on the lower Verde, I turned off to Casa Grande and Tucson, sighting the successive ranges whose essential configuration has not changed in a million years.

In June of 1886 the Summerhayes' returned to Arizona from posts elsewhere in the country.

> We travelled to Tucson in a Pullman car. It was hot and uninteresting. I had been at Tucson before, but the place seemed unfamiliar. I looked for the old tavern; I saw only the railroad restaurant. We went in to take breakfast, before driving out to the post of Fort Lowell, seven miles away. Everything seemed changed. Iced cantaloupe was served by a spick-and-span waiter; then quail on toast. "Ice in Arizona?" It was like a dream, and I remarked to Jack, "This isn't the Arizona we knew in '74," and then, "I don't believe I like it as well, either; all this luxury doesn't seem to belong to the place."

Today Fort Lowell, situated east of Tucson on the south bank of Rillito Creek, is long since abandoned, fallen ruinously to a few remnants of the old adobe walls. The great cottonwoods described by Martha Summerhayes are gone. The suburban sprawl continues to cover the valley of the Santa Cruz. There is a strong local movement, however, to restore Fort Lowell as a historical monument.

Adobe crumbles. Wood burns. Stone lasts. Thus the Mission of San Xavier del Bac, Father Kino's Dove of the Desert, stands today as Martha Summerhayes so reverently described it, when she camped for several days outside its ancient walls.

San Xavier was my last sight of Tucson, it and the red roofs of the University of Arizona, as the plane rose from the runway and set course for Los Angeles. My winter days with Martha Summerhayes were ended, during which I had driven more than a thousand miles over her trail. I held her book open in my hand, meditating on it between glimpses of the earth below, where the winter sunlight was alchemizing the ranges to amethyst; and I gave thanks to her for having written so beautifully of an Arizona as eternal as it is vanishing.

The Northland Press
in the Pinewood

THE PHENOMENON of excellence is unpredictable. Who? When? and Where? are unanswerable questions. If, for instance, I had been asked last year to forecast who would print the year's most beautiful books on the Southwest, and where they would be produced, I would have said either Lawton Kennedy of San Francisco or Ward Ritchie of Los Angeles, Roland Dickey of Albuquerque or Carl Hertzog of El Paso, all of whom have distinguished records as Southwestern printers.

I would not have predicted excellence of typographical achievement from anyone anywhere in Arizona; for the state, notable though its record has been in the production of written Southwestern literature, has never harbored a printer of the first rank.

Frank Holme's Bandar Log Press, the first private press in Arizona, which was located at Phoenix many years ago, printed only arty curiosities. Today John Beecher, the California printer, has never stayed long enough in one place to achieve any identity with a locale. Jerome, Scottsdale, Phoenix all have appeared in turn as imprints on the limited editions of his own poetry, but his latest move is back to the coast, where his roots have always been.

The University of Arizona Press in Tucson is making earnest efforts at typographical distinction under the direction of Jack L. Cross; thus far, however, except for such typographical "sports" as George Webb's *A Pima Remembers,* designed by Harry Behn (now of Connecticut), its books are distinguished more for their scholarly content than for their typographical format.

If I had been asked to name the Arizona locale of a typographical renaissance, I am sure that Flagstaff would have been the least likely place; and not because of any prejudice I have against that community up in Coconino County. On the contrary, I have a lifelong fondness for Flagstaff, from earliest childhood memories of crossings on the Santa Fe Railroad, when I stood in the open-windowed vestibule of a Pullman on the California Limited and sniffed the sweet incense of sawmill. More recently, I have enjoyed Flagstaff's piney charm while taking part in Weldon Heald's annual Writers' Conference on the campus of Arizona State College.

Yes, Flagstaff suits me fine. The Museum of Northern Arizona, the Lowell Observatory, the college—all guarded by the Sacred Peaks of San Francisco—form a cultural center of real distinction. But not typographically speaking. No printer, no press, no book production was identified with or expected from Flagstaff, at least in my experience, until . . .

Two years ago Dale Stuart King, the Globe publisher with the provocative address "Six Shooter Canyon," produced a book called *Old Father* by Pablita Velarde, an unusual volume both in format and content, produced at the Northland Press in Flagstaff. This was not a truly finished production; it lacked finesse of design and execution; it was more of an inspired amateur work, a typographical "sport"; and though bold enough in itself, it did not promise much for the future, at least in my estimation. It was chosen by the Rounce and Coffin Club as one of the best western books of the year.

Then came the third annual History Conference held at Tucson in 1962, sponsored jointly by the University of Arizona and the Arizona Pioneers' Historical Society, which featured a keepsake to commemorate Arizona's Golden Anniversary. This was Donald M. Powell's bibliography called *An Arizona Fifty*, a perceptive selection of outstanding books produced in the state during its first half century.

The quality of its *contents* did not astonish me. Ever since he came to Arizona in 1946 this Powell boy (no relative, just a friend and colleague) has been achieving renown as the state's leading bibliographer; and this latest work of his was permeated with the author's feeling for both the landscape and the literature of his adopted state.

It was the *format* of *An Arizona Fifty* that was the bombshell. Here was an impeccable piece of printing—design, paper, inking—everything was just right for eye and hand. Simple, unobtrusive, discreet, functional typography meant to be read and not used as decoration for a library table; and the pamphlet bore the imprint "Northland Press, Flagstaff."

Something was happening up there in Coconino County. There was a master printer among the ponderosa pines. I made a note to head for Flagstaff on my next Arizona field trip and see for myself who was responsible for this altogether unlikely event, for the leap forward from the amateur charm of *Old Father* to the masterful professionalism of *An Arizona Fifty*.

Before I could do this, two more books appeared from the Northland Press. If the Powell pamphlet was a bombshell, these succeeding imprints were atomic blasts. *A Navajo Sketch Book* by Don Perceval and Clay Lockett and *Torrent in the Desert* by Weston and Jeanne Lee were two of the most beautiful Southwestern books ever to appear anywhere—a statement I am fully prepared to defend, having had both eyes fixed on regional publishing throughout a book reviewing career which began in 1934.

All of my questions were answered last spring at the fourth History Conference in Tucson, when I met the man in the forest, the printer among the pines, the owner of the Northland Press, namely, Paul E. Weaver, Jr., late of Santa Monica, California; Reno, Nevada; Acapulco, Mexico; Antibes, France; the Windward Islands, West Indies; and since 1958 of Flagstaff, Arizona, where he now lives, works, and breathes that perfumed air, a happy man who needed the first thirty-five years of his life to find himself and to learn that all the world's roads led finally to that clearing in the pines up in Coconino County. I learned that the beauty of the Northland Press books is no accident; it is the reflection of a fulfilled man.

If Flagstaff was the unpredictable locale, so was Paul Weaver the unlikely producer of books peerless in Arizona's printing history, although he had inky fingers from his earliest years. Only child of Santa Monica's leading commercial printer and owner of the profitable Weaver Publishing Co., Paul Jr. seemed destined by heritage and environment to succeed his father as a successful business printer. It was taken for granted that he would get experience in the shop, go to college at near-by UCLA, make a good marriage, and settle down.

And he tried, he surely tried. He got experience in the plant, and at Santa Monica High School he showed a flair for journalism. The first signs of departure from the conventional appeared when he refused to go to UCLA—"that cashmere jungle," he called it in conversation at our first meeting in Tucson. He went off to Reno to the University of Nevada, majored in journalism, and found that he was not a true city boy. He fished the Truckee and hunted the wilds of the Sierra Nevada; and thus he determined his deepest desire for living close to nature, away from what poet Robinson Jeffers has called "the thickening centers."

It is always fascinating to go back along the road of a man's life and note the points of crisis and decision. They are not sharply marked in Paul Weaver's life. There is a good deal of blur, of forking and turning, of confusing starts and stops. He is a complex man, although what he ultimately produced is simple. Two powerful forces were working on him—loyalty to his father and the economic pull of Southern California—and it took him many years before he could spin free into his own orbit.

College was followed by a short and successful career in journalism. Young Paul Weaver owned, published, and largely wrote the weekly Palisades *Post,* of Pacific Palisades, that prosperous residential community adjoining Santa Monica to the north. The chief advantage of Palisades living, he found, was access to sailing and surfing; and as we can see when we come to examine the recent books of the Northland Press, these marine hobbies paid off.

Weaver was unable to get interested in the routine commercial printing work of his father's plant, or used to the increasing pressures of life in greater Los Angeles. His solution was to sell the *Post* and get away. From 1954 to 1957 he lived in Europe, sailing his own yawl on the Mediterranean and later in the West Indies, where he did charter work in the Hemingway tradition.

If one looked at Paul Weaver's life at this point, salt water having apparently washed the ink away, one would see no sign of the man up in Coconino County, running a press in the pinewood. Human biography, however, is less predictable than horse racing or roulette or any of those surer things.

Weaver was not destined to be an expatriate for life. He renewed contact with his father and mother and home town; and back he came to Santa Monica, sold a lot of printing for the Weaver Publishing Co., and made plans to publish his own magazine, on Latin America. *Fiesta,* it was to be called. He put money into it, but it wouldn't fly; it wouldn't leave the ground. No issue ever appeared. Weaver became desperate again and began looking around Southern California for a small-town press and paper, going as far afield as Paso Robles and, with the naive idea that it was still the small town he had once seen as a youth, Phoenix.

That frightened him. "Another San Fernando Valley," he said to himself and went to pay a courtesy call on Columbus Giragi, an Arizona counterpart of Paul Weaver, Sr., owner of the Arizona-Messenger Printing Co., one of the region's largest typographical concerns.

Here is when the roulette wheel in Paul Weaver's life began to slow for a stop; here is when his moment of truth came near. A soothsayer, an oracle, a fortuneteller would have seen omens in the air that day in the sky over the Salt River Valley, at the hour when Paul Weaver entered Giragi's office and asked him if he knew of any small-town presses for sale. Only that morning Giragi had received a call from Jack Fine, a retail merchant in Flagstaff who had just bought the commercial printing plant of Giragi's old weekly, the *Coconino Sun*. Fine, never in the printing business and dependent on a partner, found within three months that this was a bad investment and made the decision to sell it.

A phone call and a trip to Flagstaff led Weaver to his decision that he would temporarily manage the Northland Press, with an option to buy. Back he went to Santa Monica and awaited Fine's reaction to the offer he had made. A month passed and no word came. Weaver put it out of his mind and took another job, a high-paying one—and worked a single day. On the afternoon of his first day, Jack Fine phoned and said yes.

The wheel had stopped spinning. The moment of truth had come. Weaver went home and told his wife of two years, Mary Jean Sutcliffe, a successful drama teacher and coauthor of a book on the theater and a former fellow student at Santa Monica High School, that they were moving to Flagstaff. The fact that she was expecting their first child was no deterrent to either of them. (A second child has since been born to them, also in Flagstaff.)

"My wife is the hero of this saga," Weaver said to me, five years later, as we talked over lunch in Tucson. "She also has literary and editorial skills that have proved invaluable."

As master of the Northland Press, Weaver's first need was to replace obsolete and worn-out equipment and then gradually to upgrade all the work undertaken, whether it was a single business card or a complete book. Crack salesman that he was, Weaver hit the road in both directions on U.S. 66, west to Williams, Ashfork, and Kingman, east to Winslow and Holbrook, calling on old customers and soliciting new ones. The Museum of Northern Arizona and Lowell Observatory proved to be two of his best customers. For the former he redesigned their periodical, *The Plateau,* and their leaflets and catalogues; and for Lowell he likewise improved a variety of their scientific publications.

Thus far these were all things Weaver could have done in Santa Monica. The real reason he had left the shop of his father was his deep desire to print five or six fine books each year, to found a book publishing division of the printing plant.

This came about gradually in Flagstaff. The first step was securing a competent color printing man; one came in the person of Weston Lee, a Salt Lake journalist-photographer–color separation printer, who appeared providentially and decided to locate in Flagstaff. The Press's subsequent work led to a discerning article on the Northland Press in the *Western Printer and Lithographer,* written by its editor, Roby Wentz.

A chain reaction followed. The article was read by John Anderson, a peripatetic printer-designer from Philadelphia who had come West to work for Grant Dahlstrom's Castle Press in Pasadena but had his own plant at this time and, even as Weaver before him, was finding himself discouraged by Southern California's smog and traffic. He too felt the pull of the pinewood, packed his type, toothbrush, and family, and headed for Coconino County.

Now the stage was set for the production of masterpieces. The Press had a master with vision and ambition; the equipment was modern and efficient; color work could be handled superbly by Weston Lee; and in John Anderson, the Press had a virtuoso of typographical design.

Anderson had learned printing under the late Peter Beilenson of New York, founder of the Peter Pauper Press; and he brought to Flagstaff both skill and taste.

Anderson designs the way all fine designers work: by nearly endless preliminary trial runs, setting version after version of a layout, pinning all the versions up like butterflies on the wall, walking back and forth, staring, weighing, reflecting, comparing; and doing much of this after hours, playing with type in the way a pianist improvises on the keyboard, warming up to the final finished production, which sounds (or looks) so simple and is actually the result of hours of preparation.

When I learned from Weaver of this sequence of men and events in the progress of the Northland Press, I no longer wondered about the beautiful books—the Powell, the Lee, the Perceval-Lockett: they were the inevitable result of catalytic forces which brought together the right men at the right time in the right place.

"If I have any talent," Weaver confessed with characteristic modesty, "it is to recognize talent in others."

This quality in Weaver led to the book which is pure northern Arizona, the *Navajo Sketch Book*. When he saw on the walls of the Museum of Northern Arizona an exhibition of the water colors and drawings, made by Don Perceval, of the Navajo people and landscape, Weaver saw the possibility of a beautiful book. To write a text to accompany the pictures, he recognized another talented Arizonan, Clay Lockett, scion of the old Flagstaff ranching family, known throughout the state as an authority on Indian crafts and ways.

Pictures and text do not form themselves into a book. Weaver worked intensively with Perceval and Lockett and Anderson, in getting just the right combination of picture, word, and type on each page.

When it appeared, I declared the *Navajo Sketch Book* to be the most beautiful book ever produced in Arizona. This can be easily extended to describe it as one of the most beautiful of all American printed books.

Don Perceval was no new talent to me. I had been enjoying and collecting his work for many years. London-born and educated in architecture at the Royal College of Art and in life in the Royal Navy, Perceval had been working for thirty years in the Southwest, a scholar as well as an artist, accumulating a profound and accurate knowledge of Spanish and Indian costumes and crafts, drawn particularly to the Navajo and Hopi. In his own painting, Perceval was a disciple of Maynard Dixon, and in volume eight of *The Brand Book,* the annual of the Los Angeles Westerners, he had reproduced and commented on Dixon's early sketches of the Navajo country. His own Navajo drawings are in the footsteps of his master.

For the Arizona Development Board in Phoenix, Perceval, Lee, and Weaver combined their talents to produce a folded broadside on Arizona's Indians, which should be framed and hung on school walls throughout the state. In Tucson I saw the layout for a children's book on cattle brands by Don Perceval, which will be another Northland triumph.

Don Perceval also contributed end papers and maps to the Lees' *Torrent in the Desert,* that glowing pictorial on the Colorado River. He and Paul Weaver go mighty well together.

John Anderson is no longer in Flagstaff. His restlessness, and that of his wife, carried him on to Phoenix, and finally back to Philadelphia. He will continue however to design for Northland Press. Weaver believes this arrangement will prove even more efficient and productive, if somewhat less convivial.

To prove that the Northland Press is not limited to Southwestern subjects, Weaver published an unusual book called *Surfing in Hawaii,* the narrative by Desmond Muirhead and breath-taking photos by Don James, an old Santa Monica crony of Weaver's. I won't be surprised now by anything Northland does, in fact I anticipate a rich and varied change of pace in all its future work.

In the 1962 competition of finely printed Western Books, sponsored annually for the past quarter century by the Rounce and Coffin Club of Los Angeles, the Northland Press placed all three of these beautiful books: *A Navajo Sketch Book, Torrent in the Desert,* and *Surfing in Hawaii.*

Once set, the patterns of behavior in a man's life tend to repeat themselves. The compulsion which led Paul Weaver to "get out of town" and quit Southern California is being felt in Flagstaff. "I've got to get out of downtown traffic," he said to me, as we parted in Tucson. "I'm planning to move the press, and add a bindery."

"Not leave Flagstaff?" I asked.

"Oh no!" he laughed. "Just a bit deeper in the pines. I like it up in Coconino County."

The Little Package

It is your *years*, you graduates, rather than your *ears* that I seek tonight, for I speak to you across the gulf of a generation; and yet if the gap of time were closed, I would be sitting with you, not speaking to you. And I might be doing what I did thirty-two years ago at my own commencement, when I sat with my fellow seniors, my hearing aid turned off to spare me a middle-aged oracle who was speakably dull . . . yes, sat there, unbelieving, and wrote a poem, to the eucalyptus trees which backed the stage of the Greek Theater, a poem ostensibly to those tender trees—eucalyptus citriodora, they were, the sweet lemon-scented gum from Australia—but really a poem to the girl who was waiting for me in my car, a freshman girl I was in love with and to whom I am married today, a sensible creature who proved it by saying earlier to me, "I'll wait outside while you get your degree. Don't be long. I'm hungry."

And so I stand before you tonight, prepared to be short, to make sense if I can and, above all, to make you listen, for I have something to say to you. About the Little Package. What's in it? Dynamite, to blow you up. Honey, to heal you. A fire

Commencement Address, University of Arizona, Tucson, 1961.

opal, for beauty. A scarf of colored silk. Sea shells for music. River sand to filter impurities. Rose petals. Leaves of grass.

I am not being obscure. You know what I mean by "Little Package." Books, of course. I would be a poor librarian if I did not talk about my stock in trade. I know about books. I have lived with them all my life, have collected a million and a half for my university, and a few for myself. Have written some, read many; and best of all, led other people to read.

You can lead a student to the library—for it has uses not involving books—but you cannot make him read. Tonight I shall try, by throwing the book at you. It was risky of your President to give a librarian the last word. I am not sure that he knows what an explosive stockpile a library is—all those little packages stacked up and awaiting the detonation that occurs when they are touched by hand and eye and mind. And when one of them is unwrapped by the act of reading—for example, Milton's pamphlet on the freedom of the press, the *Areopagitica*, first published in 1644—then the fission and the fallout are more far-reaching than from any atomic split.

Does the President know about this dangerous place called Library? Of course he does. He has championed its growth, and won the loyalty of some of the best librarians known to me. Despite what you may have read in the *Wildcat*, you senior cats have the best university library in the Southwest, between UCLA and Texas.

So I do have the last word, before you are turned out of Paradise in the desert night, to wander the earth, and space, in search of your own Eden. I appreciate the opportunity; but frankly, it's a bit late for any more words. You have survived a four-year fallout of words; and now only a few last words hold you from your own final fallout of this air-conditioned nest.

What chance have I, in forty minutes, to undo what your distinguished faculty has taken four years to do to you? Am I wicked in wanting to diseducate you, to undermine your foundations, to reverse your fields, get you out of step, encourage you in heresy of doctrine, disbelief of dogma, and altogether demoralize you?

No. Not likely. I bring too little, too late, am a David against the Goliath of your closed minds, your molded characters, your set beliefs. You are safe. Society tells you that sheepskin is synonymous with success. As you gradually level out on the plateau of middle age, most of you will never read anything more difficult than newspapers and magazines.

Here's my warning to you. If you want to maintain your security and self-assurance, stay away from certain books. Don't open that Little Package, if you are afraid of being blown sky-high, or lulled to dreams, or dazzled by beauty. Pandora's Box had nothing on a book.

What book? I'll name a few. Some I've lived with, read, and reread, through youth and middle age. The dangerous books are not the ones the censors try to suppress. An honest book about sex—*Lady Chatterley's Lover,* for example—is not dangerous, either to the individual or to society. I like that story about the Italian printer in Florence who first set *Lady Chatterley* in type, back in 1928. Not a word of English did he know and, when a prudish friend of his, who did know English, warned him that the book was dangerous to morals because of what was done and the words used to tell it, the printer asked for an explanation in Italian. "My faith!" he replied. "We do that every day!"

The dangerous books of American literature are about such things as whales, grass, a pond in the woods, a raft on the river. Poems, essays, novels. Beware of these little packages, these bombs in sheep's binding. They slide down the throat, then explode in the stomach, whereas such obviously revolutionary books as *Das Kapital* and *Mein Kampf* stick in the throat and, if they are swallowed, produce indigestion from their lumpiness. Their time has passed. They are dead.

A book of poems, I said. Walt Whitman's of course. First published in 1855, in a small edition at the author's expense, with his own portrait as frontispiece instead of his name on the title page, *Leaves of Grass* has been continuously in print for one hundred and six years. Let me prove for you how alive it is.

This spring at UCLA we were visited by twenty of the leading

educators of Latin America. They saw everything there was to
see and, as a final sight, our bookish Chancellor, Franklin
Murphy, wanted them to see our shrine of shrines, the William
Andrews Clark Memorial Library, built of marble, travertine,
bronze, and oak, paid for with copper money from Montana
and Arizona. The Clark Library houses the world's greatest collections of John Dryden and Oscar Wilde. Exhibits were arranged of these foreign jewels; but then just before the guests
arrived, I was seized by literary patriotism. Something American
was needed. I rushed to the shelf and put out on an open table
the first edition of *Leaves of Grass,* and the most beautiful
modern edition of the book, the folio printed in San Francisco
at the Grabhorn Press.

Then the guests and their wives arrived—university rectors
and educators from Argentina, Chile, Uruguay, and Brazil. They
strolled through the building, exclaiming at the bibliographical
wonders on view—John Dryden's autograph letter to his cousin,
Oscar Wilde's sad letters from prison, the first editions of *Paradise Lost* and Newton's *Principia Mathematica.* And then the
Brazilian Minister of Education, an intense and restless man
who had wandered after the group, with eyes glazed from too
much sight-seeing—Disneyland, Marineland, Forest Lawn—saw
Leaves of Grass where I had not so innocently placed it—the
little package of the first edition, the big package of the Grabhorn reprint—and, like a hawk dropping on a mouse, he fell on
that book; and he came to life as though an electric current
had been turned on in an idle motor. He seized the book, riffled
the pages, and finding what he was looking for, called everyone around him, and began to read aloud, with a delightful
accent:

> Shut not your doors to me, proud libraries,
> For that which was lacking on all your well-filled shelves,
>   yet needed most, I bring;
> The words of my book nothing—the drift of it everything. . . .

"He is our great poet," I said, when the Brazilian had finished.

"Ours too," he insisted. "He belongs to all the Americas. Walt Whitman should be required reading in all the schools, from the primary grades on up. What better textbook for creative living?"

He put the book down. The current went out for him, and he merged with the group.

Open the little package of a paperback Whitman, and read for yourself. If there is any life in you, the current from this book will make you spin and hum like a dynamo. If you don't react to it, you are dead and don't know it, and you will live out your deadly life exactly as surveys show most college graduates to be living, subscribing to the correct magazines, belonging to a book club, absorbing cultural rations along with vitamin pills, and with predigested reading matter in every bathroom.

And this, alas, is exactly the way most of you will live, and nothing I say will affect you, tonight, or tomorrow, or ever. My hope is that, for a few of you, my words will be a time bomb, set to go off one year, five years, ten years hence; and then, one summer evening, you will be in a drugstore or a supermarket, very successful, with wife and/or husband at home, children, cars, TV, hi-fi, magazines—and, loaded with medicants or groceries, you will stop by the rack of paperbacks, and something will happen to you. At long last, this talk will explode, down by your solar plexus, and in desperation, you will spin the rack, seeking those books about grass and whales, about a pond in the woods, a raft on the river.

You will look around, to make sure no one sees you being different and then you will buy *Leaves of Grass, Moby Dick, Walden,* and *Huckleberry Finn,* all for less than a fifth of Scotch. You will put them in your cart with vitamins, cold cream, and kleenex; with the Nescafé, the Purex, the Ry-Krisp, and the soap that floats.

You will go home with your packages of tin and paper, and their contents will be consumed—vitamins, coffee, bleach, fruit, crackers, soap—and only those littlest packages will remain. Those paperbacks. You will reread these works of American literature, finding them as different as you have become different from the students who had to read them for credit; and I hope you will read them with pencil in hand, underlining passages that move you to yes or no. You can do things to your own replaceable paperbacks that you can't (or shouldn't) do to library books.

In this depleting world of ours, characterized by the conventional and the orthodox, by the quickie, the cheapie, the noisy, you will need, and will receive, the life and the light that are in these books. Don't ask me how. This is a miracle of chemistry, whereby the life of a creative writer is not lost when he dies, but is transfused into his book—and gives immortal vitality to *Leaves of Grass, Moby Dick, Walden,* Emerson's *Essays,* and *Huckleberry Finn.*

And by another miracle, equally staggering, you can tap this life, at once explosive and consoling, can plug into this source of energy and of renewal, can both dynamite and heal yourself, merely by the act of reading.

What we need to shatter is the mold of conformity into which we settle after the fluid state of childhood. A true university, and Arizona's is one, values and teaches thoughtful nonconformity. I do not mean mere eccentricity. In this struggle to find and to be yourself, the great books (neither word is capitalized) can be of help to you.

What makes a book great, a so-called classic, is its quality of always being modern, of its author, though he be long dead, continuing to speak to each new generation.

"I have written a wicked book," Melville exulted in a letter to his neighbor Hawthorne, after completing *Moby Dick,* "and I feel spotless as the lamb."

Listen to what Emerson said about language: "The short Saxon words with which the people help themselves are better than Latin. The language of the street is always strong." In the 1850s, Emerson hailed Whitman's vitality and vulgarity (qualities which often go together); and I have no doubt that if Emerson were alive today, he would be reading *Tropic of Cancer* and *The Catcher in the Rye.*

Unlike journalism, literature can never be written to order. There is no way of foretelling the time or place of the appearance of a masterpiece. The power of a work which elevates it from journalism to literature shocks the conventional and scares the timid. Efforts at censorship only serve to advertise a book. In spite of nervous parents and self-appointed censors, *The Catcher in the Rye* has taken its place as a kind of bible for the present generation. I asked a sixteen-year-old boy what he thought of it. "Man," he said, "I'd do all those things Holden Caulfield did, if I only had the money!"

Now let me become local. I was over this way last winter because of a book. My motives for travel have changed a bit since I made my first trip to this campus, thirty-three years ago, because of a bat—B-A-T, bat. No, not the kind that flies. The kind you hit the ball with. I was bat boy for the Occidental College baseball team, and I crossed the river with the Tigers to hunt Wildcats. We got clawed.

I wish I could report that it was a visit to the university library, after the ball game, that changed the direction of my life and made me what I am today. This would strike the edifying note expected of a commencement speaker. The fact is I went out on the town. I was a piano player. There was a girl in a black dress, a dancer. Daylight came too soon.

When I came to manhood, I put away my bats (and piano), and henceforth lived with books, and a record player. During the last decade I have been repeatedly in Arizona and New Mexico, and the decenter parts of Texas, and always because of books—reading, writing, collecting, and talking about, books, going with books in my baggage, books in my pocket, with books on the seat beside me and with me in the night, best of all companions to have and to read.

Because of books, I know more about Arizona than I could ever know by just traveling through it and talking with people. All the senses are heightened, widened, deepened, by reading. Multidimensional living is made possible by reading. The time barrier is broken by books. Because of books, whenever I travel in Arizona, my companions are Kino, Garcés, and Emory, on down to Ross Santee and Joseph Wood Krutch.

In the years ahead, you graduates will go to the ends of the earth, and beyond, to the realms of space. Take books with you, those little packages of American literature; you will find them good passports, and good rations. Hawthorne and Hemingway, Mark Twain and Carl Sandburg and Robert Frost, Melville and Steinbeck, Emerson and J. Frank Dobie; the genteel and the vulgar, from Henry James to Henry Miller. Foreigners will judge you by the books in your baggage. The timeless values these authors embody are also without national boundaries. In Africa, Asia, and India, as well as in Europe, you will go farther on paperback than in a Cadillac.

If we are to triumph in the world struggle, it will be because our ideas, not our arms, are the strongest; and books are the best packages man has ever found to hold his ideas. We should be telling the world that the American way, the revolutionary way of individual rights and freedom and responsibility, promises the fullest development for backward peoples; and the best way to tell our story is by the great books of our American heritage. Let them be translated into every tongue of mankind, printed in paperbacks, and sent down the rivers of the world. Huck Finn and his black friend, those children of the Mississippi, will go just as surely down the Congo, the Nile, the Ganges, and the Yellow River.

You moon travelers, put *Walden* in your pocket, if the Air Force will let you; it bulks less, yet weighs more, than *War and Peace*. Hide *Huckleberry Finn* on your person; it will export better than *Crime and Punishment*.

You graduates come from all the states of the Union, and from many foreign countries; and there might be among you, cunningly disguised, a man from Mars, or a Venus woman, soon to return from whence they came, taking with them secrets of earth. Not just plain earth. Arizona earth. Colored earth. This most beautiful Southwestern earth. And an Arizona book or two. Whoever you are, wherever you go, you will never be the same for having been Arizonans, even though for only four years; and you will take increasing pride in being alumni of this university. Life will make house cats of most of you who were once Wildcats, but not all of you.

Some of you will remain in Arizona, and become governor, senator, congressman, rain-maker, banker, lawyer, merchant, chief—and if there has to be a thief among you, let it be time that you steal, time from being successful, to remembering what I've said tonight.

And may there ever be books in your life, for there is life for you in books, the essence of all the lives man has ever lived, from Homer to Hemingway, heroic, tragic, loving, wrapped for your convenience in this Little Package called Book. Turn the leaves of Whitman and you will find these mystical words with which I close:

> I bequeathe myself to the dirt, to
>   grow from the grass I love;
> If you want me again, look for me
>   under your bootsoles.
> You will hardly know who I am, or
>   what I mean;
> But I shall be good health to you
>   nevertheless,
> And filter and fibre your blood.
>
> Failing to fetch me at first, keep
>   encouraged;
> Missing me one place, search another;
> I stop somewhere, waiting for you.

And so, good night, go far.

The Roots of Regional Literature

I HAVE BEEN WAITING all my life to speak in Las Vegas, for it is here, in a sense, that my own roots first made contact with Southwestern soil; and I have been wanting to return to Las Vegas ever since I was first here in 1906, the year of my birth.

I didn't say I was born here. I wasn't. I'm one of those stateless Americans, born in the District of Columbia. My father was a pomologist in the Bureau of Plant Industry of the Department of Agriculture, concerned with the refrigeration of fresh fruit to prevent decay in transit. The Sunkist growers of Southern California were losing millions of dollars through the spoilage of oranges en route to eastern markets. My father was assigned to this problem, and so we came west on the Santa Fe, this part of the "we" being a three-month-old baby in his mother's arms. My mother kept a journal during the last sixty-seven years of her eighty-seven-year life span, and on December 29, 1906, she wrote in it while the train was at the station here, "Baby restless. Became fascinated by Indians on the platform selling pottery."

And so all through the years of boyhood, youth, and man-

Address, New Mexico Highlands University, Las Vegas, 1959.

hood, the Santa Fe passages saw me traveling to and fro through this town on the plains, at the foot of the Sangre de Cristos; and latterly, flying over it at 20,000 feet, welcoming the red roofs of the University as familiar landmarks; or passing through on the trail of Austin T. Wright, author of that great Utopian novel, *Islandia,* who died here in hospital, after a crash on the bridge across Bernal Arroyo.

Although I have never lived in Las Vegas, or even stayed overnight, I have strong feelings about this historic town, the town wherein Kearny took possession of New Mexico for the United States, this way point on the Santa Fe trail, threshold of the capital, this place called Las Vegas—the meadows—which patiently endures the confusion occasioned by its noisy Nevada namesake.

Each word of my title is meaningful—roots and regions and literature. Not regional *writing,* but rather regional *literature;* that is to say, writing which has qualities which elevate it above everyday language, above the language of the newspaper wire services and of the slick magazines, and much academic writing. Nothing is so dead as this writing the day after it was written.

What are qualities that make language live? *Feeling* is one. A writer's ability to feel life deeply, to be responsive to it. Then *power over language,* the gift to use words significantly and to form them in ways to give them meaning and impact. Also the quality of *style,* a writer's personal way with words, as intimate a part of a good writer as the size and shape of his nose. *Knowledge* is another quality that elevates writing into literature, so that the reader is memorably informed and made aware of new worlds. *Insight* is still another quality—a writer's ability to illuminate experience, to light up the dark places so that the reader sees life more clearly. And lastly what Dobie calls *perspective,* so that in reading one is aware of relationships both in space and time.

In writing which lasts more than a season, in *literature,* we find these and still other qualities in balance. They cannot deliberately be inserted into writing, the way blood is transfused into an anemic person. They are either implicitly present or explicitly absent.

I could cite negative examples of their explicit absence to prove my point, but I would rather prove it in an affirmative way with the implicit presences, and by referring to an example of living prose from my own private anthology of life-giving literature, of language rich in vitamins and hormones.

In 1954 there came from an obscure press in Evanston, Illinois, a book of reminiscences about this region of the Southwest, a volume which I have found to be one of the most feeling and knowing and perceptive of all Southwestern books, old and new, a book to shelve next to Susan Magoffin and Erna Fergusson. It is called appropriately *Land of Enchantment*, and consists of the memoirs of Marian Sloan Russell along the Santa Fe Trail, as dictated by Mrs. Russell in her old age—she lived the long long span of years between 1845 and 1937—to her daughter-in-law, Mrs. Hal Russell.

What about *roots*? These are the deep unconscious sources on which literature feds. They reach down to the subsoil of *feeling* which lies far beneath the topsoil of *thinking*. To draw on these burial mounds of memory, a writer needs both a deep tap root and also a lateral root system, needs to be like both ponderosa and mesquite. He must go down and go out and draw up into the branches and leaves and flowers of his work the nourishing sensual elements of smell and touch and sight and sound that give reality to a piece of writing, that make great writing more memorable than life, in that in it life is focused and projected, as through a burning glass. In life, people live and die and are forgotten, countless billions of them. In literature, people live forever. Because of Homer, Helen of Troy lives; because of Petrarch, Laura. And thanks to Shakespeare, Juliet, Ophelia, and Rosalind are immortal.

In still another sense, the best writers have twin root systems, one in themselves, and one in the land of which they are writing; and the richest writing is that which is nourished simultaneously by both. Take J. Frank Dobie, for example, the Texan writer whom I have called the finest Southwesterner of them all, and his greatest book, *The Mustangs,* in which the wild horses of the West come to stand as symbols of all that is independent and free and noble in America.

Consider first, however, the ways there are to write about horses, as for example, that of a reporter on the Denver *Post,* writing about the Gunnison Horse Show—who attended and what they wore, who rode, who won, all written in simple straightforward prose that never leaves the ground, prose that leaves the reader informed but not inspired. This is journalism, and it has its place in our daily life.

Then take Dobie's *Mustangs,* its prose language written by a man with seeing eye, knowing mind, feeling heart, and mastery of language. Dobie's feeling incandesces yet does not melt, his prose leaves the runway and is air-borne.

By the word *regional,* I mean pertaining to a certain place on earth. My personal preference is for such literature about a specific place. I prefer works rooted in a recognizable region, as for example, Hardy's novels about that southwestern part of England he called Wessex; Joyce's novel about Dublin; Steinbeck's early stories of his native land, the Salinas Valley of central California.

The core of literature must be local, Yeats said, yet infinitely translatable. How does one go about writing of a region? Does he have to be a native of that region to write literature about it? Not necessarily. If he is, and has lived long where he was born, perhaps he should leave his homeland. By looking back on it, as Joyce did, from exile in Trieste and Zurich, he might achieve two things not possible when he is too close to his native habitat. I mean perspective and nostalgia. Perspective will give a better sense of form and proportion to his work. Nostalgia will increase its emotional charge.

From the vantage point of long residence in Berkeley, California, native New Mexican Harvey Fergusson looked back on his homeland and wrote his two mature novels, *Grant of Kingdom* and *The Conquest of Don Pedro.*

But it is easy to prove the opposite by citing Tom Lea, native son of El Paso, who still lives there for the simple reason that he likes it, and whose novel *The Wonderful Country* is one of the best of all regional books.

The important thing is a writer's personal equipment, meaning his sensitivity, his absorptive capacity, and his creative stamina. If these qualities are highly developed, a writer can harbor for only a season in a locale, soak up material, move on, and then write, for example, *The Silverado Squatters*, Robert Louis Stevenson's idyllic account of the Napa Valley in Northern California, where he honeymooned for a month; or write "The Princess," D. H. Lawrence's short story of the Sangres.

Harvey Fergusson's self-imposed exile from New Mexico has seen his writing about his homeland become deeper and richer and truer, perhaps because he dwells quietly in book-filled rooms in an old wooden house near the university campus in Berkeley.

There he wrote the first of the two novels I referred to—*Grant of Kingdom*, which is about the Maxwell Land Grant, those 1,715,000 acres of beautiful earth to the north of Las Vegas, which Lucien Maxwell got as dowry when in 1849 he married Luz Beaubien of Taos, and on which he lived for twenty years in feudal splendor.

It is of these acres, and of this man and woman, that Harvey Fergusson wrote his novel. In the crucible of his imagination, the mere facts of history became the supreme facts of fiction, whereby life was magnified, heightened, widened, and set free.

This is the way it *must* have been, we say when we read *Grant of Kingdom*—or even stronger, perhaps. This is the way it *should* have been. And not inconceivably, such romances of history may be all that will survive the atomic age, perhaps a microfilm of this novel, disinterred a thousand years hence from a library cornerstone, just as Homer's *Iliad* is all we know of Troy, Homer's *Odyssey* all we know of Ithaca.

This miracle was wrought by Harvey Fergusson from his transplanted root system of memories. As youth and man he hunted and fished high and deep in the Sangres, on the aspened shoulders of Truchas where the Pecos rises, in the lee of Wheeler where the little Red starts downhill. His writing is fed by these memories as the streams are fed by snow melt; and the novel flows through the fabled destiny of the Maxwell Grant as inevitably as the rivers move toward their ends.

Grant of Kingdom is literature with its roots in this region of northern New Mexico, a region which seems to this Southern Californian who sickens of too much city as close to heaven as man can come on earth.

Let me turn now from setting to sex, from landscape to love. A writer may have a very deep-rooted feeling for a region and the power to write about it movingly, yet if he does not have an equally profound feeling for human relationships, he will not write novels that will move people.

Throughout his novels, from *Wolf Song* to *Don Pedro*, Harvey Fergusson has written with restrained feeling of the eternal hunger of man for woman, woman for man. He is a master of the understatement. Without actually telling the reader all, he skillfully uses just enough words, and the right words, so that the reader imagines all. This is by far the most exciting way to write about sex. Without being nasty like Micky Spillane or mawkish like Zane Grey, Harvey Fergusson's love stories are both exciting and proper. This is fine art.

To write well of sexual recognition—the Victorians would have said of the birth of love—whatever it is called, demands insight, taste, and control. A perfect example is the opening scene of *Grant of Kingdom*, at the hot spring in the canyon above Taos, when the woman attracts the man in the most primitive way. The result is the novel. In so-called real life, the result of such powerful polarities is history.

These are often the decisive encounters in history, those between men and women of desire and power who separately might come to naught, but who when joined change the direction of history. How was it when Paris first saw Helen? Saw her whose face "launched a thousand ships and burned the topless towers of Ilium." The precise answer is lost long long ago in time.

The novelist's task is to imagine the answers; and to be convincing, his imagination must be founded on fact.

Harvey Fergusson knows the facts of New Mexican history and landscape, and he also knows what transpires in the secret chambers of the human heart. He knows the simple, profound truths of behavior of a magnetized man and woman—the shock of recognition, the mounting tension, the explosive action, and the subsequent ebb of feeling; the power, the glory, and the peace of fulfillment.

If I have dwelt at length on *Grant of Kingdom*, let me say that Frank Waters's novel, *People of the Valley*, about the Guadalupita above Mora, is equally beautiful and true. Let me praise Oliver La Farge's *Behind the Mountains*, those sketches of his wife's family place at Rociada. These books have the universal quality and appeal to people everywhere that all regional writing must have if it is to be read beyond the borders.

As for the beautiful places in New Mexico I have failed to mention, I have only begun to travel. Give me a few more years and I will enter all the counties, ascend the rivers to their sources, add Mt. Taylor to Truchas and Wheeler peaks and, in the traveling, discover something more precious than metals.

Books, for example; and the essences which they contain—truth and beauty—which will outlast all the cities of Cíbola. Why then should not one love and praise books, those creations of man which long survive their creators?

Yet I like literature no more than I do life; and what I love best is the inseparable blend of the two, in which each confirms the other. This is one of the sweetest fruits of middle age; and should be even sweeter in old age, if one can reach that state still with eyes for books.

I suppose the next most thrilling of earthly unions, after that of man with maid, is that of man with book, and at the right time and place.

My closing story is about such a union of the time, the place, and the book. It happened in Texas, and more particularly in San Antonio.

We were on the ground at the airport, en route from Houston to El Paso, a trans-Texas journey now made in a few hours, instead of the day and night it once took on the Sunset Limited.

I bought a paperback, a book by J. Frank Dobie that was new to me—his *Vaquero of the Brush Country*. Flying on to El Paso, I began to read it; and came to that rhapsody to the mesquite, the chapter on the Brush Country of Texas's heartland, over which we were flying at that moment, much of it cleared and under cultivation, yet preserved forever virgin in the pages of this book.

Dobie's prose poetry got me so excited I had to get up and walk the length of the plane. I know my seat neighbors thought I was crazy, because when reading arouses me I begin saying the words out loud and moving with the rhythm of the prose. Kinetic empathy, it's called. This chapter of Dobie's is like music, like a symphony.

It was almost incredible the changes of landscape and color I had seen since leaving Houston, and now the country was thinning out to rangeland and badlands. Crossing a river I could not name, I asked the stewardess what it was; and got the usual reply, "Sorry, I never look out." She did query the captain by intercom, and thereby loosed a lecture on landscape and history by a talkative pilot I'd flown with before on Southwestern schedules. A great reader, that man; a flight with him was like a seminar with Webb. I guess he'd been dozing, while the copilot flew the plane, and the stewardess's question undamned a flow of information worth an extra fare.

The river? The Pecos, of course, running high and dry. And then and there I experienced one of those perfect conjunctions of the time, the place, and the book, for with one eye I looked down on the country itself west of Pecos, and with the other I read the final chapter in Dobie's *Vaquero* called "Trans-Pecos."

While I read that chapter, the plane flew on toward El Paso, carrying part of me with it, and to a meeting with Carl Hertzog, the Southwest's finest printer, but the rest of me had turned off at the Pecos crossing and was heading upriver, jettisoning baggage, past Red Bluff Dam, Carlsbad, Roswell, Alamogordo

Dam, not getting very wet except at the dam sites, climbing, rising, past Santa Rosa, Puerto de Luna, and the junction with the Gallinas, the Pecos changing color with the colored earth and hemmed with green willows, finally crossing the railroad at Ribera, the little station where I once saw the eastbound-westbound Super Chiefs meet and pass, finally nearing its source in the Sangres, mother mountain, *sierra madre*, sweet-water country, swift-running, steel-colored water-over-rocks and the trout flashing (*las truchas!*) higher, ever higher toward the source far up the narrowing canyon, in the rivulets of seep and snow melt, on the aspened shoulders of Truchas, wilderness area high, wild, and handsome.

The roots of lasting literature are in earth, and earth is rock and loam, mud and sand, and also wind and rain, each with its own kind of nourishment. It takes longer for a writer to put down roots into rock than into sand. And there are hydroponic ways of raising literature—recall *Moby Dick*—and root systems in air will be a phenomenon of the space age.

To live is good. To read is good. To blend living and reading, to experience those wonderful unions of the time, the place, and the book, is almost unspeakably good.

I have come a long way through life from that twenty-eighth day of December, 1906, when on the station platform in Las Vegas baby was restless until pacified by Indians selling pottery. They say that in our beginnings are to be found our ends. To end in New Mexico, here on the meadow at the foot of the mountains, might be the best of all ends.

Act of Enchantment

New mexico, this land of enchantment, has come to be both loadstone and polestar in my life, a point of reference and orientation wherever I am, and also a source of magnetic refreshment when I am troubled by traffic and bereft of beauty. I work in a perilous city where the air is unclean, and a bounty is paid on pedestrians, and my survival is due in part to New Mexico.

In 1960 I made a flying trip around the world on behalf of the United States Air Force and the UCLA Library, to speak to librarians in Hawaii and Japan, and to collect books. It was a fast, rough trip, mostly on Military Air Transport Service planes, to Japan, Okinawa, the Philippines, Vietnam, Thailand, India, Pakistan, Arabia, and Egypt, and thence to Italy, Switzerland, France, the Netherlands, and Great Britain, grounded here by engine trouble, halted there by lack of a transit visa, getting a last-minute yellow-fever shot in order to transit India, reduced to eating K rations and worse.

Throughout the dizzy orbit I was often sustained by the act of enchantment, I mean reading of course, and by the prospect of a New Mexican *entrada* on the last leg of my journey.

Address to New Mexico Historical Society, Las Cruces, 1960.

At the most hazardous times—for example when we were five minutes out of Dhahran for Tripoli and the lights came on and the commander's voice said to the GI-packed plane, "Engine trouble, men; fasten your seat belts; we're dumping gasoline and returning to base"—and in the most exotic places—as when riding through the teeming torchlit streets of Bangkok in search of a hotel room—at such times and places, I had only to close my eyes, rub the abalone shell in my pocket, hum a fragment of Mozart, and evoke my favorite New Mexican images, and I was magically comforted and reaffirmed.

These were images of landscapes or of buildings without many people—the environs of Questa, for example; or of landscapes with people doing humble, creative things—cultivating corn in the Arroyo Hondo, repairing a roof at Acoma, kneeling in front of the church at Pecos on Corpus Christi Sunday; or of children reading in the public library at Los Alamos. If an image of group activity, then one of an Indian ceremonial rather than of an Anglo rodeo.

I suppose the anthropologists have a term to describe this kind of primitive magic, this image-evoking. Whatever they call it, I can testify that it works, for I survived and am here to tell the tale.

It began at Travis Air Force Base, near Sacramento, in whose PX I packed my zipper bag with paperbacks. A mixed bag it was too, with Shakespeare and Dante competing with Ernest Haycox and *Mamie Stover*. I never got to read them though.

On the ten-hour flight to the Hawaiian Islands, I just sat back and dreamed, and doodled in my journal, happy to be out of the maelstrom of my daily life. In Honolulu I spent a stopover talking to librarians, eating papayas, and sitting on the beach at Waikiki, outside the Moana Hotel, where years before I had played with a college orchestra.

Then on the flight from Honolulu to Tokyo, with a fuel stop at Wake Island, the GIs ran out of comics and set up a clamor for some honest reading matter—books, that is, for some stone-ground whole-wheat prose, instead of vitamin-enriched piffle. Whereupon the librarian in me triumphed over the book collector. To give books is better than to receive them, but one must get them first before he can give them. So I unzipped my bag, and went down the aisle, handing out my hoard.

Time relaxes its grip on those who read. The last eight hours passed swiftly, and the huge *C-121G* made a rainy twilight landing at Tachikawa base near Tokyo, and those GIs (and my books) melted away all over the Japanese islands. No matter. Thanks to the paperback revolution in publishing, zipper bags can be cheaply refilled all around the world.

I was too busy in Tokyo, during the workshop for armed forces librarians, to refill my bag with printed goodies. But I was not without books, hundreds of which are always with me in solution. I have never been a day without books since childhood, when *A Child's Garden of Verses* made me into a traveling reader, a reading traveler.

One day in Tokyo I was early for the evening session of the workshop; and walking from my billet to the officers' club, I fell in with a colored GI, a tall, lithe man walking with a stride I had to double mine to keep up with.

"Do you know where the library is?" he asked.

Of course I knew. I always know where the library is wherever I am, in the way Londoners knew where the nearest bomb shelter was. And as we walked along to the quonset hut which housed the Washington Heights Library, I asked the GI why he was going there.

"I always go to the library," he replied. "To improve myself and get away from it all. I'm studying accounting, and I'm fed up with group living."

As we entered the library I saw him change. He slowed up and quieted down, and tiptoed across the room as though he were walking on eggs; and I thought how much like a church a library is, in the reverent way people often make entry.

I sat there for a while in an easy chair, with men, women, and children around me, all engaged in that act of enchantment; and I rejoiced that the public library, crowded though it be, is one of the few remaining places in our culture where a man can be private.

Yes, I just sat there and watched the little library simmer. Presently I went to the shelf, and by the sheerest chance took down volume one of a two-volume set, opened it, and read:

> The valley cottonwood was the dominant and most useful tree in all the Pueblo country. Its wood was soft and manageable, and it supplied material for many objects. Its silver bark, its big varnished leaves sparkling in the light of summer and making caverns of shade along the banks, its winter-hold of leaves the color of beaten thin gold, lasting in gorgeous bounty until the new catkins of spring—all added grace to the pueblo world.

Where else on earth could that passage apply other than New Mexico? What was the book? Paul Horgan's *Great River*.

I closed the volume, and my eyes, and by that enchanted act of reading one paragraph I was back in Albuquerque, in the autumn of the year Horgan's work was published and received the Pulitzer Prize for History. It was 1954, and I had a couple of hours between meetings, and with the book on the seat beside me, I drove clear of the city—each year it takes longer to do this —and down the west bank of the river to Isleta, following the cottonwoods' stream of gold, the car radio resounding with Brahms's Third Symphony, a kind of golden pastoral music. I parked in front of the church of St. Augustine, entered with book in hand, and sat there and read for an hour—read about an ancient culture dedicated to the ways of peace; an unforgettable conjunction of the time, the place, and the book.

During my week in Japan, thoughts of war and peace were constantly in my mind, and in Kyoto I encountered an ancient community and culture which war had mercifully spared.

Kyoto lies in an upland basin, flanked by pine-clad mountains from which clear water flows. I found Kyoto reminiscent of Santa Fe. Instead of aspens, there are forests of bamboo, wind mobiles of delicate green. Instead of river pueblos of colored earth, there are wooden temples a thousand years old, and gardens of white sand and gray stone.

High above Kyoto, among the pines and bamboos, in the shade of a temple of wood, weathered to the color of earth, I sat on the edge of a formal garden of sand and stone, and meditated on the beauty and dignity and meaning of life when it is free of violence and destruction. And my thoughts were of New Mexico.

For me the sources of strength and refreshment in Southwestern history antedate the Anglos and the Spaniards, and their civilization which is shot through with violence, and I seek the communal certitudes of the earlier Mesa Verde and the river pueblos.

I would have their way of life married to our modern concern for individual responsibility and development, if such is possible. I suppose this is why I was so deeply drawn by the man Haniel Long and his works, particularly his books on Cabeza de Vaca, Walt Whitman, and St. Augustine.

They were in solution in my mind when I spoke to university students in Japan on peacefulness and good will in American literature. I had seen the students of Kyoto University demonstrating against the Treaty, and I reminded them of the terms of the benevolent MacArthur peace—of how it allowed the Japanese the freedom to speak and demonstrate against the Americans, and of how such freedom would not exist if the Russians had been the conquerors and occupiers.

In Osaka, seated on a stool at a *sushi* bar (serving only raw fish and rice), I talked about American culture with my Japanese hosts—a professor and two librarians—and we agreed that our deepest sources of both strength and consolation go back a hundred years to Emerson and Whitman; and that a hundred years from now posterity may go back to Hemingway and Faulkner for the same reasons; but that today we cannot. We may read Hemingway for excitement and Faulkner for more perverse reasons, but our true sources of inspiration, the Japanese and I agreed, are to be found in the works of the Cambridge Unitarian and the Long Island Quaker.

I was able to tell these Japanese about Haniel Long's *Walt Whitman and the Springs of Courage*, regretting that my bag did not hold a copy of this beautiful New Mexican book.

"Whitman faces us with the problem," Long writes, "which

underlies religion, art, and culture; how to unfold out of earth
and still to be earth; how within nature to become super-nature;
how to find for ourselves a natural balance in the natural chaos.
And what the world needs help upon—and from all the forms
of poetry including psychology and religion—is this same
problem; how two lives, or three lives, or all lives, are to be
woven together in life-giving inexhaustible interplay."

All the way through southeast Asia nothing recalled our
Southwest, except the cumulus clouds above the China Sea between Manila and Saigon. It was not until we were flying across
India to Pakistan that I saw arid brown earth replace the green
jungles of Indonesia, Siam, and Burma. Dry watercourses, scat-
tered mud dwellings, with only occasional trees, formed a landscape I comprehended and quickened to.

And when we landed in Karachi and I saw the buildings of
sun-dried earth and felt the dry heat like a radiant oven, I had
only to squint my eyes a bit and think I was in Albuquerque.

Throughout those long flights on MATS I was heartened
by some thoughtful servicemen I met; mostly officers in their
thirties who had stayed in service after World War II or the
Korean War, and who had been in the Orient long enough to
learn native languages and not judge a culture by chrome,
cellophane, and tail fins.

I roomed overnight with three such officers in New Delhi. We
talked for hours about America's role in the world. I wish a
recording of what they said could be played on every radio in
the land, and on our overseas broadcasts, for here was loyalty
tempered by criticism. Here was pride in an America which
values nonconformity. Here was perception which can see an
ancient wooden temple as more meaningful, and perhaps more
lasting, than the Empire State Building.

It was not until I reached Switzerland, after surmounting
perilous obstacles in Saudi Arabia and Egypt, that I felt really
secure. In Zurich I bought a Volkswagen, and with books and
maps and a few cans of apricot nectar on the seat beside me, I
took to the road in the darkness before dawn; breakfasted at
the railway station in Berne, took a *café au lait* break on the

lakefront in Geneva; and then passed through the low Alps and followed a river valley into France. I drove westward for fifteen hours of a seemingly endless day, covering 520 miles, from Zurich to Tours, in the château country, passing through a land on which many layers of culture are superimposed—a landscape, utterly unlike the American Southwest, where all the trees are green, all the rivers full, and every acre is under cultivation.

I met the Saône at Mâcon, and the Loire at Nevers, crossing from the Mediterranean into the Atlantic watershed almost without knowing it; and I recalled the long drive I once made from Questa up the Rio Grande, nearly to its source, then via the South Fork through Wolf Creek Pass and down the San Juan to Pagosa Springs—through a land in which civilization has never accumulated in depth, a land of trappers and traders, of ranchers and raiders, of nearly virgin earth as the land in Europe is no longer.

And at Pagosa Springs I had lingered at a parting of the ways, tempted westward by a sign which read Durango, on a road which would lead to the Mesa Verde. Instead I took the southeast-running road whose sign read Chama and Tierra Amarilla.

There in France, at Mâcon on the Saône, I likewise lingered at a fork in the road. To the right lay Burgundy and my old university town of Dijon, ancestral home of the dukes, of wine and mustard and gingerbread. And northwest of Dijon were two of the places in France with the strongest hold on me— Vézelay, the Romanesque basilica from whence the fiery St. Bernard preached the Second and Third Crusades; and beyond, Alésia, the place where Vercingetorix, the young Gallic chieftain from the Auvergne, made his last stand against Julius Caesar, in the year 52 B.C.

That was one of the supreme moments of history, when France fell to the Romans. The vanquished warrior was carried to Rome, driven through the streets as a captive, imprisoned, and finally killed. Today a heroic statue of him stands on the hill at Alésia, visible from the Paris train, meaningless to most, who have no sense of the past.

Of whom in New Mexican history does Vercingetorix remind one? Of Popé, of course, the Tewa medicine man who led the Pueblo Revolt of 1680. Why not a statue of him to stand where the Spaniards founded New Mexico's first capital, at Popé's native San Juan pueblo? We need to re-evaluate our historical characters. To me a Popé, whose belief leads him to fight for what he holds dear, is worth all the mercenary frontier fighters and worse.

I am sick of the scum of history—the drinkers, gamblers, and killers, the butchers of buffalo and beaver and redskins—the greater and lesser Billy the Kids who soil the pages of history with their meaningless violence.

There were brave leaders among the *conquistadores*—Otermin and Vargas, for example—and let there be statues to them too. But as for Zaldivar, the butcher of Acoma, his place in Hell is all he deserves.

As a peace-loving man, I sometimes regret that the Spaniards came first to the New World, for they were an arrogant, fanatical, and cruel people, albeit of great bravery. As Jack Forbes writes in *Apache, Navajo, and Spaniard,* "If dedicated Christians had come peacefully among the Indians of New Mexico, teaching the doctrine by means of love and high-minded examples, then many Indians might conceivably have been converted in a manner worthy of the founder of the European's faith."

I like to speculate on what would have happened if George Fox and his Quaker followers had colonized the Pueblo lands? Let me say again what a major work I hold to be that little book by Haniel Long called *Interlinear to Cabeza de Vaca,* whose doctrine is that of the power locked within us all and which can be released only with the key of compassion.

I have written often of the reading of literature as an aid to the study of history. Good uses can be made of the documents assembled by historians and preserved by various means in such centers as the Coronado Room in the University of New Mexico Library. A treasury of fact is the two-volume set of Oñate documents translated by Hammond and Rey. Creative use of these sources is being skillfully made by Irwin Blacker in a trilogy of novels to be called *The Adobe Kingdom*. Volume Two, *Taos*, has appeared, and deals with Otermin's retreat from Santa Fe. Volume One, *Acoma*, will be about Oñate, and Volume Three, *Santa Fe*, about the reconquest by Vargas.

The heroic failures of history interest me more than their successful counterparts. I have spoken of Vercingetorix and Popé. Choice between Lee and Grant is not difficult, but then as a native of the District of Columbia, my sympathies naturally lie on the south bank of the Potomac.

There are Montezuma and Cortes, a more difficult choice, posing the question, What is success? And where would either be without Bernal Díaz having written their story? Story, I said, not history.

I was at one of the last birthday parties we gave for old Henry R. Wagner, a year or two before his death at ninety-four. It was on September 27, and I had just returned from my annual pilgrimage to New Mexico where, in the Villagrá Bookshop, I had bought one of the most unusual books ever printed in New Mexico, and one of the best in a literary sense.

It was Joseph O'Kane Foster's poetic drama called *The Great Montezuma*, designed by Thomas Benrimo, and printed in 1940 at Ranchos de Taos—printed on alternate signatures of rainbow-colored papers. It is a work of lasting literature in its perception, feeling, and power of dramatic language.

I asked Henry Wagner if he had ever read it. "No," he said, "and if it is based on Bernal Díaz, I never will. That man was a scoundrel and a liar." I did not contradict old Wagner, for he was close to apoplexy. And I loved the way he spoke of Bernal Díaz, as though the old *conquistador* were a yellow journalist living just across the street.

He was probably right. Yet scoundrel and liar though he may have been, Bernal Díaz was only doing his best to remember the past, using his memory, without benefit of photostats.

We are living now in a dramatic time of the liberation of atomic power and the voyages into space—a time in which New Mexico is central. The events at Los Alamos mark a great divide in our history. The invasion by my own university's scientists of the Pajarito Pleatau is another in the chronicle of New Mexican invasions beginning with Coronado. Its subtle and indirect historian, one who was there and who could see and sense and say, is the native New Mexican Peggy Pond Church—and her two-part story of Edith Warner called "The House at Otowi Bridge," published in the *New Mexico Quarterly*, strikes me as a classic of our time.

The role of Roland Dickey and the University of New Mexico Press in publishing this quarterly, one of the most beautifully designed and written of all American periodicals, deserves the highest praise. It seems to me there could be no better use of public funds than to subsidize this press and to keep in print the classic works of Erna Fergusson, Ross Calvin, and a few others.

Sound economic health is necessary for culture to develop and flourish and be maintained, but statistics in themselves are not culture. Built on and around them must be leisure, tolerance, intellectual hunger and curiosity, and a long view of history, which can see the difference in motivation of a Popé and a Billy the Kid.

New Mexico has a proud record of cultural leadership among the Southwestern states. The university in its several branches, the museums in Roswell and Santa Fe, summer opera in Santa Fe, fiestas and ceremonials throughout the state, the devotion of such not-to-be-divorced-from-their-land New Mexicans as Erna Fergusson, Roland Dickey, George Fitzpatrick, Peter Hurd, and Paul Horgan—these cultural forces are unsurpassed. And at the risk of starting another Civil War, let me say that Carl Hertzog seems to me more New Mexican than Texan.

During the month I spent book hunting in Britain, thought of my forthcoming New Mexican *entrada* warmed the back of my mind; and then on the transatlantic flight, from London to New York, I alternately dreamed and read—and in addition to Irwin Blacker's *Westering,* what I read was a chapter in A. V. Kidder's memoirs, published in *The Kiva,* wherein the dean of Southwestern archaeologists recalled his first field work in the Southwest, a mapping of the Mesa Verde made in 1907 under the direction of Edgar Hewett by Kidder, Sylvanus Griswold Morley, and John Gould Fletcher—three young Harvard anthropology students.

Here is a sample of Kidder's enchanting prose:

> Morley and I worked here all morning, mapping the locality, exploring and measuring the ruins and admiring the skill of the stonemasons who dared build upon such narrow ledges with such abandon. . . . We rode home in an hour and a half—trot and gallop, not suffering much from the heat until we reached the McElmo and had to follow along under the bare talus slopes to sheer red rim-rocks above. These reflected the glare and radiated the heat until the little breezes that played up and down the gullies were like the breath from a dry furnace. In the afternoon I finished "La Terre" [Zola's novel, *The Earth*], lying for the most part in the irrigation ditch out of which the water had been turned, leaving delightful wet sand, also much frequented by the dogs and chickens.

It matters not where the act of enchantment is consummated, whether it be reading Zola in a *zanja*, or Kidder in a *707*, high above the Atlantic Ocean. I was in New York before I knew it, with only two thirds of the continent between me and New Mexico.

In 1950 I drove west in a Hillman; in 1957 in a Jaguar. In 1960 I let TWA fly me in a Constellation, and days were turned to hours. La Guardia Field was all but socked in by fog when I boarded Flight 263.

It was raining in Dayton, clearing in Chicago; and then blue sky all the way to Albuquerque. We came in between the southernmost Sangres and the Sandias. I hadn't been able to read for an hour or so before those landmarks appeared, so excited was I by the prospect of another enchanted entry. I just sat there with my nose to the window.

When I disembarked in Albuquerque, the sun hit me like a hammer; and I could have been back in Karachi or Dhahran. But I wasn't. I was in Albuquerque, New Mexico, on such good terms with Hertz that they gave me one of their cars, and I headed for the river road. The air was clear, and from the airport mesa I could see Mt. Taylor in the west, and the Jemez range northwest. My sense of excited homecoming was almost unbearable. Suspense too, as though I were taking the Cuba road to a uranium deposit I had dreamed of.

Whereas all I had was simply a date with Erna Fergusson. I found her right where I had left her a year before—on the screened porch of her home under the cathedral cottonwood, reading and writing and holding court. I paid my respects to your First Lady, and we began talking where we had left off.

I don't need to scold New Mexicans for not recognizing Erna Fergusson. They have. She stands for all that is old and tested and true in New Mexican culture, and I am proud to be one of the pupils in her screened-porch classroom.

Yes, it was hot and dry and familiar; and I felt utterly secure, as Miss Fergusson and I drove up the river road in the long twilight, talking of books and writing, of people and history, and of food, there in that ancient river valley so fraught with history—with New Mexican history which has been determined by water and the lack of it. And the shades I sensed in the cottonwood groves along the Rio Grande were older than any chronicles we know; were of the people of an earthly paradise who pursued the acts of peace, uncursed by war, for to live together in peace is the most enchanted life of all.

The Prospect Before Us

THE PROSPECT BEFORE US, not behind us, the forward look, rather than the backward glance. It is the cultural future of California that interests me—a future which will be the effect of past causes, which can be discerned only by its reflection in the mirror; seen paradoxically, by the backward glance. What has been now is, and will be. Prophecy can only be in terms of the past, by what is known; and thus it is with respect that I enter the storehouse of our culture to provide for the journey ahead.

If we can continue to live in peace, I believe we are on the threshold of a golden age. Culture comes from prosperity, from the tranquillity and the leisure which are the blessings of security. Poetry written on an empty stomach differs from full-bellied prose. Consider Villon and Montaigne, Poe and Emerson. California is filling up with people. If they can live in peace, they will produce wealth and an abundant economy which will give more leisure and patronage to the arts than we have ever seen.

This means new responsibilities for old institutions if they are to foster the arts. I am biased in favor of the arts—of writing

Address, Fiftieth Anniversary, Book Club of California, San Francisco, 1962.

and printing, of music and painting, architecture and sculpture. Science and economics and politics have their spokesmen, but I am not one of them. I have not the interest or the competence or the obligation to speak for them. They seem to flourish without spokesmen, once the atom was split and Frankenstein emerged from Pandora's cyclotron.

To meet their responsibilities our cultural institutions must be free of bondage to the past; must forsake the backward look, and live in the time stream, in the continuum which recognizes no barriers between past, present, and future. If we are to move forward with ease and grace, with power and authority, on all the cultural fronts, we must draw strength from our sources, our heritage, our past; and in revealing and inventorying our sources and resources, our present cultural institutions can make their contributions.

Let me indicate some of our needs, and suggest roles to be played, if we are to realize the prospect before us. Basic is a need for a new bibliography of California history and literature, on which scholarship can base its works. It was the Book Club of California that published in 1914 the first bibliography of California history, by Robert Ernest Cowan, printed by Taylor & Taylor, and reissued in 1933 by John Henry Nash; and for this pioneer work, this Club's first publication, we are grateful.

It was more a listing of Cowan's own collection than an inclusive bibliography. I do not believe he ever went very far to check other collections, even the earlier lot of Californiana which he sold to the University of California in 1897 and which was paid for by Collis P. Huntington, or the MacDonald collection which he sold to the Huntington Library in 1916.

An example of what might be called Cowan's selectivity is his listing of the pamphlets—eight in all—which led me to write my book about Philosopher Pickett. When I searched other collections—Bancroft, State Library, Huntington—I found nine more works by Pickett unlisted by Cowan, all of which had been in those libraries for years and some of which had been sold to them earlier by Cowan himself.

I came to know the old gentleman, his collection, and his

bibliography, when I joined the UCLA Library staff in the 1930s and was assigned to the accessioning of the Cowan collection. Wishing to learn more about certain items, I used to pack my bag with books and pamphlets, call on Cowan at his home near the Clark Library, take out each piece and query him thereon, making penciled notes of his replies. He was a learned man; unfortunately, most of his learning died with him. Like J. Gregg Layne, he couldn't be bothered to write it down. Like too many authors, he preferred talking to writing. How delicately he savored those fine Havanas he favored, how long their ash grew, finally to fall on his tie, on his book, on me!

To have known Cowan and Wagner, Layne, Hodge, and Hanna in the dawn of being a librarian was my good fortune. To have grown up with Ward Ritchie, to have worked for Jake Zeitlin, to have known "Father" Dawson and John Howell—these were elements of my education equally valuable with my academic preparation.

We need a bibliography of California that will go back and fill in the gaps, then push on from 1933, and record the vast output of books and pamphlets since then—probably more than the total publishing of the nineteenth and early twentieth centuries. Who will do it? Who will catch this bibliographical bull by the tail? Dauntless David could.

I am not springing anything on my friend Magee. We have discussed this needed work. He hears the call. It is at least a five-year job. May I suggest that the University of California appoint David Magee Regents Professor of Bibliography and send him state-wide? He has what it takes—scholarship, style, sympathy—all's lacking is that fourth s—subsidy.

The University of California has done much for science, for agriculture, astronomy, physics, oceanography, forestry, and animal husbandry. It has done somewhat less for the arts and letters. Is it because artists and writers are hard to housebreak? Their creations cannot be evaluated by academic measurements. When one of California's two greatest poets, now that Jeffers is dead—I mean Brother Antoninus, then known as William Everson—needed steady income, the university gave him a janitorship. It was not actually too bad; it paid $185 a month. Let him tell about it in his own words; on March 18, 1947, he wrote me:

It's a 44-hour week, from 3:30 p.m. to midnight—very good hours for me, leaving me the mornings free for my own work. In that freshness of spirit of a late arising, my poems have prospered again. By good luck I work in the library, my routine being: clean and mop the main men's lavatory from 3:30 to 5:30. From then to 10 I take care of the fourth floor—some three dozen rooms, as well as the Bancroft Library. At ten I join with an Oklahoman and we sweep the Main Reading Room, which is really a lot of work, moving all the chairs, etc.

The job is amusing in many ways—as my friend Tom Parkinson said, accosting me one day in the hall over my mop and bucket, "I don't know, but I think there's a cultural irony in this." One of my janitorial colleagues wormed my true profession from me, so all the librarians up in Bancroft know they have a poet sweeping their rooms. The professors don't though. When I enter their offices as they study at night, there is a strange relationship, they being both diffident and aloof, ill at ease, really not knowing how to cross the institutional line that makes them professors and me charman. I can't presume to try, but rather let our common humanity do its own work, and am courteous without being abject. Some of them I've never seen, but build up pictures of them from their offices. The messy ones are the best—you can tell by the butts in the ashtray a good deal about a man's intensity—that and the books sprawled open on the desk—that and the crumpled paper in the wastebasket. I lead a very covert life there, really; one that is so close to their intimacies, yet they never see me. I'm in and out again while the most of them are gone—they come back next day to find the butts removed and the heel marks vanished from the red floor, but they do not know what I've seen, nor what I know of them.

It was the Guggenheim, not the Phelan foundation, the Catholic Church, not the University, that offered this poet the security he needed for his work to flourish. The Book Club of California acknowledged him as a printer. The William Andrews Clark Memorial Library, UCLA's finest endowment, is the repository of Brother Antoninus's manuscript, printed, and spoken works.

Although Robinson Jeffers was never fittingly honored by the University, the Book Club did honor him. It published his poems. It exhibited his books. Albert Bender and Theodore Lilienthal, James D. Hart and Melba Bennett were his champions. And they did not wait until after he was dead. Jeffers' alma mater (and mine), Occidental College, also did not fail to hail the poet in his lifetime and now, led by Melba Bennett, it is making bold and imaginative plans to honor Robinson Jeffers and encourage the study and appreciation of his poetry.

Another criticism that I shall make of my employer is that since 1933, when the *University Chronicle* expired, it has not sponsored a periodical of general cultural interest, although it has spent millions of dollars for scholarly journals in specialized fields, and its University Press has issued hundreds of important monographs. Thanks to Samuel T. Farquhar and A. R. Tommassini, our University Press has become renowned for the beauty of its publications.

It was Stanford University that sponsored the *Pacific Spectator,* funded by the American Council of Learned Societies, and under humanistic Edith Mirrielees it flourished for a time. Today the Claremont Colleges are publishing a brave little quarterly which shook up that proper community somewhat by featuring an interview with Henry Miller.

Richesse oblige. Of the University of California's yearly budget of $62,000,000, not a dollar goes for a general cultural periodical to which California is entitled, which California needs, if for no other reason than to trump Texas and its new quarterly. It is as good as it is big; and it is edited by the Chancellor of the University.

If California were to found a periodical, I would propose as editor that other of the two best poets in California today, who is also essayist, translator, critic—that *enfant terrible,* Kenneth Rexroth of 250 Scott Street, San Francisco—a man of learning, guillotine edge, and taste.

A sign of greatness in a university is its inclusion of a few such genius-ridden eccentrics. Need I round up Harvard's mavericks, or name the wild men who have helped make the fame of Oxford and Cambridge? No one could have been odder than C. K. Ogden, the Cambridge don who invented Basic English, and who enjoyed conversing with cats as much as he did with colleagues.

To make such unorthodox appointments and then make them stick calls for Olympians on Olympus. The late Dixon Wecter came to the University of California with the unassailable tenure of a full professor when still a young man, and was eccentric in his avoidance of academic chores. He saw his role as critic, essayist, biographer, and he played it to the end; and when death claimed him in 1950, the University lost its most eloquent spokesman for humanism. The University also encouraged Herbert Eugene Bolton to run his one-man show called the Bancroft Factory, to the glory of Western scholarship.

I want to pay tribute to the man who was responsible for many such bold acts, the man to whom I owe my rise in the University—President Emeritus Robert Gordon Sproul. President Clark Kerr is a courageous successor, and in Chancellor Franklin Murphy, Southern California has a man to match its freeways.

One day we may see rivalries between California and Stanford, between UCLA and USC, other than athletic. Of ancient Greece, do we remember the names of any gladiators, of any Olympic winners? What did Sappho do to be remembered all these centuries? Wrote poetry.

We also need a literary history of California of the order of Van Wyck Brooks's chronicles of New England. The closest we have come is Franklin Walker's *San Francisco's Literary Frontier,* and his *Literary History of Southern California.*

A few years ago when Van Wyck Brooks was a fellow at the Huntington Hartford Foundation, hidden in the Santa Monica Mountains which guard UCLA from northern invasions, I learned that he has spent eight of the day's twenty-four hours, for forty years or more, in doing what? In just reading—thousands on thousands of books, drawn from the Sterling Library at Yale, near which he lives. Another eight hours he spends in writing, leaving a full eight hours for such incidentals as eating and sleeping. The perfect regimen, I would call it, free from the distractions of pleasure, from such follies as bridge and golf, cocktail parties and banquets.

We need book reviewing free from the pressures that see the amount of space available determined by the amount of advertising that must be accommodated. I was an admirer of the late Joseph Henry Jackson and of Paul Jordan-Smith, and while I do not question the integrity of their successors, William Hogan and Robert Kirsch—they do wonderfully well within the limitations of the newspapers which employ them—I do say that if California is to go on making what the Indians call "Big Mouth" about its size as the number-one state in the Union, it should endeavor to found and support a literary periodical of equal stature.

Great works—and if California is to be truly great, and not merely in the number of its inhabitants, it must now produce masterpieces of bibliographical and literary scholarship—great works, I say, will come only out of unusual and favorable conditions, by recognizing creative persons of the first rank and freeing them to read and reflect and write.

Princeton's Institute for Advanced Studies is an example of what can be done. The Guggenheim fellowships are without strings. The Huntington Library gave Robert Glass Cleland the freedom to write those good books of his ripe years. It could happen again.

I want to praise the Sierra Club and what it is doing to keep California from being bulldozed under. Its role in the annual Wilderness Conferences, its publications, and its magnificent work for wilderness conservation owe much to the vision, courage, and eloquence of its secretary, David Brower.

More than half of the hundred volumes published thus far by the Book Club of California were printed by the Grabhorn Press. All of them explode in that perfect fusion of the elements that go to make a book triumph—something worth saying in a form worth seeing. I do not believe the corporate structure or the committee system can be credited for this. I see rather the quiet presence of a few civilized Californians who, by their taste and intelligence, their energy and devotion, imagination and creative vision, have done more for the fame of San Francisco and this Club and, by the radiation of their achievements, for the entire state, than all the boosters and beaters of drums among us: W. R. K. Young, Alfred Sutro, Albert Bender, Flodden Heron, and Morgan Gunst; Oscar Lewis, Edwin and Robert Grabhorn, George Harding, Florence Walter, Elizabeth Downs, James D. Hart, David Magee, and Joseph Bransten.

I mentioned radiation, that is the emission from a central point of light and heat, of life and joy. The Book Club of California has been such a radiator, sending its magnetic rays even through the thickest Tehachapis, inspiring the late Gregg Anderson and Ward Ritchie to make pilgrimage to San Francisco, to Nash and to the Grabhorns, when they sought to become printers. It was Gregg Anderson who founded the Rounce and Coffin Club, a fiery group which has been to Southern California something of what the Book Club has been to the center of the state—a loosely organized band of creative people, free of institutional bondage.

In the years ahead, what must happen if this kind of creative individualistic society is to flourish? Patrons must appear who will make it possible for writers and editors, illustrators, designers, and printers to work in peace and freedom, with ease and grace. I am afraid the universities, the way they are governed now, are not the place, although UCLA has offered haven to California's most brilliantly individualistic scholar-printer, Will Cheney. When his telephone-booth-sized print shop on La Cienega was marked for destruction, two of Cheney's oldest patrons, Glen Dawson and Jake Zeitlin, asked the university to rescue Cheney. The William Andrews Clark Memorial Library offered him sanctuary from the angelic maelstrom, and installed him in the gatehouse as printer to the library.

I know that Will Clark would have approved this act—Clark, the patron of John Henry Nash. I am not sure that *Nash* would have approved. He liked to print big books. Cheney doesn't. He likes to print little books. The Clark Library accommodates books of all sizes: Nash and Cheney, Updike and Armitage live at peace within its walls. We have sought particularly to collect the work of the contemporary printers of Southern California.

If what has been called the California renaissance of fine printing is to continue, new printers must appear, be recognized, patronized, and kept fruitful. We cannot expect the miracle of the Grabhorns to happen again. This seems to me the greatest challenge of this Club's years ahead—to see that fine printing does not die out.

How can this be done? Let the Book Club of California, the Roxburghe Club, the Zamorano Club, and the Rounce and Coffin Club band together and offer prizes, awards, commissions, fellowships, every possible encouragement, to creative young people in the graphic arts. We cannot expect the academic communities, or commercial printing groups, to do this.

Nor can we depend only on the clubs I have named. There must be individual patronage, such as that extended by Will Clark and Albert Bender. Book clubs, such as the several I belong to, have some men of means among their members who do nothing to encourage the graphic arts, who take and give not, who are content to achieve status merely by belonging. This is immoral. When eating and drinking and sleeping through speeches becomes the main interest of the majority of members, that club is moribund.

And so what *is* the prospect before us? The growth of a commonwealth of material abundance, of wealth and leisure and opportunities for learning and creative achievement, which if given leadership and standards of excellence might see the flowering of a new culture in the next fifty years.

The first fifty years of this Club are a fair model. I would warn against the blight of gentility, of respectability for itself alone, of imitation and conformity and rigid organization, of the proliferation of committees—of all the forms that kill the spirit.

The recognition and encouragement and patronage of young turks and mavericks—name your own—the willingness to experiment, and the glorification of the individual artist, not the group —these are the things to aspire to, if we wish this Elizabethan age of the Book Club to be followed by another, perhaps even greater one. Such an age will not leap full grown from the Franciscan brow. Its flowers and its fruit will come only from today's seed, from what we plant in the soil of our culture, from the care with which we cultivate our state-wide garden.

"There will be, in time, such poems to hold the immensities of California in a brief compass," wrote Genevieve Taggard in *Continent's End*, the anthology of California poetry published by this Club in 1925; and then she continued, in a blaze of rhetoric, "If we hang our meditations in her trees, and our impulses from her precipices, and stir her dust with the whirlwinds of our desire, some swarthy Keats or electric Shelley will come, in a hundred years or so, and find the land alive."

This is the prospect before us.

Part VI

ON THE MALIBU COAST

Ocian in View

WILLIAM CLARK was a better explorer than speller. When he
and Meriwether Lewis had made their way across the Missouri
and down the Columbia and had come at last in sight of what
they had been so long in finding, Clark wrote in his journal,
"Ocian in view. O, the joy!"

Ocean is in view as I write, our watery front yard, ruffled by
the westerly which blew away the overcast. Close at hand the
water is sandy, then the calm of the kelp bed, and beyond lies
the dark sea with wind-horses running wild on its surface.
Farther out, a tanker from El Segundo is heading upcoast, riding nearly awash, taking explosions of sea over the bows, sight
of which recalls my own life at sea, which began with a voyage
round the world when I was eighteen.

Mountains I love and desert and a few cities, but I have
chosen to live what's left of my life here at continent's end, on
the hem of the sea, where the water nibbles away at property
to which man holds tenuous title.

Great poetry has been written about the sea, from Homer
through Shakespeare, to Melville and Matthew Arnold, Dana,
and Robinson Jeffers. Only geniuses or fools write poetry about

it, and I know I am not the one and hope I am not the other. Keats had its discoverer staring at it silent in wild surmise, but then Balboa (not Cortes) was exploring, not essaying. And yet living beside it, seeing and hearing, smelling and feeling the Pacific Ocean, finds me moved to words, hopeful of communicating the role of ocean in my life.

Buried first memories cannot be dredged up, even for the sake of an essay. They go back to my infancy for, though born in the east, I came each year to California as a baby, either to Riverside or Newport Beach; and when we finally moved for good to South Pasadena, our summers were spent on that spit of sand between sea and bay at Newport-Balboa.

My father liked to fish. He also had means to buy soft-shelled crabs for bait. I dug and screened and imprisoned them live, then sold them to him for pocket money. He was a surf fisher, while I preferred harpooning sharks in the shallow water over mud flats in the bay. I liked to go alone on the incoming tide clear to the backwaters known as The Lakes, deep in the Irvine Ranch, harpoon and fish there for hours, then drift home on the outgoing tide. Later I went to sea with my father and Cap'n Adams, in the latter's motorboat *Skipjack,* and we trolled for albacore in the Catalina Channel, and caught 'em too, big ones who preferred our jigs to being canned as Chicken of the Sea.

When I was fifteen my father died; we had less money then, and there were no more summers at the beach. Years later my girl and I used to go down to the sea again on winter weekends, to a house on the bay front, built of somber redwood, full of sweet smells and windy noises. There was no one on the beach, and all the wood and shells were ours to glean.

The round-the-world voyage came after my freshman year in college, and was taken for recuperation from a summer siege of flu. I went as a member of the ship's orchestra on the Dollar Liner, *President Harrison,* sailing from San Francisco November 5, 1925, on a gray afternoon when the swells began to lift the bow even before we had cleared the Golden Gate. Liner? Passenger-carrying freighter.

During the four-month voyage we called at twenty-six ports,

including Hong Kong, Singapore, Port Said, Genoa, New York, Panama—places of squalor and beauty, of poverty and riches, all of which made lasting impressions on me, who had been an avid boy-reader of the little blue school geographies by Carpenter; and yet the most lasting of all impressions was that made by oceans and seas, seen at all hours, and different seasons, and in all weathers. I recall the rain-swept run from Honolulu to Kobe, the first tropical sunsets between Manila and Singapore, the lonely waters of the Indian Ocean, and the crowded Mediterranean hemmed with colored stuccoes; and the North Atlantic in January during one of the worst storms ever measured, when the waves and the troughs between them were of vast dimensions, and the ship took a pounding. We were three days late on the run from Marseilles to Boston.

During the summer of 1928 I worked again as ship's musician, this time on the *Yale,* that slim white steamer with the thin black stacks which plied with her sister ship, the *Harvard,* between San Diego, San Pedro, and San Francisco. We used to sail from the latter port twice a week at four o'clock, and by sundown were abeam the Santa Lucias, then picked up the lights of Sur and Piedras Blancas, as the darkness and the wind fell together.

The next long voyage came when I sailed for France on board the French Line freighter *Orégon,* San Pedro for Le Havre, calling at La Libertad and the ports at either end of the Panama Canal. It was the first time I had ever been a paid passenger on a ship, and I relished that twenty-eight-day voyage, reading and writing, eating well, learning French, sun-bathing on the forward-deck cargo of squared Douglas fir or lying on the ledge at the apex of the bows, looking down at the cutwater and curl of ocean, as we drove through summer seas, awed once by sight of a shark as it followed the ship for hours, rolling over to show its teeth. Rainbow-colored jellyfish floated on the surface. Flying fish with iridescent wings flew on deck.

I came home from Europe in the *Majestic,* crossed the Atlantic again years later in the *Queen Elizabeth,* and returned in the freighter *American Scientist,* ever in love with ocean life, eager for the voyage to continue indefinitely, sensitive to changes of sea and sky, both subtle and sudden, delicate and brutal, addicted to the master smell of oil-hot machinery, and so conditioned by the pulse of the propeller shaft that when the engines were turned off, I felt that the ship had died, its heartbeat stopped.

Such are the memories that rise in me when I sit at cliff's edge and look down and out to sea.

The wind has risen to the degree described by mariners as "fresh," by no means a gale, but of such force as to lift the kelp fronds, which usually lie on the surface, and fly them like amber banners. The sea birds have given up and gone to roost on the lee side of the rock cliffs; and if it were not for a pane of glass between me and the wind, I too would be driven into the roost we call house.

A large anthology could be compiled of sea poetry and prose, a job for my old age, when I hope I will be better read than fifty finds me. If I had now to pick the one example which pleases me the most, it might well be the cry of William Clark—"Ocian in view. O, the joy!"

The Move to the Coast

WE MOVED TO THE MALIBU, twenty-eight miles from campus, and my wife hasn't yet recovered from the shock. For years we lived close to the library, and I was scornful of those who chose to inhabit such outlandish communities as West Covina, Compton, and Canoga Park, and had to spend hours each day in fighting traffic. Although she always wanted to live at the beach, my wife had lost hope, for the near-by ocean resorts were too built up to satisfy her desire for a large yard and semiwild garden, and she had come to take as gospel my claim that I would never become a commuter.

What happened? It began with the stand of bamboo outside our bedroom window, planted originally for the lullaby of its rustle. Then the weather seemed to worsen (all changes in weather are blamed on The Bomb, aren't they?) and the movement of evening air slackened and finally ceased, and there was nothing but smog by day and its stagnant after-mist by night, while the bamboo stood somnolent. I longed for the mild aerial turbulence Southern California once enjoyed.

There were other factors too in my change of feeling, such as the growing up of our sons, which made it no longer necessary that we live near schools, and my discovery that the library got along nicely without my presence every day, which had been my bad habit during the years we lived near campus.

And so it came to pass that one day, in obedience to the inner voice, I went home early and said to my wife, "We're going house hunting." She sat in amazed silence as I drove along San Vicente Boulevard (reminiscent of the Santa Monica road races of my boyhood), down canyon to the coast highway, thence northwest beyond Topanga and Las Flores canyons, Malibu Lagoon and the movie colony, the strand at the mouth of Corral Canyon which some Floridan corrupted to Coral Beach, then Látigo Canyon (accent on the primary, if you please, it's Spanish for whip), past Paradise Cove and over the neck of Point Dume (also a corruption, from Fray Dumetz, one of the Franciscan missionaries in the eighteenth century), thence to the county beach at Zuma, and the adjoining Trancas and Encinal colonies, where the coast curves east and west—coast of the prevailing westerly, to which windbreaks of blue gums and cypress bear witness.

Only then did I slow up and sniff the air, pungent with sea wrack and conifers, mesembryanthemum and geranium, and we looked at one another. I wet my finger and held it out the window.

"This will make the bamboo rustle," I said. "Now to find a place suited to our needs. I know it's here, but where?"

"You mean way out here?" my wife asked. "You'd be willing to live way out here?"

"It's still in the county, isn't it?" I countered.

She was speechless—and pleased.

The realtor had nothing for sale, but as we were leaving, his phone rang. Someone calling in to list a house. It sounded possible. The three of us went to investigate, and found it off the highway on the coast between Lechuza and Sequit points. We entered the yard through a grape-stake fence, beneath untopped cypresses, and found ourselves in a secret garden, planted to roses and lilies, dropping to terraces of geraniums, hedged by pine, eucalyptus, and *Pittosporum crassifolium,* the silvery-gray-leafed Australian which resembles the pineapple guava.

The garden grew to the brink of the palisade, bushed with wild bladder, salt bush, and wild buckwheat, and ankled a hundred feet below with sandy beach and blue water, and a few rocks to relieve the monotony. A cliff's edge *cabaña* promised smoky cooking. The sheltered patio was bright with bougainvillaea, hibiscus, fuchsias, camellias, and pacified by an olive tree.

It was a winter day, and we could see Santa Barbara Rock, forty miles due south, while the islands of Santa Catalina, Anacapa, and Santa Cruz lay closer on either hand. Behind us and to the west, the skyline of the chaparral-covered Santa Monicas was high and curving. Through a break in the trees, highway traffic could be seen but not heard.

I stole a look at my wife, and caught her stealing a look at me. She nodded. I nodded. The shock of recognition, and we had yet to enter the house. Surely not the way Benjamin Franklin would advise one to acquire property: to know you wanted it before you had even examined it. Or does he have a paragraph on instantaneous perception as a business asset?

Inspection proved the house fairly well suited to our needs and wants. If the kitchen was too small for her, so was the study too small for me; each sympathized with the other, thus maintaining the balance necessary for marital bliss. At least the garage had an ocean view window, which would please our car-loving younger son if, during hours spent on visits home, he ever emerged from the bearing straits and looked out.

A series of obstacles, chiefly in selling our house in Palms, delayed the deal, but we never doubted, for we knew that house was meant for us; and thanks to patience and banker friends, the obstacles were overcome, and we moved to the Malibu.

"But isn't it windy?" our friends ask. "Don't you find the fog depressing? And what about that long drive into the sun, both morning and night?"

So I explain to the city dwellers that windy air means fresh air, and how responsive we and the transplanted bamboo are to it. Our stretch of coast, more sheltered than Zuma and Dume, receives a brooming nearly every afternoon; and in the gray hours before the westerly has swept the mist away, we hear the foghorns of the fishing boats, speaking of the need for cautious movement. Back in 1912 an Englishman named J. Smeaton Chase camped on the Malibu while riding horseback from Mexico to Oregon, and wrote in the book he published afterward called *California Coast Trails,* "The breeze was strong and keen, and an inexhaustible freshness was in the air, as if the world had been created within the week." No change in the weather.

And the sixty-mile round trip? Not bad. The fast highway is a safe road if one keeps his eyes more on it than on the scenery. There are only a few signals between home and campus, and a neighbor tells us that if one finds favor in the Lord's eye, he can make all of them in green sequence. The Diesels that roll between Los Angeles and San Francisco run interference for a Hillman, and when the setting sun dazzles, one can seek the shady slip stream of a Fruehauf and let the truck driver face the music.

Mornings I coast to work on the momentum of sound sleep and good breakfast, while the drive home in the evening brings me to the place a wag suggested we christen El Sea Powell more relaxed than my wife found me when we lived close to campus, the reason being that the forty-five-minute drive home is just the time needed for the administrative sediment to settle.

Reading on the Malibu

AFTER THE MOVE to the Malibu my reading suffered a corresponding change, both sea and sierran. The coast beyond Point Dume is beautiful for its sandy beaches, kelp beds, crumbling palisades, and curving line of the Santa Monicas; so immediately beautiful that our television has been dark since we moved. All the hours are lovely in their lights and colors, wind and calm; and if one isn't gardening or gleaning wood on the beach, swimming or walking, he is content to sit and watch the passage of time over the earth.

The only way to get any reading or writing done in this environment is to retreat to my study at the back of the house, pull the curtains to shut out sight of the mountains through the leaves of the olive tree, and sit facing the wall, yellow pad on my lap, blue pencil in my fist, and hope.

In moving to the new house my wife and I had twin hopes, she for a larger kitchen, I for a study that would shelve all of my books. Neither was realized. Her ship's kitchen was even smaller, my study nearly the same size as before, 9 by 12, a mere three-foot gain.

Though lacking a panoramic view, it has a blue-green shed-roof ceiling and golden pine walls which accommodate assorted pictures and prints, including Tom Craig's water color of the tawny hills back of Stanford, haired with oak, a mezzotint of Rembrandt's son Titus, and Conrad Buff's oil of Maynard Dixon's cool house in southern Utah, with its blue door, blue sky, and shimmering cottonwoods. An Oriental floor rug, two prayer rugs, and a pair of Asia Minor saddlebags, all from my father's collection. Two religious pictures in hand-carved olive-wood frames he brought from Florence half a century ago and which serve as a link between me and him, dead now nearly as long a time. A rose jar, put down in 1910, sweet as ever. Two abalone shells, heaped with smaller shells sent by my brother Clark from the shores of the Indian Ocean. Book truck. Work-table. Chair. Pallet for guest bed. Cherry-wood case for small books. Two oakwood sections holding a thousand volumes. "The Ellwood Queen," Joseph Muench's photograph of the lemon-scented gum at Goleta. A Greek dancing maiden, equally queenly. The Dollar Line insignia from my musician's cap. Pig bank. Radio. Pictures of Fay, two of Mozart. Material possessions. Talismans. Warders-off of evil. Things beloved, things fugitive. Mine for a time, then someone else's, then no one's, all doomed to "leave not a wrack behind."

There out of sight but not sound of the sea, breathing the pungent fragrance of the neighborhood, what have I been reading? Books about the new environment, the old Spanish Rancho Topanga Malibu Sequit. On the day of the opening of the coast road in 1928, after the long fight to gain a public right-of-way, I drove over it in a topless Hupmobile roadster from Santa Monica to Oxnard and back via Calabasas, an all-day trip, and even then the beaches were withheld by barbed-wire fence. I can still recall the sense of discovery I had during that first day on the Malibu, three hundred eighty-six years after Cabrillo.

Happy Days in Southern California by Frederick Hastings Rindge (1898) is a rare work by the former owner of the rancho, filled with details of shore and ranch life. Thus the owner had only himself to blame for having commenced the advertising which led people to come and squat on his land.

When I called for the book in the library's rare book room, I was startled to see by the accession number—286063—that it was one of the first volumes I handled upon joining the UCLA staff in 1938, when I was given the task of accessioning the recently acquired Cowan collection. This copy was presented by the author to Robert Ernest Cowan.

Another example of a coming event casting its bibliographical shadow occurred in the second Malibu volume I read—*Sondelius Came to the Mountains,* by Madeleine Ruthven, a pamphlet of poems published in 1934 by the Primavera Press when I was one of its directors (assigned to the shipping room), along with Jake Zeitlin, Ward Ritchie, Phil Townsend Hanna, and Carey McWilliams. I had not reread it since, and did not seem to own a copy. I found out why when I called for the UCLA copy: on August 11, 1938, it had been presented to the Library by L. C. P., and in the seventeen ensuing years it had been uncalled for.

The poems are about the folklore and flora of the back country from where we now live: Big Sycamore Canyon, Boney Ridge, Triunfo Pass, and the Yerba Buena road. Along with Hildegarde Flanner, W. W. Robinson, and C. F. MacIntyre, Madeleine Ruthven is one of the few poets who has looked at the mountains of Southern California with eyes both sharp and loving.

During vacation we varied days on the beach with explorations of the back country Miss Ruthven wrote about, and were pleased to locate many of the landmarks just as she described them. The great stone house, whose creation she tells so beautifully, still stands on the sage-covered hill facing the battlements of Boney Ridge.

This end of the Santa Monicas, from Malibu Canyon west to Big Sycamore Canyon, a distance of perhaps twenty miles, and of a depth of ten or twelve from ocean to Ventura Boulevard, is lonely country. Too unspectacular to draw tourists, too dry to support many settlers, it slumbers undisturbed with few to breathe the incense of chaparral or to see the gray fox cross the road, the hovering hawk, and the rare hunter without firearms, taking advantage of a special deer season limited to the bow and arrow.

At the foot of Boney Ridge, approaching Triunfo Pass, the road traverses a stand of the brush known as red shanks, which in August was in feathery bloom. To learn more about this member of the chaparral family I reread one of the best of all botanical works of Californiana, *The Elfin Forest of California* by Francis M. Fultz (Los Angeles, Times-Mirror Press, 1923), a small book with more than one hundred photographic illustrations, which is entirely about the chaparral and small pines of the Southern California mountains.

Botanically accurate and charmingly written, this book by a retired educator and forester who lived in Highland Park deserves reprinting. His death a few years ago brought Fultz's papers to the UCLA Library, through the generosity of the author's widow and the good offices of Glen Dawson.

Let me quote what he says about the virgin stand of red shanks we came upon in our wanderings:

> A sister of the Chamise flourishes in the southern part of the Elfin Forest. It is *adenostoma sparsifolium,* the specific name indicating one of its distinctive characteristics—thinly leaved. It is often called "red-shanks," from the color of its trunk. It keeps shedding its bark in long, thin shreds, which gives it a rather untidy appearance. But this characteristic serves as an unfailing mark of identification. It is a much more robust shrub than its sister, the greasewood, growing to double the diameter and nearly twice the height. It is plentiful about the western slope of Mt. San Jacinto, and from there southward. The only place that I have seen it north and west of the San Gabriel Valley is in the Santa Monica Mountains, where there is a patch of unusually fine specimens near Saddle Peak.

In his *Southern Sierras of California* (1924) Charles Francis Saunders has a chapter on the Santa Monicas which includes several pages on the flowers of Malibu Creek, whose gorge is now traversed by a road cut in the rock face by convict labor.

Dana was also on my summer rereading list, and I savored once again his *Two Years Before the Mast*. His descriptions of the coast from San Diego to Monterey are timeless. Holder's *Channel Islands of California* was consulted to see if it gives the flashing intervals of the Anacapa Light (it doesn't), and finally I returned to Chase's *California Coast Trails* to read again what he said about the Malibu:

> Turning, then, westward, a few miles of pleasant road brought us to the entrance to the Malibu Ranch, a long strip of land lying between the southward-facing foothills of the Santa Monica Mountains and the shore. At the gate was posted a warning that Trespassing was Strictly Prohibited. I knew that public right of way through the ranch had long been contested by the owners, and I had been warned that I might find my way disputed by their myrmidons with shotguns. But there was nothing except the passive placard to prevent my entering, and I passed on with little doubt of making an equally peaceful exit at the western end.

Chase camped that night by the lagoon at Trancas Canyon, and to this day one of the Rindges' range rider's shacks stands near-by, boarded up and ruinous. The following night he slept on the beach farther upcoast.

> I was up at four o'clock, and broke camp early. The breeze was strong and keen, and an inexhaustible freshness was in the air, as if the world had been created within the week. After a few miles more of alternate shore and cliff, we crossed the line into Ventura County, and at the same time bade adieu to the Malibu and its cantankerous but futile placards.

Where the Mountains
Meet the Sea

MY BOYHOOD AND YOUTH were nourished by the San Gabriels and the San Bernardinos, which ranges wall out the desert from Southern California. It was not until I went to work at UCLA and moved near to the campus that allegiance was transferred to the Santa Monicas, a less spectacular range which rises in Hollywood and extends fifty miles northwest to a marine ending at Point Mugu.

From living in Beverly Glen, I came to love the surrounding range of chaparral, oak, and sycamore. It was a good place for our sons to live as boys, and now that they are grown to manhood they find their subconscious minds full of memories of their mountain boyhood.

Although, as I have already written, I discovered the western-most part of the range in the poems of Madeleine Ruthven, it was not until a decade later, in 1944, that I came actually to know this remote area. At war's end my friend Gordon Newell, the sculptor, acquired land on the north slope of the mountains, overlooking Seminole Hot Springs, and it served me as a kind of retreat from too much city. From driving and walking and talking to Newell, I came to know and to love his land and the sea of chaparral which enislanded it. The north slope of the Santa Monicas is green the year round from springs, one of which he had deepened and rock-lined, so that it was an unfailing source of cold water, even in the driest summer. Through the years I watched him quarry honey-colored flagstone, sift and sack oak leaf-mold, breed Nubian goats, keep bees, carve wood, and cut stone, while his wife Emelia fashioned delicate jewelry and airy mobiles, and their children thrived in a kind of twentieth-century Theocritean idyll.

It takes time to assimilate the essences of a land. When after years of residence in Inyo County Mary Austin wrote *The Land of Little Rain,* her publishers wanted her to move around the country, writing similar books about other places of residence. Her reply was that it would take her ten years in a locale to be able to evoke its spirit, as indeed she did later for Arizona-New Mexico in *The Land of Journeys' Endings.*

Thus although we moved to the Malibu, in the seaward lee of the Santa Monicas, as recently as 1955, I brought to the land years of slow-growing knowledge and deepening love for this country "where the mountain meets the sea"; and I was ready to write about it not as a stranger. In fact it was this long background of reading and seeing that motivated our move—that and the feeling we have always had for the seashore. Plus something else, instinctive, mysterious, and right.

So it was a kind of magnetic homecoming, this move to the Malibu, and now our leisure time is divided between shore-line walks and mountain drives.

On this coast the seasons merge imperceptibly into each other. When the rainy season is regular, then it is easier to know the time of year. When drought comes, how is one to know summer and fall from winter and spring? By the stars to be sure, and the position of the sun—those heavenly clockworks that transcend earthly times of wet and dry.

In the late autumn the evening wears Vega like a blue-white diamond. Arcturus has set long before the sun. Capella comes up over the mountain, brightest of the northernmost stars, and toward midnight, when Sirius is well risen, there directly below it, just above the horizon, appears the sky's number-two glitterer, the southern star Canopus, never rising high enough to get beyond the city's atmosphere which lends it a baleful light.

The sun, which in summer set behind the mountain, has moved out to sea, dropping from sight at the point where San Nicolas Island lies, if we were high enough to see it. See it we did from the crest of the mountains, on one of the day's end drives which conclude our otherwise stay-at-home Sundays, lying between Santa Barbara Rock and the Santa Cruz–Anacapa conjunction, eighty miles out, dark whale on the blue sea, never to be seen from shore line.

Living on the Malibu one can choose between many peaceful things to do—stay at home and read or write or garden and other chores, or just sit; or drive in the hills; or walk on the beach. There is choice too among the hill drives—whether it be up the Decker Road along Mulholland, and down the Arroyo Sequit to the sea again, or up Little Sycamore Canyon on the Yerba Buena road, over Triunfo Pass with a view to Lake Sherwood, then down past the lake, through Hidden Valley, over the hills and down Long Grade Canyon to Camarillo and the coast highway; or west from Little Sycamore along narrow roads leading into cul-de-sacs, where one sees foxes and hawks, and water flowing out of rock face—all of this within fifty miles of Los Angeles, unknown to the millions.

In the autumn of 1955, when the first of two fires swept over the mountains from the valley, leaped the crest of Boney Ridge, and devoured the forest of red shanks which graced that mountain's southern slope, we feared a long bareness for the burned flanks. Winter rains brought a myriad of flowers in places where the sun had not penetrated for years, and then in the spring we rejoiced to see rise from the base of the burned chaparral delicate new growth. The fire had not proved mortal, though ten years would be needed for the forest to recover.

Summer's flowers succeeded spring's pinks and blues and whites—orange monkey flower, red gooseberry, and larkspur, and the purple sage, bee heaven on earth—while the arroyos became *seco* and sand choked the creek mouths.

By summer the winter's creek wood had all been gathered, and the gleaning was again of plank wood cast up by the sea, that and shells and fragments to serve as gravel on the garden paths. All these years I had remembered the crushed abalone shells with which Una and Robinson Jeffers graveled their paths at Tor House, and now I began to strew our walks with shells and bones and jeweled bits from the seashore.

The Chumash who dwelled here were jewelry makers, and the Southwest Museum preserves examples of their necklaces of tide-line treasures. Now I see why. The wash of water renders all things smooth, and after high tide recedes one finds the beach strewn with beautiful fragments. Westward I walk, stooping, picking, filling a cloth bag, until it becomes leaden and the way back weary. And when at last I empty it out on the path at home, the scattering iridescences and pearly bits—blue-black of mussel, flesh-pink of cowrie, purple of abalone—make a display Tiffany's should envy, and I am moved to acquire a polishing wheel, a cutter and a borer, a ball of cord, and become a necklace maker. The abalone shells of this coast were prized by the Hopis far to the east, who ground them for dye tincture. These Mollusca are rarely exposed by even the lowest tide, seeking the safety of deeper water, and even then skin divers need powerful leverage to pry them loose, and woe to the man whose hand is caught. Freshly caught and sautéed in butter they are delicious, and their shells remain forever beautiful.

Indians are buried everywhere from Mugu Lagoon to Malibu Creek. Every bulldozing operation brings their bones and artifacts to light, as one did just across Broad Beach Road from us —a dozen huddled skeletons, four or five hundred years old, taking no notice of their noisy resurrection. Our geranium garden, falling to Encinal Creek, is sure to be a burying ground, the diggers tell us. Mary Austin writes of the residue of personality that always haunts a place once inhabited by man. Jeffers' poetry is full of these hauntings. But I cannot say that I have encountered spirits here on the Malibu. Perhaps the Diesels drive them away. I have no fear of them however. The Chumash were a gentle people, living on shellfish, roots, and acorn meal. We who are carnivorous may leave a different residue. Sometimes I wonder who will follow us here, and what they will make of our artifacts—books and disks and Scriptos and, less tangible though perhaps more lasting, our love for this marine mountainscape called the Malibu.

Manna from the Sea

ALONG THE MALIBU there has been good aftermath of the storm, and the coast has been gathering manna. Mushrooms and other edible fungi rose overnight, and lived briefly in the light of day before consummating a buttery union in the skillet. Mustard greens likewise had a short life span before they too yielded up on the stove. Last year's stalks were rooted out by the wind and piled like skeletons against the fences, to make room for the new growth now in its head-high yellow prime.

Mussels also are in season—no delicacy, true, but few meals are more satisfying than a mess of them, gathered at ebb tide in the twilight, then steamed open and dunked in lemon-butter, salty, sandy, tough little guys, tasting of kelpy iodine, an atavistic feast linking us with our predecessors on this coastal shelf, who gave names to many of the places, from Anacapa and Hueneme to Mugu, Malibu, and Topanga.

Now we know why they inhabited the lagoons at the creek mouths, for when the rainy run-off swells these *arroyos secos* to savage streams, the rivers break their summer sand bars and run to the sea, bearing treasure to the tidelanders. We live on the cliff by the estuary of Encinal Creek, and at the height of the storm, when we went down with shovels to divert ravenous run-offs, we saw the little watercourse, long barred from union with the ocean and held in stagnant continence, changed to a torrent, and raging out of the Santa Monicas to an eager consummation with the sea.

The Pacific was belying its name, roiled up for a mile offshore, wind-blown, coffee-colored, perilous to all but its native denizens —and I doubt they were pleased with the turmoil. We dwell on an open coast, with few shelters for small craft, and the shore line is that seen by Cabrillo, Drake, Vancouver, and Dana, and in our day by the crews of purse seiner, tuna clipper, and tanker. The Catalina and Santa Barbara channels afford scant protection from southwesterlies, and the islands themselves are mostly steep and forbidding on both their leeward and windward sides.

Life on the Malibu is richest at the creek mouths, the Chumash knew; and so did we, after the storm was over and the run-off from the mountains washed upon the beaches. What a haul of firewood for the gleaning! We envy our neighbors the Brents, whose open fireplace will take logs up to ten feet in length. Ours is only twenty-four inches wide, which means that sawing, chopping, and splitting must follow gleaning and hauling.

It is years since the hills received such a scouring, yielding logs and stumps, burned roots, and rotting branches of oak, sycamore, red shanks, and chamisal, much of it smashed to fireplace length in its fall down the stream beds, and sculptured into beautiful shapes.

The sea itself casts up wood, smoothed by wind and wave— empty packing cases of water chestnuts from Hong Kong and ammunition boxes from navy vessels, flawed planks of pine, Douglas fir, oak, and redwood, cast overboard from lumber schooners, flotsam, corks from fishermen's nets, an occasional Japanese glass float, battered lobster traps, and sundry jetsam not worth its salt.

The first step is to cache the wet wood and let it dry, before carrying it up the path to the cliff top. If one posts his pile with a sign reading "Blest be he who leaves my logs; curst be he who steals my sticks," he is certain to find it when he returns, and just half its weight.

The joy of gathering beach wood is matched by that of burning it, although an occasional twinge is felt, like eating one's pet rabbit, when a shaft of skin-smooth chaparral is reduced to silvery ash. This wild wood's smoke has its own smells, different from those of domestic firewood—oak and walnut perfumy, eucalyptus acrid, orange bittersweet, and juniper like incense— and unless it has been submerged a long while, it does not burn with a blue flame. One twelve-foot length of 2 by 4 was difficult to identify. From its weight and grain and color I called it oak. When I began to saw it, I realized my error. The fragrance was like the interior of our clothes closet. Cedar! The smoke from its burning was even sweeter. Once I found a broken mast or boom, stamped with Chinese characters. On sawing, it proved to be camphor wood, so pungent that I kept a section of it in my clothes closet.

Characteristic of this coast is the offshore wind that blows after dark, very faintly, a mere breath of mountain air suspiring delicately toward the sea, bearing smells of sun-warmed brush and stream bed with smoke from our chimney, ghosts of the beach wood, drifting down over the dark sand and water, residue of fire, liberated energy, sweeter far than incense of cathedral.

Now winter's constellations are risen high, Sirius ruling the zenith and fiery Canopus, describing his short arc above the southern horizon. In the west the lighthouse opens like an eye, then closes, leaving the night darker than before. In the east, when it is very clear, the Point Vicente light can be seen on the Palos Verdes and, nearer, the light buoy off Point Dume. These smells and sights assure one that one can leave the world to the wakeful and seek one's bed, with the final thought that another storm will find us in the wood business.

Fire!

Life on the malibu is not without its hazards. Rainstorm is one. When ten inches fell in thirty-six hours, the cliffs grew sodden and began to slide, and we learned the uses of sandbags. Then fire. As one who grew up in Southern California, I thought I knew all there was to know about forest and brush fires. From our house in Pasadena I had watched the wide face of the mountains burn. Later I fought fires in the San Bernardinos near Forest Home. In La Crescenta during the autumn of 1933, we saved Poet MacIntyre's cabin from the flames, only to lose it to flood on New Year's Day. In Beverly Glen we taught the boys the peril of open fires and wind, and all of us were relieved when we quit the canyon for the open plain.

On the ocean edge of the westernmost Santa Monicas, we seemed to be protected from fire by three roads and fields which separated us from the mountain, and also by the prevailing wind, which would drive fire back over the mountain away from the shore.

It was wind that nearly brought our ruin—not the westerly wind, though, but the hated north wind, whose name in Southern California is the Santa Ana. All fall it blew, often for days at a stretch, bringing the brush to explosive dryness. No rain had fallen since spring.

Christmas Day was dry and clear, and from indoors the sea was beautiful, driven offshore by the air which came in gusts from the north, so that one could see the wind devils whirling over the water in clouds of spindrift, finally disappearing out to sea.

While waiting for the lamb to roast, I ventured a shell-gathering walk at low tide. My naked body felt the blown sand like a whip, and at the fiercest, I had to brace myself to keep from being blown away. Gulls were soaring and swooping, and cormorants rode the wind like jets, headed eastward to their feeding beds. A couple of the curlewlike birds known as marbled godwits took off ahead of me with foolish cries, their outspread wings changing their drab appearance while feeding to the black-and-white splendor which gives them their name. I took shelter behind a rock, directly beneath the ruin halfway up the cliff of one of the "depots" on the old Malibu railway.

The wind was still savage when we went to bed at ten, the sky swept clear, aglitter with stars. Anacapa flashed its warning light. The cypresses, pines, and eucalyptuses were noisier than the surf. Cats' fur threw sparks when stroked. We slept in spite of the sinister atmosphere.

I awoke abruptly at four to see a fierce glow in the sky. I arose instantly, knowing what it meant. Fire. From the bedroom's west window, the point of origin seemed north. I went to my study and looked out the window through tossing foliage. What I saw made me shout, and brought my wife on the run. Fire? God, the whole face of the mountain was burning, in a long line just below the summit, and moving toward us on the wind. Fear dried my mouth. I knew doom when I saw it.

Swiftly I dressed in shirt, pants, and shoes, while my wife, equally silent, corraled the four cats and one dog in our bedroom and shut the door.

In the patio we could smell the smoke and feel the heat. While I began to couple our garden hoses and prepare to wet down the cypress, potential torches, and the garage section of our roof not covered by tiles, my wife called the County Fire Station at Zuma Creek to ask if a general alarm had been sounded. "At 2:30," the operator said. "Haven't you been alerted to evacuate?" We hadn't.

Our neighborhood and the highway were silent. Of the ten houses in our colony, only three were inhabited. The others had gone away for Christmas. Next to us, new occupants, the man convalescing from an operation, took our advice and left by the highway west to Oxnard. It was still dark.

Then we phoned James Hartzell, a neighbor who was at his other home in Beverly Glen, thirty miles away. Half an hour later he had arrived and joined us on the hose line. Fell in back of a sheriff's car, he said, and made a fast run. Eventually we owed more to him, and the Killinger brothers, than to anyone else.

Sparks came like bullets on the wind, as the fire neared the highway. Occupants of two houses at the very foot of the mountain were setting backfires, their horse and burro beginning to whinny and bray in terror.

We made our decision not to load our animals in the car and leave, as others were doing, but instead I drove the station wagon down the road to the foot of the cliff in front of us, and we prepared to carry the cats down and lock them in it. Pippin, the big orange male, was too wild to hold, and ran off and hid. While carrying the two young males, Junior and Joey, down the path through the geraniums, my wife turned her ankle and dropped the cats, and they too hid. So we ended with me carrying Besa, the toy poodle, and she carrying Mei-ling, our old Siamese.

Back up at the house we found it enveloped in smoke and sparks, and once again we were driven to the beach below, abandoning everything except Fay's handbag and my brief case.

From the beach we saw fire on both sides and in back of our house. A neighbor's wife joined us, carrying a bottle of water, a jug of brandy, and a revolver, and leading the horse and Sugar, the burro, from higher up. These latter I took charge of, and tied them to a post at the foot of the cliff, both docile as long as they were not separated.

My wife reconnoitered along the beach and returned to report a holocaust to the east of us. To the west the fire had come down Encinal Canyon and the neighbor was certain her house was burning, in spite of the valiant fight being waged by her husband to save it. Ours seemed doomed. We were somehow calm and resigned, having passed the point of concern for material possessions. Of a thousand beloved books, save which few? Pictures, records, clothes, the Steinway? Absurd. The detached mind said, Let them burn. But the eyes turned away, unwilling to watch.

Still I ventured a look at our house on the cliff, little low white-board-sided dwelling, with slanting red-tile roofs, clinging to the earth in the dark grove of trees, and I saw it was not yet burning. The wind had veered due west. So I wrapped a wet towel around my face and went up, and just in time. The *cabaña* was beginning to catch fire from a burning mattress laid alongside it for sun-bathing. I dragged the mattress to the middle of the lawn, just as Pippin made a flying leap and landed on my shoulder, his favorite riding place. So I took him down and shut him with Mei-ling and Besa in the station wagon. Later Joey and Junior came safely out of hiding.

Then we went back up to the house and joined Hartzell in fighting the fire, which had reached our very road, and was burning fences, cypresses at their base, weedy lots—everything but the houses themselves. We used dribbling hoses—water was giving out—shovel, hoe, wet sacks, anything, for we knew that if one house caught fire, all would be lost. The Brents and the Clarkes came from upcoast and helped. We lost track of time. The sun rose, blood red through smoke. Presently my wife came hobbling among us with a tray of lamb sandwiches and milk, a goddess of plenty, no less.

When we had control of these small fires, Hartzell and I moved along the front and found the four Killingers, down from their homes high on the Decker road, fighting to save the houses toward which the fire in the cliff brush was being driven by the changed wind. They seemed to be up to their waists in flame. This was what my wife had seen burning and what made her think all the houses were afire, so thick was the smoke from flaming cypresses. By some miracle our trees had not caught fire, perhaps because the wind was so fierce, though they were scorched.

Get a pumper engine! they cried, and I ran back to the west, where Hartzell reported a county engine had arrived and was trying to save the two houses at the mouth of Encinal Creek. They had been successful. Only trees and outbuildings were burning. One was the old range rider's shack.

The engine captain, come all the way from Downey in the eastern part of the county, would not heed my plea, having been ordered to stay put until danger was passed. But he used his radio to ask for another engine to be sent to the other danger point. Sheriff Ray Rowe and his wife were fighting to save their house, and lost only an outbuilding, thanks to the help of a pumper.

So back I ran, to find the Killingers and Hartzell, all but afire themselves, joined by two Edison Company linemen bearing a chemical tank with which they laid down a fireproof line on the brush. Down on the beach I saw a blundering possum. Most of the wild life had fled in the other direction.

It was then eight o'clock in the morning, and the worst was over on our stretch of Broad Beach Road. All day, though, we fought flare-ups, and by midafternoon Hartzell and I were down in Encinal Creek, seeking to quench a stubborn fire in the mesembryanthemum that had just reached and ignited a neighbor's board fence, leading like a fuse to a grove of cypress against the house itself.

From its thick green look, one would think that ice plant would not burn. Wrong. Under the green fleshiness are the old dry stalks through which fire spreads, slowly dehydrating the green growth above, until finally all is consumed.

We had commandeered all the garden hoses in the colony, and

coupled them in two long lines, each of which dribbled water, but enough.

A couple driven out of Encinal Canyon by the advancing fire came by in their pickup truck, and showed us what they had chosen to save: their dog and parrot, the man's stamp collection, an extra pair of shoes for him (both lefts, one brown, one black), and his wife's cleaning rags (mistaken for her drawer of silk underwear). Later they returned and found their house had been saved by a heroic pumper unit from Zuma Fire Station, specially dispatched by the captain for whom the man had once done a carpentry favor. Bread cast upon the waters. . . .

Our telephone was dead, so we drove to Zuma Lifeguard Station and got through to my secretary to spread the word to family and friends that we were safe. Our sons never did succeed in getting through the roadblocks until the fire was out.

Late afternoon we drove west to the Brents' and found the fire coming down the mountain to the highway and the houses beyond, just as it had to us twelve hours earlier. There had been ample warning, however, and animals had been evacuated, including thirty-eight dogs from a kennel, and many Ventura County pumping units were present. No houses west of us were lost, save back in the canyons—Sequit and Little Sycamore—which were burned out, all but the winter-bare sycamores along the stream bed. Those lovely arroyos lay in blackened ruin, the birds and small animals dead or homeless.

There was nothing we could do to help, and we barely regained our neighborhood before the fire reached the road and swept across it to the very sand and sea.

Still the wind blew, savage and unrelenting, hour after hour. Our hair was gray with ashes, our eyes red from smoke. There was no water for several hours. The sour smell of burned brush was everywhere. All evening I patrolled the cliff and the cypress windbreaks with hoe and shovel, seeking to keep the wind from scattering the embers of chaparral roots and redwood fence posts. Hartzell returned to Beverly Glen at sundown, with my assurance that I could control the situation.

Milk and coffee were our only food, as between patrols my wife and I sat at the west window and watched the fire burn away from us along the coast—a fireworks display such as we never wish to see again. It was also going northward over the mountain, and we had a guilty feeling of security in knowing that, except for our immediate trees, there was nothing left to burn for miles around.

Throughout the night I kept on the alert, making half-hour sorties around the deserted neighborhood, shovel on my shoulder. Down in Encinal Creek oak and sycamore trunks were still burning. We were alone, except for an occasional Highway Patrol car, on guard against looters. Eight houses on the beach were burned; scores more on toward Point Dume.

Sometime after midnight I had a fright when I saw a glow in the cypress trees and thought they were afire. It was the rising moon seen through smoke. My mouth went dry again with a recurrence of the morning's symptom.

After twenty-one hours on her feet my wife went to bed and slept, the animals gathered around her—a most beautiful still life. I blew out the candle she had lit, unable to bear any sight of fire, and tiptoed away. The wind would not let me even doze. Cold milk was my sustenance.

At four o'clock the wind finally dropped, twenty-four hours after we had awakened. I lay down in my dirty clothes on the sofa in the living room and slept for two hours.

Coffee at six was the best drink of my life. I felt equal to the day's work. It was another day before my body began to ache. By noon deputy sheriffs had arrived, and our roads were sealed off by round-the-clock sentries from the curious and the would-be looters. I would have had no compunction in shooting any trespasser, so savage were my feelings from the horror of destruction. Rats from the hills were beginning to overrun the coast. Our cats now earned their keep, while Besa served as a pointer.

Later I drove downcoast to Zuma Fire Station, headquarters for the fighters and their machines, which had arrived from as far away as San Diego and San Luis Obispo, and found it like a scene behind battle lines—hundreds of men arriving and leaving, eating and resting, with heavy equipment of all kinds, some pieces with engines idling, the air full of a rumbling at once fearful and reassuring. The county services had performed heroically.

This was fire on the Malibu in Christmas week of 1956. A hundred dwellings were burned. There was no consolation in the words of the County Fire Chief, who said, "There is only one thing certain. It will happen again."

The Round of Hours

AFTER FLOOD AND FIRE things are peaceful again, hills green-ing after rain, the round of hours beautiful with the harmony of life. This is what all men seek and few men find. Now I know what Jeffers meant in speaking of his life at Carmel, before the death of Una, when he said, "I should be glad to live like this for several centuries; but good and evil are very cunningly bal-anced in the most favored lives, and I should not consider myself ill-used if I were to die tomorrow, though it would be very annoying."

In order to maintain this balance in my own life and to pro-pitiate evil, I have devised rituals of prayer and offerings, aimed at keeping myself thankfully in a state of grace for the blessings the Malibu has brought—a primitive practice which should not offend the ghosts of the aborigines.

Looking back on it now, our escape from the fire was mi-raculous. Or was it because we had passed the point of concern for material possessions that the Lord allowed us to keep our homes?

What next? Cliff slippage? Earthquake? Drought? Plague? War? All have visited the earth at some time in history. South-ern Californians should not expect immunity forever.

Returning to Jeffers, he once explained his poetry as a means of warding off evil by creating poetical characters who would divert bad spirits from his household. Now I understand his intention. My prayers are said out of doors, uninsulated by wood and tile; my litanies are launched on the night wind before I go to bed. The outer magnificence here makes ridiculous indoor worship.

In New Mexico and Arizona *sky determines;* on the Malibu *ocean determines.* When city people ask silly questions, I realize that although they live in Los Angeles, ostensibly a seaport, they have no relationship with the ocean, other than to dip in it when the radio tells them the temperatures of sea and sky are safe for their health. Between Santa Monica and Big Sycamore, a distance of thirty-five miles, there are often several variations of weather in the course of the hour's drive. I could not say which I like the most, a day of sun, when the heat radiates from even the water, or one of blown sand and spindrift, or the smother of windless fog, or mist, or driving rain. My wife feels differently. Gray weather depresses her, because she is a practical woman and wants sun for growing flowers and drying clothes.

I rise in the darkness before dawn, build up the fire from the night's coals, turn cats out, leaving dog to sleep, and sniff the air for the day's smells. Visitors have remarked that our colony smells like Carmel. That would be because of sun-warmed or fog-wet cypress, pine, and geranium.

Then I make coffee, sit in front of the fire, and consider the state of the world. If it seems able to revolve without my help, I begin to write—correspondence, reports, reviews, or a talk, and continue until the light shows in the east. If it is clear day, then sunrise over Point Dume is beautiful, Catalina dark against the sky. The newspaper hits the gate around seven. I take it with coffee to my wife in bed, then I breakfast on milk and fruit, and begin to think about the change to city man.

Since living on the Malibu, I go to work earlier and leave for home sooner than before. Unless there are evening demands, I try to leave campus by four thirty, and when I turn off San Vicente Boulevard and corkscrew down Santa Monica Canyon into 101A, see the ocean on my left, never the same shade of blue or green—peacock, slaty, milky, turquoise, opalescent, amethystine—halcyon or wind-capped, and the curve of the mountains around the bay to Point Dume; then I love the route, every mile of it, in both directions, at any time of day, the ribbon of road between sea and sierra, past Topanga and Las Flores, the Colony, Malibu Lagoon, and the canyons and coves clear to the Point, and then up and over its neck and the fall to Zuma Beach—another world, a better world.

In winter I reach home at sunset, shed suit for wool shirt, slacks, and sandals, then have a drink with my wife, and watch the sea and sky change and darken, as the animals come in for the night. When the days lengthen, there is time for a walk on the beach before dinner, or a swim. Lacking a dining room, we eat at a candlelit table by the sea window, or by the fire. The cormorants go by on their westerly way, moving as fast as head wind allows, urgently bound for their island roosts. In contrast, the gulls float gracefully to their near-by cliff dwellings, while down on the beach sandpipers tarry till dark, rolling in and out as though on invisible wheels, with the come and go of the water, dining on crustacea. Or pelicans, dropping like doom on their dinner.

Our animals come close, but don't beg. They get handouts when they are good. There is Princess Mei-ling, our little Siamese, born in April, 1943, and still as temperamental as ever; the Orange Pippin, with his fondness for riding on my shoulder and scuffling with our younger son when he is home overnight. The two toms, Joey and Junior, which my wife found as abandoned kittens on the beach, look upon Besa as their mother, and she rules them with loving authority. She is a good watchdog too. Sometimes in the still of a moony night, when sea lions surface and bark, Besa explodes like a pack of firecrackers. Newest addition to our little menagerie is Emily, a miniature Hungarian sheep dog of the breed called golden puli.

Sundays are the best days, and the round of hours revolves from dark to dark with beautiful things between. Then I often write till midmorning. If it is the page for *Westways,* I work in

my study, where the books are piled, and where the store of
memorabilia—books, pictures, relics from different periods of
my life, all of which I once consigned to the flames—makes
good medicine and the words stream from the Scripto.

The rest of Sunday is for pruning, weeding, sweeping, and
raking, or chopping and sawing. Our land is an acre, all
planted, and we are the only gardeners. Roses bloom the year
around, the eucalyptus seems to flower whenever it feels like it,
the geraniums are dormant in summer, then explode into bloom
when it rains. Springtime brings sweet alyssum, breaking over
the yard in waves of fragrance. Camellias—the beauty called
Colonel Fiery. Bougainvillaeas. *Copa de oro.* Purple and yellow
lotus blooms of the mesembryanthemum. Along the cliff the
coreopsis gigantea, most of the year a dead stalk, feathers out
green and bears the golden flower that gives it its name.

Each spring the same mockingbird has returned to entertain
us with his repertoire of imitations: crow, quail, meadow lark,
duck, frog, dog, cat. We are waiting confidently for him to mock
the "song" of Sugar, the burro. In summertime the migrating
monarch butterflies drift by in orange-colored argosies.

Sundays are also for neighborly visiting and tea. We don't
deal cards or shake cocktails, and so we move in the slower set
that values talk above tippling and shuffling. Much of our talk
is about community problems in this changing area of sub-
dividing and urbanization. We have a local homeowners' group
known as the Malibu Encinal Association, headed by Catherine
Barlow. There are similar ones for Trancas Beach, Point Dume,
and Zuma Canyon. All are joined in the West Malibu Community Council, which I serve as an officer. Grass-roots politics.
Differences of viewpoint on land between those like us, who own
only the piece on which they dwell, and those owners of large
tracts, to whom land is a speculative asset.

Sunday is also the time to glean wood in the wake of the fire.
Bare limbs of sumac, killed down to the root, are light and easy
to cut into kindling. The new growth is already greening their
bases, and after the rains the spaces between are lush with wild
cucumber vines and rye grass, springing from helicopter-sown

seed. We watched the "whirlybirds" at work, trailing seed like smoke. Lupin and poppy make blue and gold blankets on the bare shoulders of the hills. Brodiae, Indian paintbrush, Mariposa tulips, hairy phlox—"all the flowers of the spring meet to perfume our burying."

One could write a book about the people alone and their reasons for living in the country, starting with old-timers such as the Deckers who came long ago to ranch beyond the limits of the Rancho and to hunt wherever the deer roamed; or later ones who built along the shore in the 1930s when the Ranch was first subdivided. The Country Store at Trancas is the place to see them, and my wife has good eyes for people-watching, plus a charitable heart toward all, and someday she and I will write a novel about Malibu Man, of which there are more and more each year, alas. The longer one has lived here, the more painful it is to watch urbanization spreading like a rash.

I don't know which is sweeter, the morning when the day's work is ahead, or the evening with the prospect of sleep. After dinner I usually work by the fire. I rarely write in the evening because of the difficulty in turning off my mind once it begins to work. I prefer slowly to run down. No television. No radio. The phone doesn't ring often because people don't want to make a toll call. In their thrift is our peace. My wife is in our bedroom with her own listening and reading, and assorted animals. I have long-playing records to choose from and, stretched out on the couch at the sea window, listen to music by firelight and the sound of the surf. My romantic taste ranges from Bloch, Copland, Gershwin, and Bartók, to Scriabin, Liszt, Dvořák, and Schumann, back to Mozart, and Bach's Goldberg Variations. I have experienced a revulsion for Beethoven, even his quartets, whose music, with its hammering themes and violent pianofortes, sounds coarse, after Mozart.

The latter's piano works have come to mean more to me than any other music—the concertos, sonatas, and other pieces for solo instrument. In his music occurs the resolution of the discords of life. By his mastery of composition Mozart made symbols of the reconciliation of the human tragedy which, in his own life, he was unable to avert. His clarity and form and taste, permeated with his own loving nature, make Beethoven sound rough and clumsy. Beethoven for the young, Mozart for the middle-aged, Bach for the old. So it sounds to me at fifty.

As I lie there in the flickering light, in the room with the golden walls and turquoise roof, this best of all music washes away the last of the day's dirt and bears me to sleep. Outside the window pass the lights of the northbound trucks, red and orange, and far off gleams the jewel on Anacapa—diamond, topaz, or ruby, depending on the atmosphere.

One final turn out of doors before going to bed, giving Besa her last run. Now all is quiet save for the wash of water, and the cry of night birds, and sometimes the swoosh of an owl. When the sea is phosphorescent, the kelp beds are milky and the breaking waves flash like neons. When the sea is high, the surf strikes the sand with hammer blows which make the cliff shake. Sometimes fog drifts in like smoke. In the dark of the moon the purse seiners string out in a carnival of lights. The full moon's track on the water is dazzling, and once we saw an eerie lunar eclipse. Always there are planes overhead, en route to and from San Francisco, or navy helicopters from Hueneme, whirling by at nearly eye level, while the Milky Way bands the sky from south to north. Lastly, the shine of city in the east—that monster which feeds on countryside, and which will eat us all in the end. But not quite yet.

Mind the long drive? Need I answer?

Index

About the Author

Lawrence Clark Powell was born in Washington, D.C., in 1906, of Quaker parents, and soon moved to South Pasadena, California, where he attended public schools. He is a graduate of Occidental College in Los Angeles, and received his Doctorate in Letters from the University of Dijon, having written his dissertation on Robinson Jeffers. His professional training for librarianship was at the University of California at Berkeley. He has been awarded honorary degrees by Occidental College, Juniata College, and the Carnegie Institute of Technology. Dr. Powell's experience in the book trade, before entering library service, is reflected in several of his writings, including *Recollections of an Ex-Bookseller, Vroman's of Pasadena,* and *. . . & Brown.* By his writings and his speeches he has served internationally as a catalytic agent among librarians and booksellers. For seventeen years he was University Librarian on the Los Angeles campus of the University of California, during which time the library led the country in rate of growth. In 1960 he became Dean of the newly established School of Library Service at UCLA, and he continues as Director of the William Andrews Clark Memorial Library, which he has made into a hive of bibliographical activity. Dean Powell has been a visiting professor at Columbia University and has lectured on such varied campuses as Yale University, Carleton College, University of Michigan, New Mexico Highlands University, and Clemson College. In 1957 he gave the British Library Association's Annual Lecture at the Conference in Harrogate. In 1960 he made a flying trip around the world to lead a workshop in Japan for U.S. Air Force librarians and then to buy books in Asia and Europe for the UCLA libraries. Another trip abroad in 1963 increased the flow of research materials to California. Through his field work UCLA has been enriched by such great modern collections as those of Michael Sadleir, C. K. Ogden, and Isaac Foot. Whenever in London he is called upon to address the Antiquarian Booksellers Association. In 1960 Dean Powell was the first recipient of the Clarence Day Award by the American Library Association for his encouragement of a love of books and reading. Dr. Powell was a member of the committee which in 1963 selected a library for the White House. He has been a Guggenheim Fellow, president of the Bibliographical Society of America, the California Library Association, and the Zamorano Club of Los Angeles, and is also a member of the Roxburghe Club of San Francisco, the Caxton Club of Chicago, and the Grolier Club of New York. He is internationally acclaimed as a fluent and forceful speaker in the bibliohumanistic tradition.

Dean Powell's writing embraces more than a dozen books, scores of pamphlets, and hundreds of articles and reviews. He has been translated into Japanese, Dutch, and Scandinavian, as well as French, German, and Italian. His books classify roughly into two categories: about books, book collecting, and reading, of which *The Alchemy of Books, A Passion for Books,* and *Books in My Baggage* are the best known; and about Southwestern literature and landscape, including *Books West Southwest, Heart of the Southwest,* and *Southwestern Book Trails.* He is one of those rare Southern Californians who is *persona grata* in Arizona, New Mexico, and Texas; in other words, a true Southwesterner.

Even before the establishment of the UCLA library school,

Dr. Powell was known as a teacher and trainer of bookish librarians, and today former members of his staff occupy leading positions in major libraries throughout the country; and now the graduates of his school are going out in increasing numbers to work for the improvement of library service.

When their two sons, Norman and Wilkie, had grown up, he and his wife, Fay Ellen, moved to the Malibu coast, thirty miles northwest of Los Angeles, where their hobbies are gardening, cooking, beachcombing, and music, their companions the cats and the dogs of this book's dedication.

THIS BOOK WAS SET IN

BASKERVILLE AND PERPETUA TYPES BY

HARRY SWEETMAN TYPESETTING CORPORATION.

IT WAS PRINTED AND BOUND AT THE PRESS OF

THE WORLD PUBLISHING COMPANY.

DESIGN IS BY LARRY KAMP.